CHALLENGE
TO THE COURT

SOCIAL SCIENTISTS
AND THE DEFENSE OF SEGREGATION,
1954-1966

I. A. Newby

LOUISIANA STATE UNIVERSITY PRESS • BATON ROUGE

To the memory of
my mother

NOMIE BELL FLOYD NEWBY

1899–1965

She would not have agreed with all the views expressed in this study. She would, however, have been proud of my accomplishment in expressing them.

PREFACE

The Negro's struggle for equality is one of the heroic episodes in American history. It rightly claims the attention of the American people, and a large measure of their support, too. Americans of both races contribute their resources and energies to this struggle, vote for public officials sympathetic to the Negro's cause, and make heroes of men as diverse as Martin Luther King, John Lewis, and James Baldwin. They debate the civil rights struggle, its strategy and tactics; they read about it, write about it, and make it an object of perpetual concern.

All this is as it should be. The attention heaped upon the civil rights movement has made the American people, or at least the most concerned among them, aware of the Negro's plight and appreciative of his protest. But in their understandable preoccupation with the problems and aspirations of Negroes, Americans too often neglect the other side of the story. They too often ignore segregationists, or, more accurately, too hurriedly dismiss them as nothing more than unreasoning demagogues or cruel and selfish bigots. As a result they misunderstand and underestimate their adversary. Epithets such as "demagogue" and "bigot" may in fact be apt descriptions of many segregationists, but name-calling is an unsatisfactory substitute for thoughtful analysis of the segregationist mind. It is also unconducive to understanding the strength and tenacity of anti-Negro ideas in America. In their zeal to further the Negro's cause, the national press, the communications media, and other molders of mass opinion invariably present segregationists and their ideas in the worst possible light, and more often than not select irrational persons with a Ku Klux mentality to present the anti-Negro point of view. The result is to ridicule segregationists to the amusement and satisfaction of integrationists, but not to help Americans understand the appeal of racist ideas or the tenacity with which white Southerners cling to those ideas. Nor does it induce segregationists to question their own racial views.

This is not to suggest that segregationists be treated with indulgence. After all, they often advocate racial policies of a most callous and exploitative kind, and would deny to Negroes many of the rights and privileges inherent in American citizenship. But this is not the point. Regardless of the offensiveness of the ideas they profess and the policies they advocate, segregationists must be taken more seriously if they are to be understood. Racist ideas are as rational, systematic, and convincing to segregationists as equalitarian ideas are to integrationists. Yet if racial harmony is to be achieved in this country, those racist ideas must be exploded and the racial attitudes of segregationists radically changed. To do this, anti-Negro thought must be understood, which is to say it must be systematically analyzed and subjected unemotionally to tests of logic, reason, history, and science. And the process must be continuous. It is not enough to say that racist ideas are invalid; it is more important to demonstrate their rationale, their logic, their premises, and spell out their implications for American democracy as well as for racial policy. In this way their weaknesses will become apparent and their appeal, hopefully, diminished. Nor is it enough to say that racist ideas have already been refuted or that they fall from their own absurdity, although they have been refuted (or revealed to be value judgments which permit no objective refutation) and many of them are patently absurd. Anti-Negro literature circulates widely among segregationists, who accept much of it at face value and from it derive assurances that their racial policies are correct. One of the integrationists' most pressing tasks is, or should be, to analyze and evaluate that literature, challenge its premises, logic, and data, and point out its real nature to segregationists.

In this spirit I offer this study. Proponents of civil rights and racial integration have, I believe, done their cause a disservice by giving too little attention to anti-Negro ideas and the workings of the segregationist mind. Yet it is those ideas which motivate segregationists and explain their implacable opposition to racial integration. As a practical matter, or so it seems to me, segregationists are segregationists because they are convinced, first, that Negroes are racially inferior to whites, and, second, that this alleged inferiority is genetically fixed and transmitted by heredity. They thus believe that racial intermixture, which they assume is the logical consequence of social integration, will be a racial—and national—catastrophe. Of course, the psychological and sociological dynamics behind Southern racism are profound and complex and are the ultimate source of anti-Negro racism. But the conviction that Negroes are inferior—and the parallel one that whites are superior—is the immediate motive force behind segregation.

Anti-Negro thought is an amalgam of history, religion, and science reinforced by a reactionary social philosophy and a backward-looking view of politics and economics. The relative significance of these factors has differed from time to time, as has the intensity with which segregationists defend their position, but each has endured as an element of racist thinking. In recent years one of the most important and curious features of anti-Negro thought has been a renascence of scientific racism, of the use of science and social science to defend racial segregation. This development, an outgrowth of the Supreme Court's use of psychological and sociological authorities in the decision of *Brown v. Board of Education of Topeka* (1954), is a little-known facet of the racial controversies which now engross this nation, but it is an important element in the South's efforts to prevent racial integration, especially in public schools.

The purpose of this study is to describe the use of science by segregationists since 1954 and to analyze the ideas and the literature which scientific racists now use to defend segregation. To do this, I have focused upon the small group of academic social scientists who are largely responsible for the recent resurgence of scientific racism, and I have discussed their major works in some detail. Since their effort was a direct response to the Brown decision, I felt obliged to discuss the social science evidence presented in the Brown cases. Segregationists use science for two reasons, one of them general—to justify racial segregation—and the other specific—to overturn the Brown decision—and I have emphasized both. I have stressed the *ideas* of scientific racism rather than the uses which segregationists made of those ideas, for my primary objective was to illuminate the segregationist mind and to understand why some Americans so tenaciously defend discriminatory racial policies. Understanding the segregationist mind will not eliminate the necessity for continued Negro protest, nor remove the need for "outside" pressure upon the white South. It will, however, give integrationists a better idea of what it is that they shall overcome.

It seems appropriate at the outset to comment upon the problem of personal bias or "prejudice." In writing this study I found it necessary to play the dual role of historian and commentator. In the former, I sought to relate as straightforwardly as possible the major ideas of scientific racism, and to do so in a factual, objective manner. In the latter, I attempted to discuss and evaluate those ideas (most of which I consider scientifically unsound and socially unwise) within the framework of what seems to me to be sound social science and necessary social policy. In this, I was unable (and, indeed, rather unwilling) to avoid all subjective judgment. In any case, I endeavored to keep the two roles separate and prevent my own convictions from interfering with an accurate presentation of the ideas of scientific racists. The reader must judge for himself the extent to which I succeeded.

In the final analysis, one's attitude toward racial integration, racial equality, interracial marriage, and a multitude of related subjects rests upon basic assumptions and value judgments concerning such debatable issues as human nature, heredity and environment, the nature of democracy, the relationship of the individual to society, and, indeed, the nature and significance of race itself. To say that an individual is "prejudiced" is to say, in part at least, that his assumptions concerning these subjects differ from one's own. Scientific racism, the chief concern of this study, rests largely upon several such assumptions or value judgments—that human nature is fixed by heredity and immune to environment, that behavior characteristics (morality, criminality, ethics) as well as intelligence are genetically determined and directly related to race, that racial differences are relevant to the formulation of public policy, that race, in short, is the basic reality of life.

Given the present state of scientific knowledge and methodology, these assumptions cannot be absolutely disproven, and this, of course, is a major source of strength for those who accept them. Scientific racists are convinced that the assumptions are valid, or probably valid, and base their conviction on what they consider the best available scientific evidence. Most social scientists, however, who are not racists and who reject the major ideas and value judgments of racism, believe those assumptions are false, or largely false, and they, too, base their position on what they accept as "the teachings of modern scientific authority." The disagreement between scientific racists and their critics is thus first of all a disagreement between rival value systems, and the disagreement cannot, unfortunately, be resolved to the satisfaction of everyone by an appeal to objective scientific data. The available data are subject to different interpretations, even by well-meaning men. There is a body of data which *may* be interpreted as evidence of racial inequality, just as there are other data which seem clearly to indicate that races are equal, or potentially equal. Scientific evidence, however, is only one part of a larger whole, and here the logic of the situation seems clearly to favor equalitarians. Scientific racists look to science for guidance in formulating public policy. However, constitutional, legal, and political factors, as well as democracy, justice, and human decency, would seem to be much more important than science in defining the civil rights of Negroes and their proper role in American life. A philosophy of race relations based exclusively upon science is clearly inadequate.

I do not mean to say or imply that the merits of the debate between scientific racists and equalitarians are purely relative, or that the merits depend exclusively upon the validity of the initial assumptions of each side. As this study will show, I believe emphatically that the mass of scientific evidence is such that it is reasonable to assume that races are approximately equal. I recognize, however, that innate racial equality has never been objectively demonstrated by scientists (and neither has innate racial inequality). I am convinced that considerations of racial equality or inequality are of little relevance to the basic issue involved in either the Brown decision or the civil rights struggle. The basic issue is the civil rights which Negroes are entitled to as American citizens, and those rights rest on constitutional guarantees, not scientific data.

Finally, a word about terminology. A major difficulty in writing about race is the problem of "loaded" terms. Segregationists reject as invidious such terms as "racism," "scientific racism," and "racist." As I have used it here, "racism" suggests a belief in innate racial inequality, including the corollaries of Negro inferiority and white superiority. However, most of the individuals discussed in this study insist that they are not racists, that they believe only in racial *differences,* not racial *inequality.* I have therefore applied the term "racist" to anyone who advocates racial policies such as segregation, civil disabilities against Negroes, and prohibition of racial intermarriage—policies which are meaningful only if the races are inherently unequal. A "racist" is thus anyone who believes in racial inequality and/or advocates the above racial policies, and a "scientific racist" is one whose racism rests chiefly upon science or pseudoscience. Virtually all the individuals described in this study as racists or scientific racists object to the descriptions and deny that they are racists.

I wish to express my appreciation to Professors Theodore Saloutos, Roger Daniels, and Ralph Turner of the University of California at Los Angeles, Professor Lawrence B. de Graaf of California State College at Fullerton, and Richard H. Levensky of Hollywood, California, each of whom read all or parts of the manuscript and offered many helpful suggestions for improving it. I alone am responsible for any errors which remain.

I. A. NEWBY

CONTENTS

CHALLENGE TO THE COURT

1

BEFORE THE BROWN DECISION

On May 17, 1954, the Supreme Court of the United States delivered an epochal opinion. On that date the Court issued its long-awaited decision in the series of cases [1] by which the National Association for the Advancement of Colored People had challenged

---

[1] *Briggs v. Elliott*, 95 F. Supp. 529 (E.D. S.C. 1951); *Brown v. Board of Education of Topeka*, 98 F. Supp. 797 (D. Kan. 1951); *Davis v. County Board of Prince Edward County*, 103 F. Supp. 337 (E.D. Va. 1951); *Gebhart v. Belton*, 87 A. 2d 862 (D. Del. 1951); and *Boling v. Sharpe*, 347 U.S. 497 (1954). The Supreme Court decision discussed here is *Brown v. Board of Education of Topeka*, 347 U.S. 483 (1954).

the constitutionality of racial segregation in the public schools of this country.

As Chief Justice Earl Warren read the decision to a hushed, crowded courtroom, its significance became immediately apparent. Flanked by the eight associate justices of the Court, each of whom endorsed the decision he was reading, Warren first surveyed the background of the cases, touching briefly upon the history of racial segregation and the role of public education in American life. He then examined the judicial history of the Fourteenth Amendment, emphasizing its relevance to public education. Finally, he reached the heart of the decision. "Does segregation of children in public schools solely on the basis of race, even though the physical facilities and other 'tangible' factors may be equal, deprive the children of the minority group of equal educational opportunities?" he asked, almost matter-of-factly. His answer was forthright: "We believe that it does." To segregate Negro pupils "from others of similar age and qualifications solely because of their race generates a feeling of inferiority as to their status in the community that may affect their hearts and minds in a way unlikely ever to be undone."

To support this interpretation Warren turned directly to the findings of a lower federal court in one of the cases at hand. "Segregation of white and colored children in public schools," the lower court had held in the case of *Brown v. Board of Education of Topeka,* "has a detrimental effect upon the colored children. The impact is greater when it has the sanction of the law; for the policy of separating the races is usually interpreted as denoting the inferiority of the Negro group. A sense of inferiority affects the motivation of a child to learn. Segregation with the sanction of law, therefore, has a tendency to retard the educational and mental development of Negro children and to deprive them of the benefits they would receive in a racially integrated school system."

This obviously is a statement of sociology or social psychology and not of law, but the Court made no attempt to conceal its reliance upon social science authority. On the contrary, the decision proceeded on a consciously psychological note. "Whatever may have been the extent of psychological knowledge of the time of Plessy v. Ferguson," [2] the Chief Justice continued, "this finding is amply

2 *Plessy v. Ferguson,* 163 U.S. 537 (1896). This decision, which wrote the separate-but-equal concept into American law, was set aside by Brown.

supported by modern authority." To substantiate this sweeping statement, the Court inserted the famous footnote number eleven, around which a long and bitter controversy later swirled. The footnote, a list of references to some of the latest and most authoritative research on the effects of segregation on personality development, was an integral part of the Brown decision, and represented an effort by the Court to buttress its legal case with expert nonlegal authority. Although some supporters of the decision later attempted to play down the footnote and dismiss it as an unimportant aside by the Court, it was clearly intended to supplement the legal basis of the decision, and to blunt the adverse reactions the decision was expected to produce. Enlarged to include complete citations, the footnote read as follows:

Kenneth B. Clark, *Effects of Prejudice and Discrimination on Personality Development* (Midcentury White House Conference on Children and Youth, 1950); Helen Leland Witmer and Ruth Kotinsky, *Personality in the Making, The Fact-Finding Report of the Midcentury White House Conference on Youth and Children* (New York: Harper and Brothers, 1952), Chapter VI, "The Effects of Prejudice and Discrimination," 135–58; Max Deutscher and Isidor Chein, "The Psychological Effects of Enforced Segregation: A Survey of Social Science Opinion," *Journal of Psychology*, XXVI (October 1948), 259–87; Isidor Chein, "What Are the Psychological Effects of Segregation Under Conditions of Equal Facilities?" *International Journal of Opinion and Attitude Research*, III (Summer 1949), 229–34; Theodore Brameld, "Educational Costs," in *Discrimination and National Welfare* (New York: Harper and Brothers, 1949), ed. Robert M. MacIver, 44–48; E. Franklin Frazier, *The Negro in the United States* (New York: Macmillan, 1949), 647–781. And see generally Gunnar Myrdal, *An American Dilemma* (New York: Harper and Row, 1944).

On the basis of these authorities and a mass of expert testimony in the lower courts, the Supreme Court concluded that "separate but equal" has no place in the field of public education. "Separate educational facilities," the Justices ruled, "are inherently unequal." [3]

As anticipated, the decision evoked an outcry against the Court. One of a series of "liberal" decisions which have adapted American law and constitutional interpretation to recent socioeconomic and technological changes, the Brown ruling was denounced by a multitude of critics—segregationists, advocates of states rights,

[3] *Brown v. Board of Education*, 347 U.S. 483 (1954). The text and footnotes of the decision are reproduced in Kenneth Clark, *Prejudice and Your Child* (2nd ed.; Boston, 1963), 156–65.

strict constitutionalists, and a varied group of social and political conservatives. The decision was a milestone in the Negro's stride toward equality, and as such was especially offensive to segregationists and white supremacists. However, the Court's inclusion of social science authority and its implicit endorsement of the testimony of social scientists who testified for the NAACP in the lower courts, introduced a novel element in the response to the decision.

The segregationists' immediate reaction was shock and dismay, but after recovering their composure they began a broad, concerted counterattack. Initially, they stressed legal and constitutional factors, accusing the Court of ignoring the principle of *stare decisis* and resorting to judge-made law. Southern legislatures passed interposition resolutions designed to nullify the Brown decision by 'interposing' the authority of the states between their citizens and the federal government. Lawyers and politicians "exposed" the Fourteenth Amendment and questioned the legality of its inclusion in the Constitution. A multitude of new laws and ordinances appeared upon the statute books in the South, each in some way designed to defy the Court and frustrate the Negro's achievement of equality. "Respectable" segregationists organized State Sovereignty Commissions or Citizens' Councils, seeking thereby to avoid the image of bigotry and violence which attached to the Ku Klux Klan and compromised its effectiveness. The Citizens' Councils, "uptown Klans" in Thurgood Marshall's telling phrase, channeled Southern energies into economic boycotts, thought control, and community pressures for conformity. They watchdogged public leaders, both elected and otherwise, purged school books of unacceptable ideas, and warned the South and the nation that integration would be a calamity. As part of a general educational or propaganda effort, which was by no means confined to Citizens' Councils, though their leadership was important, segregationists attacked the social science—and social scientists—which the Court utilized in the Brown decision.

The attack was multifold. It was in part negative: an effort to undermine the scientific validity and personal integrity of authorities cited by the Court. It was in part positive: an effort to provide an alternative body of scientific data sufficient in quantity and authority to convince the skeptical that there are rational, scientific justifications for racial segregation. To achieve these ends, a small but articulate cadre of social scientists, who were convinced of the desirability of segregation, especially in "delicate" areas of social relations, began soon after 1954 to formulate a scientific defense of segregation. Their effort inevitably provoked a controversy with other social scientists. Though the controversy involved men of science on both sides, it was waged with a vehemence and intensity dismaying to the layman. The displays of public denunciation and name-calling to which both sides on occasion resorted are timely illustrations of the problems involved in the study of man and society, and demonstrate anew the difficulty man has in studying himself objectively. The two groups approached their studies with divergent assumptions about the concept of race and with differing views on the social implications of race. Segregationists and scientific racists stressed its importance; integrationists and equalitarians played it down. As a result, the two groups drew basically different conclusions, not only from their own research but from general scientific knowledge in the field of race. In every case, apparently, researchers on the subject of race reached conclusions which confirmed their initial assumptions. There seems to have been no instance of a segregationist scientist whose research and study led him to alter his views toward race in any fundamental way. Likewise, no equalitarian scientist was ever led to question his basic assumptions as a result of study and experimentation. If the researcher was convinced at the outset that racial differences are so important that social segregation and racial purity are vital to national survival, his research reinforced that conviction. If, on the other hand, he was convinced that racial differences are superficial and irrelevant to public policy, this conviction was reaffirmed by his research.

Social scientists study controversial and troublesome things: the origin and nature of racial characteristics, the workings of the mechanism of inheritance, the relative importance of heredity and environment, the problems of interracial contact and conflict. The very nature of such subjects makes it impossible for social scientists to speak with the assurance of chemists or physicists. The social scientist must frequently qualify even his most important conclusions. "As far as we now know," "the preponderance of scientific opinion holds," "we can not speak on this point with absolute certainty," "on the basis of this experiment"—such statements appear regularly in his writings. He must, if he is honest, admit that the precise nature of racial differences is not always understood, that the workings of inheritance are not precisely known, that in a host of similar vital areas scientific knowledge is incomplete.

And this is the heart of the problem. The areas of limited

knowledge provide an opening for speculators. They enable both racists and integrationists to inject a substantial element of interpretation, of value judgment, into the most rigorous social science experimentation. In the social sciences, data often mean different things to different men, and the racist (or, again, the integrationist) is enabled thereby to utilize valid data in invalid ways. When a racist is also a social scientist who speaks under an academic or scientific mantle, his authority is notably enhanced, not only among designing bigots but among unsophisticated laymen as well. For this reason scientific racists are important spokesmen for racist causes.

To repeat a truism, the twentieth century is an age of science and education, and any theory of social relations which clothes itself in scientific authority and academic respectability is thereby greatly strengthened. The recent outpouring of scientific racism is evidence aplenty of the segregationists' recognition of this fact. Today a significant element among their number relies chiefly upon science instead of states rights or strict constitutionalism in attacking integration. Exploiting a widespread fear of the possible consequences of racial integration, they tell white Americans that "science" has proven that races are unequal, that Negroes are inferior to whites, and that racial inequality is perpetrated by heredity. They tell them also that integrated schools are but a prelude to the Negro's real goal, racial intermarriage, which is itself a preliminary to mongrelizing the American people and destroying American civilization.

Scientific racism is not a new phenomenon. The Negro's "place" in this country, whether in or out of the South, whether slavery or segregation, has always been based, in part at least, upon science or pseudoscience, and, until recently, scientific racism always had wide support among scientists. Before the Civil War, science was a major ingredient in proslavery thinking.[4] Such dissimilar scientists as Josiah Nott of Alabama, Samuel George Norton of Philadelphia, and Louis Agassiz of Harvard were convinced that Negroes are innately inferior to white men, and based their convictions on the most up-to-date scientific authority. Supported by the latest research and most authoritative speculation in anthropology and anthropometry—sciences which study racial origins and compara-

4 William Stanton, *The Leopard's Spots, Scientific Attitudes toward Race in America, 1815–1859* (Chicago, 1960).

tive racial differences—and even phrenology, egyptology, and bibli-
cal criticism, ideas of racial inequality enjoyed complete scientific
respectability before the Civil War. What is equally important,
George Fitzhugh, Thomas R. Dew, and a host of other proslavery
spokesmen took these ideas and upon them erected a social philosophy, a "sociology" resting on the cornerstones of slavery and racial
inequality.[5]

Nor were scientific attitudes toward race significantly altered by
emancipation of the slaves or by Reconstruction efforts to give
equality to the freedmen. As Professor Thomas F. Gossett has
recently shown, the mainstream of scientific thought after 1865 continued to accept racial inequality and Negro inferiority as undis-
puted facts.[6] And Darwin's evolutionary hypothesis brought new authority to racist opinion. To older arguments of racial inequality it
added the idea that racial characteristics are adaptations to the
environment in which the race evolved. In the Negro's case, this
meant adaptations to the hot, steaming jungles of tropical Africa.
To protect themselves from the burning sun, so this idea ran, Negroes developed thick, dark skin, a thick skull, woolly, matted
hair, and a capacity for perspiring profusely. This hot, humid environment prevented the development of superior racial qualities.
Food was plentiful and readily obtainable; shelter and clothing
were unnecessary, or virtually so. As a result, life was easy and
Negroes were not forced to develop the qualities which a more
rigorous environment produced in other races. The white man
evolved in the challenging, invigorating climate of the far north,
where he was forced to think for himself, to plan for tomorrow,
to reason, to organize, to brave the elements, to conquer nature.
In his case evolution produced constant improvement and, ulti-
mately, superiority. The Negro, however, stagnated.

In the half century after Reconstruction several new scientific
disciplines also added to the growing authority of scientific racism.
Psychology and sociology, joined presently by eugenics and genetics,

[5] See George Fitzhugh, *Sociology for the South* (Richmond, 1854) and
Cannibals All; or Slaves Without Masters (Richmond, 1857); Henry Hughes,
A Treatise on Sociology (Philadelphia, 1859); Thomas R. Dew and others,
*Pro-Slavery Arguments as Maintained by the Most Distinguished Writers of
the Southern States* (Charleston, 1852).

[6] Thomas F. Gossett, *Race, The History of an Idea in America* (Dallas,
1963), 253–86.

opened whole new vistas in the study of race, and soon they too were offering "proof" of racial inequality and Negro inferiority, reinforcing the evidence of anthropology, ethnology, anatomy, and physiology. In all of these disciplines notable scientific advances occurred in the late nineteenth and early twentieth centuries. It is a striking and chastening fact that the remarkable progress made in this period in scientific knowledge and methodology increased rather than destroyed the prestige and authority of racism.[7]

The net effect was that men of science in the early twentieth century found racist ideas generally acceptable. As applied to Negroes, those ideas went something like this: *Race* is not merely a convenient means of grouping members of the human family; it is instead the ultimate fact of life. To speak of individual traits and potentialities is but to speak of racial traits and potentialities. Racial (individual) characteristics are permanent and unchangeable except by the slow, sure workings of evolution. The physical manifestations of race can be isolated, measured, and used to define racial groupings. Head shape, cephalic index, brain size, facial prognathism, skin color, hair texture—such features are racially determined, and individually or collectively reflect the relative quality of different races. The significance of race, however, is not limited to physical features. Indeed, differences of mentality and psychology are greater than physical differences, and far more important. Racial instincts account for the childishness, joviality, irresponsibility, and other traits which are popularly attributed to the Negro.

Whether physical or psychological, however, racial characteristics were products of centuries of evolution during which the races were isolated from each other. This long period of intraracial inbreeding, undisturbed by "foreign" genes from other races, produced genetic harmony, an equilibrium in the genetic characteristics of the individual and the race. Preserved and transmitted by heredity, this equilibrium is upset by the injection of new and alien genes, which occurs when races interbreed. The halfbreed, a mixture of discordant genes, lacks genetic harmony, and is likely to be unstable and malcontented. The mulatto, the offspring of white

7 These ideas are discussed more completely in I. A. Newby, *Jim Crow's Defense, Anti-Negro Thought in America, 1900–1930* (Baton Rouge, 1965), 19–51.

and Negro intermixture, is usually erratic, high strung, nervous, troublesome—and a leader of "equality" movements.

The racial mongrel, however, is only one result, although a tragic one, of the inexorable workings of genetic laws. Morality, social behavior, physical constitution are also genetically determined, or largely so. The high rates of illegitimacy, broken families, unemployment, murder, rape, crimes of violence, and even tuberculosis, among Negroes are outward manifestations of inborn qualities. Put another way, the Negro's position in American life, whether social, economic, or political, is the logical and inevitable result of his racial inferiority. Because of limitations inherent in his nature, he is unable to appreciate or derive full benefit from Caucasian civilization, the institutions of which are products of the white man's unique racial genius. Political democracy, constitutionalism, Christianity, free enterprise economics, modern technology are beyond the limits of the Negro's racial capacity, and he cannot compete in a society based upon them.

Carried to a logical conclusion, these ideas posit a direct correlation between race and civilization, a thesis which has been central to racist thought since Gobineau.[8] Each race, so the thesis runs, creates its own civilization, a civilization which expresses or reflects its unique racial genius. To the extent that races differ in this innate genius, so will the civilizations they create differ, and to that extent one race will be unable to absorb the civilization of another. Civilization is, in short, a product of race, that is, of genetic inheritance, and no civilization can survive large scale racial intermixture. Indeed, mongrelization will destroy a civilization more thoroughly than conquering armies, as the history of Greece and Rome vividly proves. Such examples are perpetual reminders of an inexorable law: when mixed, racial characteristics, like water, seek the lowest possible level. White-Negro intermixture will thus result in the inundation of superior white genes in a flood of inferior black genes.

The usefulness of these ideas to white supremacists, especially in the South, is apparent. Segregation, subjection, ignorance, and disfranchisement, they assert, are natural states for the Negro.

[8] Gobineau, Arthur de, *The Inequality of Human Races,* trans. Adrian Collins (London, 1915); originally published as *Essai sur l'Inegalite des Races Humaines* (4 vols.; Paris, 1853–55).

Abolishing racial distinctions, especially social and political distinctions, only risks destruction of American civilization, at least where Negroes are congregated in large numbers. To provide Negro and white children with the same education programs makes a mockery of the education process. The Negro's intelligence is too low, his brain is too small, too primitive, too generalized to enable him to master an education program adapted to the capacities of a superior race. Public policy, whether it involves education, the right to vote, social relations, or legal status must reflect racial realities, which is to say it must reflect scientific truth. Segregation and attendant policies do this, or so segregationists claimed. In their view segregation is grounded in the authoritative principles of sociology, psychology, anthropology, and genetics and acknowledges the principles of Darwin and Herbert Spencer. And what scientists endorse as good policy, so also do clergymen, educators, historians, political scientists. "Science," insisted segregationists, merely reinforces what the Bible suggests, what history illustrates, what experience makes manifest—that Negroes are inferior to Caucasians and are likely to remain so in the foreseeable future.

Thus read the scientific racism of the early twentieth century. Significantly, every one of the above ideas, though often embellished by new authority or restated in more plausible and sophisticated language, has reappeared in racist literature since 1954.

Such ideas do not exist in a vacuum. On the contrary, they graphically illustrate the social philosophy of those who accept them, a social philosophy based almost exclusively on racial determinism. One cannot accept the "fact" that Negroes are racially inferior without also accepting social, educational, and political policies which reflect that "fact." As a matter of course, the architects of Southern race policies have always based their racial ideas to one degree or another upon "science," and have assiduously cultivated "authorities" to serve this purpose. It was the fashion among opponents of the Brown decision to decry the Court's use of social science, and to look upon "sociological jurisprudence" as another example of the modern tendency to discard time-honored and proven principles. It all began, they declared, when Louis Brandeis introduced extraneous evidence in his "sociological brief" in *Muller v. Oregon* (1908), and the Supreme Court used his brief, which detailed the harmful effects of long hours on working women, as one justification for upholding the constitutionality of an Oregon law limiting the work day of women to ten hours.

"Sociological jurisprudence," however, goes back much further than 1954 or 1908. The use of sociological evidence has always been implicit, if not explicit, in the South's (and the nation's) treatment of Negroes, whether in or out of the courts. Certainly the Dred Scott decision conformed to pro-slavery "sociology," as did the long list of Supreme Court decisions which defined the Negro's place in this country after the Civil War. In ruling that racial discrimination in public accommodations is not a violation of the Fourteenth Amendment, the Supreme Court in 1883 rejected the Negroes' contention that such discrimination implies a condition of servitude or inferiority for members of their race. "Can the act of a mere individual," asked the Court in the *Civil Rights Cases* of that year, "the owner of the inn, the public conveyance, or place of amusement, refusing the accommodation, be justly regarded as imposing any badge of slavery or servitude upon the applicant?" Certainly not, was the answer. Free Negroes before the Civil War had suffered a multitude of legal, social, and political restrictions, yet nobody had considered such restrictions a mark of servitude or slavery. "No one," the Court said, "thought that it was any invasion of his personal status as a freeman because he was not admitted to all the privileges enjoyed by white citizens, or because he was subjected to discriminations in the enjoyment of accommodations in inns, public conveyances and places of amusement. Mere discriminations on account of race or color were not regarded as badges of slavery." [9] Nor could they be so regarded in 1883. Whatever the legal and constitutional merits of this decision, it conformed nicely to the sociology of white supremacists.

Even more revealing was the decision in *Plessy v. Ferguson* (1896), a decision which segregationists repeatedly praised while denouncing the use of social science in the Brown ruling. As a recent study points out, "sociological and psychological theories controlled the Court's decision" in the Plessy case. That decision, writes Barton J. Bernstein, in the *Journal of Negro History*, "wrote conservative theory and the prevailing social science 'truths' into law. The court explained that the standard of reasonableness is determined 'with reference to the established usages, customs, and traditions of the people. . . . Law is reasonable when it follows custom." [10]

[9] *Civil Rights Cases*, 109 U.S. 3; 3 S. Ct. 18.
[10] Barton J. Bernstein, "Plessy v. Ferguson: Conservative Sociological Jurisprudence," *Journal of Negro History*, XLVIII (July, 1963), 196–205.

The issues in Plessy were similar to those in the Brown cases fifty-eight years later: Does enforced separation of the races stamp Negroes with a badge of inferiority? Are segregated facilities inherently unequal? Are they in the final analysis intended to remind the Negro in a degrading and humiliating way that his is a race apart, that associating with him even in public places is repulsive and demeaning to whites? The Court answered these questions with an emphatic "No," and incorporated in its answer a generous sprinkling of sociological theory. The Plessy decision thus merits quoting at length:

> The case reduced itself to the question whether the statute of Louisiana [requiring segregated railroad cars] is a reasonable regulation, and with respect to this there must necessarily be a large discretion on the part of the legislature. In determining the question of reasonableness it is at liberty to act with reference to the estimated usages, customs and traditions of the people, and with a view to the promotion of their comfort, and the preservation of the public peace and good order. Gauged by this standard, we cannot say that a law which authorizes or even requires the separation of the two races in public conveyances is unreasonable, or more obnoxious to the Fourteenth Amendment than the acts of Congress requiring separate schools for colored children in the District of Columbia. . . .
>
> We consider the underlying fallacy of the plaintiff's argument to consist in the assumption that the enforced separation of the two races stamps the colored race with a badge of inferiority. If this be so, it is not by reason of anything found in the act, but solely because the colored race chooses to put that construction upon it. . . . The argument . . . assumes that social prejudices may be overcome by legislation, and that equal rights cannot be secured to the Negro except by an enforced commingling of the two races. We cannot accept this proposition. If the two races are to meet upon terms of social equality, it must be the result of natural affinities, a mutual appreciation of each other's merits and a voluntary consent of individuals. . . . Legislation is powerless to eradicate racial instincts or to abolish distinctions based upon physical differences, and the attempt to do so can only result in accentuating the difficulties of the present situation. If the civil and political rights of both races be equal one cannot be inferior to the other civilly or politically. If one race be inferior to the other socially, the Constitution of the United States cannot put them upon the same plane.[11]

This is replete with the ideas of late-nineteenth-century social science. Law, it says, must follow established customs and usages, for as William Graham Sumner was then insisting, social mores are

11 *Plessy v. Ferguson*, 163 U.S. 537 (1896) .

immune to the tamperings of social theorists and reformers. There is, it also says, no assumption of inferiority inherent in segregation laws and customs. If any inferiority is involved, it exists in the minds of Negroes and not in the law itself. Besides, questions of racial inferiority and superiority are beyond the reach of law. Inferiority and superiority are earned; they can not be decreed by legislative enactment or judicial fiat. Nor can law eradicate racial instincts, a term which, incidentally, smacks more of psychology than of law. Nowhere was the Court's acceptance of late-nineteenth-century social science more explicit. Racial instincts, it said, are just that—instincts. They cannot be ignored or altered, and to attempt to do so is to invite trouble. The object of law, however, is to avoid trouble, even though this must sometimes be achieved over the objections of one part of the citizenry. This view of the law was quite narrow, and concerned form rather than substance. The law of Louisiana required segregation but did not, in the Court's opinion, permit discrimination or servitude or fix upon Negroes a badge of inferiority. The law, or so the Court interpreted it, prescribed legal equality. That was all it could do. Social relations and feelings of inferiority were beyond the law's concern.

The Plessy decision in particular and Southern race policies in general, then, reflected the social science of segregationists. For this reason their attack upon the use of expert testimony in the Brown decision appears paradoxical at first sight. Certainly everyone agrees that the law must be reasonable, that it must reflect the accumulating knowledge of mankind. Yet knowledge is just that—accumulating, growing, progressing—and to keep pace with it the law must evolve. Law, as even segregationists admit, is not static. Its meaning and uses change as society evolves. Certainly it must reflect scientific truth, for to deny such a principle is, presumably, to say that truth is irrelevant to law.[12]

The socio-legal views of segregationists who attacked the use of social science in the Brown decision were unambiguous. Segregationists admit that the law changes through evolution, that is, through interpretation and custom, but they insist that it can properly change only in specified ways and within exceedingly narrow limits. Since they are a minority in the nation and oppose the major trends of scientific opinion on the subjects of race and race

[12] See the discussion on this point in Clark, *Prejudice and Your Child*, 206–35.

relations, they insist upon a strict interpretation of the Constitution, at least of those sections which serve their ends, and a rigid adherence to legal precedent. These, of course, are the methods best suited to preserve the constitutionality of policies which conform to their sociology. Their position is approximately this: Law must reflect scientific truth, but the social sciences are inexact, and the truth on racial topics is difficult to ascertain. In these areas the courts must use social science with the utmost caution, and recognize only those principles and data which are universally accepted. In cases in which there is any significant disagreement, legal precedent and strict constitutionalism must prevail. This will result in perpetuating racial policies which rest upon old (and, to integrationists, outmoded) social science data and theory. The old data and theory, however, are already incorporated into legal precedent and constitutional law, and need not be subjected to the careful scrutiny which newer data and theory must withstand. The burden of proof rests upon those who espouse the newer findings. The Supreme Court said in 1896 that segregation does not impose a mark of inferiority upon Negroes, and that segregated facilities are not inherently unequal. By virtue of this decision, segregationist sociology was the law of the land, and the law of the land cannot be changed for light and transient causes. The Plessy verdict can be set aside only when integrationists have proven their case so conclusively that the effects of segregation are no longer a matter of debate; that is, when they have proven to the satisfaction of segregationists that segregation is per se inequality, that its purpose is to mark Negroes with an inferior status, and that it violates the equal protection clause of the Fourteenth Amendment.

Segregationists eventually came to understand, once they reflected upon their position, that their objection to the use per se of expert social science testimony in the Brown decision was invalid. Within a few years after 1954 they shifted their ground, and today they object not so much to the use per se of social science testimony as to the use of what they feel is false and invalid social science testimony.

It would seem that everyone must accept as facts certain assumptions about segregation—that Jim Crow laws reflect a belief in Negro inferiority, that social segregation is based on an assumption by whites that racial equality is undesirable, that disfranchisement and civil inequality indicate an assumption that Negroes are incapable of discharging the responsibilities of citizenship, that Negroes are, in other words, a degraded and inferior race. If such assumptions are not valid, segregation would seem to have no *raison d'etre*. But such, it seems, is not the case at all, for the Negro's status under American law before 1954 rested on the premise that those assumptions are false. The law, in other words, was based on a fiction, the fiction that segregation implies no discrimination against Negroes and no assumption of Negro inferiority.

The widespread acceptance of this fiction indicates the magnitude of the task which the NAACP undertook in the Brown cases. Attorneys for the Association had to prove an obvious truth, but a truth which was unrecognized by the law and thus irrelevant to it, namely, that racial segregation is inherently discriminatory and marks the Negro with an inescapable badge of inferiority. Yet how can such a truth be proven, especially in a way which meets the rigid requirements of evidence in a court of law? Since the Brown cases involved public school segregation, would it be necessary to prove the detrimental effects of the single factor of school segregation? Would it be possible to do so? Can one facet of racial segregation be isolated from all others and measured objectively? Can the effects of school segregation be separated from the effects of economic discrimination, housing discrimination, or any one of the thousand ways in which society tells the Negro he is inferior? And must the effects of school segregation be demonstrated in the case of each individual Negro child involved in a suit?

Such were the questions facing the NAACP when it instituted the Brown cases. The Association's position, however, was not without hope. In a series of decisions going back to the 1930's the Supreme Court, though upholding the separate-but-equal principle, insisted upon an increasingly rigorous definition of "equal facilities," and made serious inroads on racial segregation in graduate and professional schools. As early as 1938 the Court held [13] that "equal facilities" must be within one's own state, thus relieving Negroes of the obligation of accepting out-of-state tuition grants at the discretion of the states. A decade later the Court held that facilities for Negroes must be available as soon as those for whites—constitutional rights, in other words, are here and now.[14] In 1950 the Court

[13] *Gaines v. Canada,* 305 U.S. 337 (1938).
[14] *Sipuel v. Board of Regents,* 332 U.S. 631 (1948).

went further in two important decisions. In *McLaurin v. Oklahoma State Regents*,[15] the court ruled that once a Negro student is admitted to a public institution he is entitled to use all facilities of the institution on the same basis as white students. The state of Oklahoma had assigned McLaurin, a Negro who was admitted to the University of Oklahoma by court order, a designated place in the classroom, library, and dining room. This, said the Court, deprived McLaurin of equal protection of the laws, even though his facilities were in the same room as those of whites. Such restrictions, it held, artificially inhibited his ability to study, to exchange views with other students, and to learn his profession. The state could not deprive an individual of the opportunity to gain acceptance on his own merits.

Also in 1950 the Court issued its most significant decision affecting school segregation before 1954. In *Sweatt v. Painter* [16] the Court ruled that a law school built especially for Negroes by the state of Texas was not equal to the University of Texas Law School, and ordered the admission of Sweatt to the University's law school. The Court based its decision not only on tangible factors such as quality and reputation of the faculty, size and quality of library holdings, and variety of courses offered, but also upon intangibles such as the school's reputation in the state, its traditions, the influence of its alumni, and the quality of educational experiences it offered. On this basis the Court found the University's law school superior to the one provided for Negroes. The Court was insisting that graduate and professional schools meet such rigid standards of equality that segregated facilities for Negroes would virtually always be found unequal.

To be sure, none of the decisions before 1954 applied specifically to the public schools, but they did indicate that the Supreme Court was increasingly willing to listen to evidence concerning the effects of segregation upon the individual and the quality of his education. Accordingly, in 1951 the NAACP in cooperation with a group of psychologists, sociologists, and educators undertook to prove in the courts that racial segregation in the public schools is per se discriminatory and that the effects of discrimination are manifested on all educational levels.

15 *McLaurin v. Oklahoma State Regents,* 339 U.S. 637 (1950).
16 *Sweatt v. Painter,* 339 U.S. 629 (1950).

2

THE BRIGGS CASE

An assault upon the legal and constitutional bases of the separate-but-equal principle was a natural outgrowth of the Sweatt and McLaurin decisions. In those decisions the Supreme Court took cognizance of expert social science testimony and looked beyond mere physical facilities in applying the separate-but-equal doctrine. That doctrine, after all, did not *require* segregation; it *permitted* segregation when the facilities available to the two races were equal. Nor had the Supreme Court defined the term "equal," at least not definitively. In fact, the Court had studiously avoided a direct review of the separate-but-equal principle, though it had applied the term "equal" in such a way that eleven of the seventeen states permitting racial segregation in public education had been ordered to admit Negro students to previously all-white graduate and/or professional schools. On these levels, at least, separate facilities had become almost by definition unequal. The Court was gradually shifting the grounds upon which segregation cases were being decided, and the shift was in the direction of arguments offered by NAACP lawyers and endorsed by social scientists who testified in the Sweatt and McLaurin cases.

In 1951, however, the process was incomplete. The separate-but-equal principle remained the law of the land, and the increasingly rigorous definition of "equal" facilities had not been applied to public schools, where the vast majority of Negro students were found. Integration on the graduate and professional levels affected only a handful of Negroes. To be at all meaningful, educational integration had to be extended to the public schools. Moreover, most social scientists who had studied the problem were convinced that the worst effects of school segregation occurred during the earliest years of the child's education.

In the years following World War II social scientists gave ever-increasing attention to the study of racial segregation in this country, especially to its effects upon the motivation, self-respect, and personality development of Negroes. A voluminous literature on these subjects had appeared by 1950,[1] and most social scientists agreed that segregation was harmful to individual Negroes and to society as a whole.[2] In utilizing expert social science testimony to challenge the separate-but-equal doctrine, the NAACP was merely bringing to the attention of the federal courts a body of knowledge and a set of principles which those social scientists already endorsed.

The story of the social science testimony in the Brown cases begins with a report which psychologist Kenneth B. Clark prepared in

[1] For a brief summary of the legal implications of this literature see "Grade School Segregation: The Latest Attack on Racial Discrimination," *Yale Law Journal,* VI (May, 1952), 730–44.

[2] See Max Deutscher and Isidor Chein, "The Psychological Effects of Enforced Segregation: A Survey of Social Science Opinion," *Journal of Psychology,* XXVI (October, 1948), 259–87.

1950 for the Midcentury White House Conference on Children and Youth.[3] This report, the first item cited in footnote eleven of the Brown decision, discusses such subjects as the manner in which small children become aware of race and prejudice, the impact of this awareness upon them, and the reactions, especially among minority group children, to exposure to prejudice and discrimination. In preparing this study Clark utilized not only his own extensive research on the subject but that of such authorities as Gunnar Myrdal, Gordon Allport, Max Deutscher and Isidor Chein, Otto Klineberg, Allison Davis, Mary Ellen Goodman, Ruth Horowitz, and others. In his brief, succinct report is found many of the basic ideas which social scientists later presented in testimony in the Briggs, Davis, Brown, and Gebhart cases.

Clark was first concerned with determining the extent to which children between the ages of three and seven are aware of differences in skin color. This he accomplished by two ingenious tests, his famous doll test and a coloring test. In the doll test, the results of which he described several times in testimony in the Brown cases, Clark presented to a group of children four dolls exactly alike except that two were white and two were brown. He told the children: "Give me the white doll." "Give me the colored doll." "Give me the Negro doll." Among three-year-old Negro children more than 75 percent were aware of the difference between white and colored, and Clark concluded that racial awareness was already developing among Negro children by the age of three. Similar experiments among older children indicated that the extent of racial awareness increased until all Negro children are aware of race by age seven.

Having established this fact, Clark carried his experiment a step further, asking each of the children to point out the doll "which is most like you." Thirty-seven percent of the three-year-olds and 87 percent of the seven-year-olds answered correctly, though light-skinned Negroes had more difficulty than dark-skinned ones. Clark then requested of the children: "Give me the doll that you like to play with." "Give me the doll that is the nice doll." "Give me

[3] Kenneth B. Clark, *Effect of Prejudice and Discrimination on Personality Development* (Midcentury White House Conference on Children and Youth, 1951). The report is reprinted as Parts I and II of Clark, *Prejudice and Your Child.* In the discussion which follows, the quotations from the report are from *Prejudice and Your Child,* 17–65.

the doll that looks bad." "Give me the doll that is a nice color."
His purpose here was to determine the extent to which the children associated "white" with "nice" and "Negro" with "bad." He
found that a majority of Negro children at each age indicated an
unmistakable preference for the white dolls and a corresponding
rejection of the brown. The majority was greatest among three-
year-olds, but even seven-year-olds still preferred the dolls with
white skin, thus evidencing in Clark's opinion a desire to identify
themselves with the white dolls. "The fact that young Negro children would prefer to be white," he stated, "reflects their knowledge that society prefers white people. White children are generally
found to prefer their white skin—an indication that they too know
that society likes whites better. It is clear, therefore, that the self-
acceptance or self-rejection found so early in a child's developing
complex of racial ideas reflects the awareness and acceptance of the
prevailing racial attitudes in his community."

To Clark, "prevailing racial attitudes in his community" was
the heart of the matter, the taproot to which he traced all the ill
effects of segregation and discrimination. Children, he wrote, get
their attitudes toward Negroes "not by contact with Negroes but
by contacts with the prevailing attitudes toward Negroes," from
parents, friends, and neighbors, from religious and educational institutions, from the communications media, from social mores in the
community. As the child becomes aware of racial differences he is
made to see racial symbols throughout society. He sees Negroes living in ghettoes, attending dilapidated schools, assigned to segregated sections of public facilities or excluded altogether. He sees
them shunted into the lowliest occupations, working as domestics,
janitors, and menials. He sees them in movies, on television, in
newspapers and comic strips often cast in the role of menial, syco-
phant, or comic. The entire social milieu forces him toward the
conclusion that Negroes *are* inferior and their proper place in society is lowly and dependent. So effective is the process that
Negro children themselves are adversely affected; they, too, often
display negative attitudes toward themselves, their race, and other
Negroes.

According to Clark's findings the warping, stultifying effects of
segregation are already apparent when the five- or six-year-old Negro
child enters a segregated school. By assigning the child to such a

school, society tells him that race is an important factor in education, and this just as he is beginning to comprehend the significance society attaches to race. It is impossible, therefore, or virtually so, for the Negro child to appraise himself except in terms of
racial identity. He is made to understand that his school is segregated because he is a Negro, and he sees for himself that Negro
schools are inferior to those reserved for whites. He thus comes
to understand that society views him and his race with disdain, even
to the extent that whites quarantine their children from him. This
awareness, at so early and impressionable an age, is likely to do
permanent damage to his ego. The standards of society become
"reality" to him, even though "reality" makes him a pariah. His
sense of reality is distorted and his self-respect destroyed. The
seeds of personality damage and emotional disturbance are sown.

Clark supplemented the results of his doll test with a coloring
test designed to further measure the impact of racial awareness
upon young children. After determining that a group of 160 five-to
seven-year-old Negro children understood the color of things (by
having them color a leaf, an apple, an orange, and a mouse), he
gave them the following assignment: "See this [outline drawing of
a] little boy? Let's make believe he is you. Color this little boy the
color that you are." (The wording was appropriately changed for
girls taking the test.) The results were instructive. All the very
light-skinned children colored the figure representing themselves
white or yellow, which Clark interpreted as accurate. However, 15
percent of the children with medium-brown skin and 14 percent of
those with dark brown skin also colored the figures representing
themselves white or yellow or some bizarre color such as red or
green, and this despite the fact that they had correctly colored a
leaf, an apple, an orange, and a mouse. "Their refusal to choose
an appropriate color for themselves," Clark remarked, "was an indication of emotional anxiety and conflict in terms of their own
skin color. Because they wanted to be white, they pretended to be."

Results of the second half of the test were even more striking.
Clark asked the children, "Now this is a little girl [or boy]. Color
her [or him] the color you like little girls [or boys] to be." Forty-
eight percent of the children chose brown as the preferable color,
37 percent white, and 15 percent a bizarre or irrelevant color. Thus
52 percent rejected brown or black as the preferable color, a fig-

ure which Clark interpreted as supporting his findings in the dolls test that 60 percent of the children tested preferred the white doll or rejected the brown one.

In his experiments Clark discovered significant differences in the responses of Northern and Southern Negro children. The differences were quite large and later became the basis of some of the most effective criticism of his tests and of the data he presented in the Brown cases. His interpretation of the differences is therefore important. "Nearly 80 percent of the southern children," he found, "colored their preferences brown, whereas only 36 percent of the northern children did. Furthermore, over 20 percent of the northern children colored their preferences in a bizarre color, while only 5 percent of the southern children did." The two groups also differed in their reactions during the course of the tests. "A record of the spontaneous remarks of the children," wrote Clark, "showed that 82 percent of the southern children spoke as they worked, but only 20 percent of the northern children did so." The latter sometimes reacted with "open demonstrations of intense emotions" when confronted with the choices which the experiment forced upon them, though none of the Southern children showed such reactions. "The Southern children when confronted with this personal dilemma [of making choices based on color] were much more matter-of-fact in their ability to identify themselves with the brown doll" even after they had selected a white doll as the "nice" one or the one they would like most to play with. Some of the Southern children laughed or giggled self-consciously as they identified themselves with the brown doll. "Others merely stated flatly: 'This one. It's a nigger. I'm a nigger.'"

The conclusions Clark drew from these reactions were the focal point of much of the criticism later directed against him.

On the surface, [he wrote] these findings might suggest that northern Negro children suffer more personality damage from racial prejudice and discrimination than southern Negro children. However, this interpretation would seem to be not only superficial but incorrect. The apparent emotional stability of the southern Negro child may be indicative only of the fact that through rigid racial segregation and isolation he has accepted as normal the fact of his inferior social status. Such an acceptance is not symptomatic of a healthy personality. The emotional turmoil revealed by some of the northern children may be interpreted as an attempt on their part to assert some positive aspect of the self.

This conclusion pointedly reveals the dependence of Clark upon his initial assumptions. He was convinced that racial segregation has detrimental psychological effects upon Negroes, effects which manifest themselves as soon as the Negro child becomes aware of racial differences. From the perspective of this conviction, his conclusions regarding the reactions of Northern and Southern Negro children is not only plausible but eminently reasonable. To anyone who rejects his initial assumptions, however, an entirely different conclusion—"that northern Negro children suffer more personality damage from racial prejudice and discrimination than southern Negro children"—is just as reasonable. The value of Clark's findings is due not to the fact that they substantiate the conclusion quoted above—this they do not do in any conclusive, objective way—but to the fact that they corroborate what common sense suggests and experience makes manifest: that the practice of racial segregation in this country is demeaning to Negroes, and an organized means of exploiting and suppressing the race. And as a practical matter, this is what Clark concluded.

Clark's testimony in the Brown cases relied heavily upon his doll and drawing tests. The tests were not designed to determine the specific effects of school segregation as distinct from other forms of segregation; he intended them to show how Negro children are affected by life in a society which is generally prejudiced and segregated. The authority of his report to the Midcentury White House Conference rested upon these tests and upon the scholarship of other authorities, of which he made substantial use. In general, his conclusions may be said to represent the most advanced scholarship on the psychological effects of racial segregation, and his report helped crystallize social science opinion on that subject. Minority group children react to segregation "with deep feelings of inferiority and with a sense of personal humiliation," Clark wrote. "Many of them become confused about their own personal worth" and "develop conflicts with regard to their feelings about themselves. and about the value of the group with which they are identified." As a result they rationalize their internal conflicts in order to accommodate the discrimination and rejection they receive from society with their imperative need for racial and personal respect. The results of their effort vary greatly among individual Negroes, ranging all the way from withdrawal or resignation to hostility and violence. The reactions of an individual depend upon a myriad of personal and environmental factors; in almost every instance, however, it produces damage to the personality and ego.[4]

Clark's stature as a pre-eminent authority on the psychological effects of prejudice and discrimination,[5] his dedication to the principle of racial equality, and the fact that he is himself a Negro [6] made him the logical choice to direct the social science aspects of the Brown cases. In February, 1951, Robert L. Carter of the legal staff of the NAACP asked Clark "whether psychologists had any findings which were relevant to the effects of racial segregation on the personality development of Negro children." [7] The NAACP, Carter explained, "had decided to challenge the constitutionality of

[4] Clark's testimony on the psychological effects of discrimination upon small children is fully supported by the research on the subject since 1951. See Mary Ellen Goodman, *Race Awareness in Young Children* (New York, 1964), 248–68.

[5] See for example the following works by Kenneth B. Clark: "Group Violence: A Preliminary Study of the 1943 Harlem Riot," *Journal of Social Psychology,* XIX (May, 1944), 319–37; "Racial Prejudices among American Minorities," *International Social Science Bulletin,* II (Winter, 1950), 506–13; "Social Science and Social Tensions," *Mental Hygiene,* XXXII (January, 1948), 15–26; Clark and Mamie P. Clark, "The Development of Consciousness of Self and the Emergence of Racial Identification in Negro Pre-school Children," *Journal of Social Psychology,* X (November, 1939), 591–99; Clark and Clark, "Emotional Factors in Racial Identification and Preference in Negro Children," *Journal of Negro Education,* XIX Summer, 1950), 341–50; Clark and Clark, "Racial Identification and Preference in Negro Children," in T. M. Newcomb and E. L. Hartley, (eds.), *Readings in Social Psychology,* (New York, 1947); Clark and Clark, "Segregation as a Factor in the Racial Identification of Negro Pre-School Children," *Journal of Experimental Education,* VIII (1939), 161–63; and Clark and Clark, "Skin Color as a Factor in the Racial Identification of Negro Pre-school Children," *Journal of Social Psychology,* XI (February, 1940), 159–69. See also Clark, *Dark Ghetto, Dilemmas of Social Power* (New York, 1965), a distillation of the report Clark and others prepared for the President's Committee on Juvenile Delinquency and for Harlem Youth Opportunities Unlimited (HARYOU).

[6] Clark was born in the Panama Canal Zone, where his father was employed by the United Fruit Company. At the age of four he moved with his parents, who were West Indians, to New York City. He was educated at Howard and Columbia universities, receiving his Ph.D. in psychology from the latter in 1940. In 1960 he was president of the Society for the Psychological Study of Social Issues, a branch of the American Psychological Association.

[7] This author's account is taken from Kenneth Clark, "Desegregation: An Appraisal of the Evidence," *Journal of Social Issues,* IX (No. 4, 1953), 1–76; Clark, "The Role of the Social Sciences in Desegregation," Appendix V of *Prejudice and Your Child,* 207–15; and Clark, "The Social Scientist as an Expert Witness in Civil Rights Litigation," *Social Problems,* I (June, 1953), 5–10.

state laws which required or permitted racial segregation in the public schools." Specifically, the Association would challenge the Plessy decision and the separate-but-equal doctrine on grounds that segregated facilities are inherently unequal, that social scientists have empirically demonstrated the detrimental effects of racial segregation, and that the concensus of social science opinion is that racial segregation is unjustifiable. Carter invited Clark to collaborate with the NAACP legal staff "in planning for the most effective use of social psychologists and other social scientists in the courts of first instance and appeal." His effort was fourfold: to marshal all relevant social science data and opinion, to assist in making the best use of those data and that opinion, to collect information on previous instances of racial integration in order to determine whether and under what conditions integration can be accomplished peacefully and without lowering educational standards, and to arrange for expert testimony by appropriate authorities in the several cases.

Clark was assisted in his tasks by some of the nation's foremost social scientists. Among those who testified in one or more of the cases were Clark's wife Mamie, a psychologist in her own right; psychologists David Krech of the University of California, Helen Trager and Brewster Smith of Vassar, Alfred McClung Lee of Brooklyn College, Isidor Chein of New York University and the American Jewish Conference, and Otto Klineberg of Columbia; sociologists John J. Kane of Notre Dame University, Frederick B. Parker of the University of Delaware, and Kenneth Morland of William and Mary College; and psychiatrist Frederick Wertham. Other expert witnesses included Horace B. English of Ohio State University, Wilbur B. Brookover of Michigan State University, Louisa Holt of the University of Kansas and the Menninger Clinic, Bettie Belk of the Workshop in Human Relations at the University of Kansas City, Jerome S. Brunner of Harvard, and George Gorham Lane of the University of Delaware.

In each of the cases covered by the Brown decision, there was lengthy testimony by social scientists and educators, so that given in one case necessarily overlaps or repeats that in the others. The most comprehensive presentation of evidence was made in the Briggs and Davis cases, and a brief review of those cases will indicate the nature and scope of the testimony as a whole.

The case of *Briggs v. Elliott* [8] grew out of the efforts of Negroes in Clarendon County, South Carolina, to improve the educational facilities available to their children. Located in the heart of the South Carolina low country, Clarendon County is typical of those areas of the deep South where Negroes are most heavily concentrated. By attacking school segregation in this black belt country, the NAACP was challenging the Southern way of life at its very roots. In one respect the Briggs case was an assault upon school segregation in its most vulnerable area, for the Negro schools of Clarendon County met none of the standards which the Supreme Court had enunciated in the Sweatt and McLaurin decisions, nor indeed of the standards implicit in the separate-but-equal principle itself. In other respects, however, the institutions and customs of segregation were nowhere stronger or better protected than in Clarendon County or in School District No. 22, the district directly involved in the Briggs suit. The people of Clarendon County, or the white minority at least, were united to a man in their determination to protect racial segregation, which they rightly regarded as the cornerstone of their way of life. To outsiders, they presented the appearance of a monolith determined to resist anything which might alter the pattern of race relations in their community. In 1955 *The Nation* described the county as a place where whites "talk of Citizens' Councils and the 'economic squeeze,' where the Ku Klux Klan met with Bryant Bowles, head of the National Association for the Advancement of White People, as a featured speaker, where integration is freely referred to as a 'Communist-Catholic-Jewish plot,' where a place of business displays the latest newspaper clippings showing crimes of Negro against white, where private citizens discuss the hated Ford Foundation along with the price of tobacco, where the NAACP has only a small chapter and where you hunt long and hard for a defender of the Negro." [9] A measure of the determination—and success—of Clarendon County whites is the fact that their schools, including those of District No. 22, remained segregated until 1965, ten years after the District was enjoined by the federal courts from discriminating against Negro pupils on the basis of

---

[8] 98 F. Supp. 529 (E.D. S.C. 1951).

[9] Quoted in Howard H. Quint, *Profile in Black and White* (Washington, 1958), 12–13.

race. In the fall of 1965 six Negro children finally "integrated" the white schools of District 22. [10]

In 1951 when the Briggs case began its long journey through the federal courts, the population of Clarendon County was approximately 31,000, of which perhaps 23,000 were Negroes. Public school enrollment totaled 6,531 Negroes and 2,375 whites, though expenditures for the last school year had been $395,329 for white schools and $282,950 for Negro schools,[11] which amounted to approximately $166 for each white student and $43 for each Negro. In District No. 22, 298 white and 2,259 Negro students were enrolled in 1951. The inferiority of Negro schools in the district was glaring, and the first objective of the Briggs suit—to demonstrate the physical inequality of Negro schools—was easily achieved. The point, in fact, was not contested by attorneys for South Carolina and District No. 22. Instead, they admitted the inequality and based their defense upon the fact that the state and district had already undertaken an emergency construction program to bring Negro schools up to white standards.

The NAACP, however, had a more fundamental objective, which was to show that racial segregation in public education is in and of itself psychologically damaging to Negro children and segregated Negro schools are thus per se inferior to white schools. This, attorneys for the state and school district would not concede.

The chief object of the social science testimony in the case was to prove this contention. Kenneth Clark testified first and at greater length than any other expert witness in the Briggs case.[12] He introduced the most significant of the social science arguments against school segregation, and presented the data he had discussed in his report to the Midcentury White House Conference on Children and Youth. "I have reached the conclusion," he testified, "that discrimination, prejudice and segregation have definitely detrimental effects on the personality development of the Negro child. The essence of this detrimental effect is a confusion in the child's concept of his own self-esteem—basic feelings of inferiority, conflict, confusion in

10 James Leeson, "Desegregation," *Southern Education Report*, I (September-October, 1965) , 32.

11 Quint, *Profile in Black and White*, 12.

12 For Clark's testimony see *Briggs v. Elliott*, 98 F. Supp. 529 (E.D. S.C. 1951) , transcript of record, in transcript of *Brown v. Board of Education*, 347 U.S. 483 (1954) .

the self-image, resentment, hostility towards himself, hostility towards whites, . . [or] a desire to resolve his basic conflict by sometimes escaping or withdrawing."

Clark was careful to point out that this and his other observations were not his alone. Anticipating later charges that he was a special pleader who allowed personal prejudices to interfere with his scientific detachment, he showed convincingly that an overwhelming majority of social scientists in this country believe that educational segregation is psychologically harmful to Negro children. In 1948 a survey of the attitudes of social scientists on this point was made by psychologists Max Deutscher and Isidor Chein.[13] Their survey, which the Supreme Court cited in footnote eleven to the Brown decision, was based upon responses of 517 anthropologists, sociologists, and psychologists to questionnaires designed to determine their attitudes toward racial discrimination. They were asked whether in their opinion "enforced segregation" even with equal facilities had "detrimental psychological effects" upon Negroes and/or whites. Ninety percent replied that in their opinion enforced segregation was harmful to Negroes, and 83 percent thought it also was harmful to whites. The results were remarkably consistent for sociologist, psychologists, and anthropologists—Southerners and non-Southerners. "Substantial majorities of social scientists who may be said to have competence with regard to the matters under inquiry," Deutscher and Chein wrote, "agree that enforced segregation is psychologically detrimental to both the segregated and enforcing groups even when equal facilities are provided." [14]

Clark also had responsibility for answering specific objections to the social science testimony in the Brown cases. One of the most plausible arguments which segregationists made against the testimony was that witnesses spoke in such general terms that their testimony failed to meet minimum standards of relevancy and admissibility. The witnesses spoke of the ill effects of segregation upon Negroes in general or upon "the Negro" in abstract, but did

---

13 Deutscher and Chein, "The Psychological Effects of Enforced Segregation"; and Chein, "What Are the Psychological Effects of Segregation Under Conditions of Equal Facilities?" *International Journal of Opinion and Attitude Research,* III (Summer, 1949) , 229–34.

14 Deutscher and Chein, "The Psychological Effects of Enforced Segregation," 268.

not, charged segregationists, prove that individual plaintiffs had suffered specific, demonstrable damage from *de jure* school segregation. In making this charge, segregationists were insisting that social science evidence be narrowly construed by the courts and that it be required to meet the same tests of relevancy and admissibility as evidence in a criminal prosecution. In this manner they sought to have it thrown out altogether or, failing this, to have its usefulness to the NAACP severely restricted. The latter could be achieved by having the court reject all social science testimony not directly relating to specific injuries to individual plaintiffs. Under such a procedure an order admitting individual Negro plaintiffs to white schools would not apply to other Negroes. It would instead require each Negro who sought admission to a white or integrated school to demonstrate in court specific injuries which he had personally suffered from segregated education. Such a ruling would be virtually worthless to Negroes and would neutralize almost all the testimony of the social scientists.

To answer the segregationists on this point, Clark insisted repeatedly that the particular effects of school segregation could not be isolated from the effects of other forms of segregation. The personality of a segregated child, he pointed out, is molded not by his educational experiences alone, but by the totality of his environment, by all the varied influences touching his life. A child's earliest experiences are his most important insofar as lasting impressions are concerned, and the Negro child suffers the ill effects of segregation long before he enters a segregated school. Segregated education is only one facet of life in a segregated society. The major evil is the general system of segregation, not the specific practice of segregated schools. This emphasis upon the ill effects of the broader issue rather than the narrower one was characteristic of much of the social science testimony of the Brown cases, and it suggests the NAACP was fighting segregation itself and not just segregation in public schools. But surely, countered segregationists, local school boards cannot be held responsible for the effects of community customs and practices, even though those customs and practices might adversely affect the child's personality development and his ability to learn in school.

Attorneys for the NAACP rejected the arguments of segregationists on these points, and insisted instead that the relevancy and admissibility of social science testimony be construed in the broadest possible way. But they also attempted to show that the ill effects of segregation, including segregated education, are particular and individual as well as general. A few days before he testified in the Briggs case, Clark conducted one of his doll and coloring experiments upon the Negro children involved in the case. He asked sixteen children between the ages of six and nine the same questions he had asked in earlier experiments. Each of the children correctly identified the white and Negro dolls, and their reactions to the dolls were similar to those of other children Clark had tested. Ten of the sixteen chose the white doll as preferable to the colored; eleven selected the brown doll as "bad" and only one chose the white doll as "bad." (The others made no choice.) The experiment indicated, or was so interpreted by Clark, that segregation had produced in the children "basic confusion" about themselves and conflict in their self-images. When asked to color a figure representing herself, one of the darkest of the children colored it flesh colored, and seven of the sixteen children picked the white doll as the doll most like themselves. "This must be seen," said Clark, "as a concrete illustration of the degree to which the pleasures which these children sensed against being brown forced them to evade reality—to escape the reality which seems too over-burdening or too threatening to them." He added later, "The conclusion which I was forced to reach was that these children in Clarendon County, like other human beings who are subjected to an obviously inferior status . . . have been definitely harmed in the development of their personalities; that the signs of instability . . . are clear, and . . . that every psychologist would accept and interpret these signs as such." [15]

The significance of Clark's testimony in the Briggs case is apparent in the Brown decision. The Supreme Court incorporated many of his views in the decision, and cited his works and those of other authorities to whom he referred in his testimony. For this reason it is significant that the attorneys for South Carolina and School District No. 22 made no effort to rebut his testimony through witnesses of their own. Their only rebuttal witness was E. R. Crow, superintendent of schools in Sumter County, South Carolina, and chairman of the State Education Finance Commission, an agency recently created to equalize the educational facilities of the two

15 *Briggs v. Elliott,* transcript of testimony, 86, 127.

races. Crow was not a psychologist but he did have considerable experience as a public school administrator. He was obviously intended to be a "practical" spokesman who recognized the impossibility of integrating the schools of South Carolina and who therefore contrasted sharply with the "academic" and inexperienced, and thus impractical, Clark.

This illustrated one of the major devices of defense attorneys in the Brown cases—to attempt to discredit the social science testimony on grounds that the witnesses had no experience in the public schools of the South and could not therefore understand the practical problems of school administration and policy formulation. Tolerance, equality, and brotherhood might be praiseworthy principles, argued the attorneys, but they present insurmountable problems to Southern school officials if they can be achieved only through racial integration. The public schools depend upon public support, they continued, and the arbitrary imposition of racial integration without regard to popular feelings would undermine that support and might even destroy the school system. "The existence of the feeling of separateness between the races of this state," Crow testified, "would make it such that it would be impossible to have peaceable association with each other in the public schools." [16]

Clark's testimony was supplemented by that of David Krech, who testified concerning the psychological consequences of legalized segregation. Through legalized segregation, Krech declared, society defines the individual Negro and his legal rights in racial terms and tells him thereby that race is a factor of overriding significance in life. The message, however, is not restricted to Negroes. It is made equally clear to whites that theirs is the preferred race, the superior race which must be protected from the contamination which comes from associating with Negroes. Both races are made to consider racial factors pre-eminent, and whites especially are inculcated with feelings of racial prejudice. In fact, Krech suggested, legalized segregation is the single most important source of racial prejudice and of the belief among whites in racial inequality. "No one," he declared, "unless he is mentally diseased . . . can maintain any attitude or belief unless there are some objective supports for that belief. . . . Legal segregation, because it is legal, because it is

[16] *Briggs v. Elliott,* transcript of testimony, 113.

obvious to everyone, gives . . . environmental support for the belief that Negroes are in some way different from and inferior to
white people, and that in turn . . . supports and strengthens
beliefs of racial difference [and] racial inferiority." Segregation in
the public schools is an especially important facet of legal segregation for it separates white and Negro children at a critical point
in their psychological development. Just as they begin to form
views of the world and of the people in it, they are placed in
an artificial situation. They come to look upon themselves as a
people apart, and to view persons of the other race not as individuals but as members of a strange and alien group. The result
is distortion—and prejudice. Psychologists have long since given up
the notion that IQ is independent of education and experience, said
Krech in illustrating his point. Inadequate education, which is implicit in segregation, especially for Negroes, results in a lower (or
less well developed) IQ and in lesser ability to cope with the problems of life. Through segregated education "we build into the
Negro the very characteristics, not only intellectual, but also personality characteristics, which we then use to justify prejudice." [17]

These ideas were further developed by Helen Trager of Vassar
College.[18] Mrs. Trager, an educational psychologist, had conducted
extensive tests and interviews in Philadelphia with white and
Negro children between the ages of five and eight, and her testimony was a discussion of her research. She had found children of
both races aware of racial differences by age five, but she noted
that this awareness produced different reactions among whites and
Negroes. White children talked freely about race and race differences; Negro children on the other hand showed "obvious discomfort" discussing these subjects, and accordingly sought to avoid
them. Both groups, however, "saw being Negro as a disadvantage." White children recognized that theirs is the preferred group
in American society, and they answered "yes" when asked if they
thought Negroes would prefer to be white. Negro children dis-
played unmistakable signs of conflict and tension on this point,
and answered Mrs. Trager's query by stating "that Negro children

17 *Briggs v. Elliott,* transcript of testimony, 133–34.
18 *Briggs v. Elliott,* transcript of testimony, 138–47. For more detailed discussion of her research see Helen G. Trager and M. R. Yarrow, *They Learn What
They Live: Prejudice in Young Children* (New York, 1952).

liked to be Negro but that Negro children would [also] like to be white." To Mrs. Trager this contradiction seemed "terribly important," representing as it did "a conflict and an inability to accept one's own group and yet [manifesting] the psychological need to accept what one is."

Interestingly enough, as Mrs. Trager pointed out, both white and Negro children understood "Negro" as meaning the same thing: "that you are not liked by people, that you won't be asked to play, that you won't be allowed to do things that other children can do." Both groups had fears and misconceptions about each other, and gave "the weirdest, and most frightening and inaccurate explanations" of the meaning of "race." But unlike the white children, the Negro children "showed a tendency to expect rejection," and the expectation increased sharply between ages five and eight. "At 5 a Negro child would indicate that he expected Negroes not to be accepted and would give as the reason 'Because he isn't white,' or 'Because he is black,' or using the vernacular 'Because he is a nigger.' " At eight, however, explanations were "evasive, avoidant," and accompanied by definite feelings of discomfort. Now the explanations were: "Because he can't play the way they can"; "because he doesn't live near them"; but not "because he is colored." Mrs. Trager concluded that segregation and discrimination frustrated the Negro child's basic emotional need for self-respect. "A child who expects to be rejected," she declared, "who sees his group held in low esteem, is not going to function well[.] He is not going to be a fully developed child[.] He will be withdrawn, or aggressive in order to win the acceptance he doesn't get."

The testimony in the Briggs case had little effect upon the three federal judges who heard it. Chief Judge John J. Parker of North Carolina, whom Herbert Hoover once nominated for the Supreme Court only to have the nomination rejected by the Senate in part because of NAACP opposition, and Judge George Bell Timmerman of South Carolina, whose son was later governor of that state, rejected the plea of Negro plaintiffs. They ruled that segregation in the public schools of Clarendon County did not violate the Fourteenth Amendment, now that efforts were underway to bring the physical facilities of Negro schools up to the standards of those available to whites. The third member of the Court, J.

Waties Waring, also a South Carolinian, but one who had a record of decisions favorable to Negroes, dissented vigorously.[19]

Although the social science testimony made little impression upon the court, attorneys for both the NAACP and South Carolina dealt with the testimony at length in their briefs to the Supreme Court, to which the NAACP promptly appealed the lower court's decision. The appellees' brief,[20] which the South Carolinians submitted to the high court, is perhaps the earliest statement of the ideas of scientific racism which the Brown decision helped to crystallize. Despite their failure to call expert witnesses of their own, the South Carolina attorneys now challenged the social science testimony, and did so vigorously. This in itself was noteworthy, for it indicated they now considered the testimony important and feared its impact upon the Supreme Court. Their challenge centered largely around the contentions that (1) the witnesses had no responsibility for decisions in educational policies and no experience in the public schools of South Carolina or the South, (2) the empirical data offered to the court did not prove that public school segregation was psychologically and educationally detrimental to Negro children, and (3) spokesmen who understand racial mores in the South recognize that large-scale integration of the public schools is impossible, even undesirable, and a court order to integrate would likely destroy the public school system there.

The South Carolina attorneys drew a distinction between the general effects of racial segregation and the specific effects of *de jure* school segregation, and asked the Court to concern itself only with the latter. They argued, for example, that the testimony of Mrs. Trager, which was based upon studies made in Philadelphia, was thus irrelevant to the issues in the Briggs case, for the public schools of Philadelphia were by law integrated.

[19] "From their testimony," Waring wrote in his dissent in reference to the NAACP witnesses, "it was clearly apparent, as it should be to any thoughtful person, irrespective of having such expert testimony, that segregation in education can never produce equality and that it is an evil that must be eradicated. This case presents the matter clearly for adjudication and I am of the opinion that all the legal guideposts, expert testimony, common sense, and reason point unerringly to the conclusion that the system of segregation in education adopted and practiced in the State of South Carolina must go and must go now."

"*Segregation is per se inequality.*" *Briggs v. Elliott,* transcript of record, 206–08.

[20] Brief for Appellees, No. 2 *(Briggs v. Elliott),* transcript of *Brown v. Board of Education* 347 U.S. 483 (1954).

They dealt with the testimony of Kenneth Clark at greater length. The crucial point of Clark's testimony was his contention that the "symptoms" which his doll tests and interviews revealed among Negro children demonstrated the ill effects of segregation. Here the appellees challenged Clark by quoting one of his own studies against him.[21] In analyzing the results of a study he and his wife had made a few years previously, Clark had offered a detailed comparison of the reactions of Northern and Southern Negro children to his tests, and here as elsewhere had found some differences. In this instance 69 percent of the Southern children identified themselves with the colored doll, compared to 61 percent of the Northern children. Seventy-two percent of the Northerners chose the white doll as "nice," compared to 52 percent of the Southerners. Seventy-one percent of the Northerners likewise chose the colored doll as "bad," compared to 49 percent of the Southerners, and 63 percent of the former chose white as the "nice" color, compared to 57 percent of the latter. To the South Carolinians these figures indicated "that Negro children in the South are healthier psychologically speaking than those of the North."

Moreover, the "conflicts" which Clark found in Negro children in Clarendon County, continued appellees, were unrelated, except in an indirect and tangential way, to school segregation. "Negro children are already aware of race and accompanying value judgments at the preschool age," and the possibility "that the schools play an initiating role in creating psychological conflicts" is thus eliminated. Nevertheless, they continued, "the age of starting school is a crucial one in the development of the child's ego structure." At this time the child "is especially sensitive to the accepted social values of his larger environment, because he seeks group identification and personal self-esteem," and it is questionable whether a Negro child, at such a tender age, should be forced into the tense and uncertain atmosphere of an integrated school, there to compete with white children whom he more likely than not regards as his superiors. Such an issue, the South Carolinians suggested, is "fraught with difficulty" and requires "the most careful and painstaking consideration, necessarily involving study of the accumulated data which the most thorough, impartial and scientific research can supply." It must be resolved in the child's best

21 Clark and Clark, "Racial Identification and Preferences in Negro Children."

interest and without regard for impractical theorists or outside pressure groups. It is an issue "for the legislative and educational authorities of the state to decide and not for the courts."

On these points the South Carolina attorneys made their most effective criticisms of the social science testimony. They did not prove the testimony false nor demonstrate empirically that their own position was valid, and in discussing the problems of race relations they treated the symptoms rather than the malady itself. They did, however, point out some of the limitations of the testimony. They based their arguments largely upon two contentions, each of which is partially valid: that empirical data on the psychological effects of segregation are piecemeal and inconclusive, and that scientific research on the subject is still experimental and likely to be influenced by the researcher's prejudices. In other words, after attacking the social science testimony as internally contradictory, they suggested it was not what it appeared on the surface to be. The implication was that the witnesses, each of whom was committed to the principle of racial integration, had allowed this commitment to influence their research and prejudice their conclusions. The issue, they suggested, is still open; the conclusions of expert witnesses are only their opinions and entitled to consideration on that basis alone. The witnesses might have acted from the loftiest of motives and might be convinced that their testimony is valid, but this is not reason enough to overturn the legal basis of the South's racial policies.

To support their position the attorneys summoned "the opinion and judgment of leading sociologists and educators who, unlike the witnesses for appellants, have . . . years of research, observation, and practical experience in states where the two races live in the same area in great numbers." This seemed to promise that they would cite authorities of their own, matching in stature and reputation those who testified for the NAACP, but such was not the case—with one notable exception. The "leading sociologists and educators" turned out to be (other than E. R. Crow, who was mentioned previously, and Howard Odum, who was indeed a leading sociologist and is discussed below) Frank P. Graham, then president of the University of North Carolina; Colgate W. Darden, former governor of Virginia and in 1951 president of the University of Virginia; Hodding Carter, the Mississippi author and newspaper editor; and, surprisingly, W. E. B. Du Bois and Gunnar Myrdal.[22]

Graham, Darden, and Carter, especially Graham and Carter, were well known throughout the nation as Southern liberals on racial matters and as representatives of the best elements in public life in the South. As such, their opinions carried weight among liberals and moderates outside the South, and to quote them was an effective move on the part of appellees, even though none of the three was a scientist or social scientist. According to a statement by Graham, race relations in the South are expressed in social mores which reflect history, the large number of Negroes in the section, racial differences, a "universal consciousness of kind," and "the economic competition of the low income groups." These mores, he admitted, sometimes produce discrimination against Negroes, a fact he deplored, but improvement can be effected only by "a new emphasis on the influence of religion, education, personal kindness, decent respect for the human dignity of persons, and voluntary cooperation of people of good will for better relations in the local communities, in the long haul of the generations for justice on this earth." Hodding Carter added in a similar vein, "It will be tragic for the South, for the Negro and the nation itself if the government should enact and attempt to enforce any laws or Supreme Court decisions that would open the South's public schools and public gathering places to the Negro. The one saving factor would be the Southern Negro's own common sense refusal to implement the law." The Southern Negro, Carter continued, "by and large, does not want an end to segregation in itself any more than does the Southern white man."

The comments reflect the viewpoint of many Southern white liberals in 1951 and pointedly illustrate the dilemma in which men of liberal views have often found themselves in the South. Graham and Carter and thousands of other Southern whites like them were (and are) men of good will with a sincere interest in improving

[22] The appellees quoted a statement by Myrdal that Negroes were divided among themselves on questions of school integration, and cited an article in which Du Bois had suggested that Negro children might suffer more from the hostile atmosphere of integrated schools than from inferior facilities in Jim Crow schools. See Gunnar Myrdal, *An American Dilemma* (New York, 1944), 901–02; and W. E. B. Du Bois, "Does the Negro Need Separate Schools?" *Journal of Negro Education*, IV (July, 1935), 325–35.

race relations and bettering the condition of Negroes in their region. Historically, however, the liberal Southerner has been particularly vulnerable to attack from segregationists. In proposing any change in race relations or the status of Negroes, he runs the risk of losing whatever influence in public life he might have. He has therefore been forced to speak the language of moderation and endorse the larger policy of segregation in order to achieve the lesser goal of improving the Negro's status. The expediency might well have been necessary, and Negroes would certainly have benefited had the views of Graham and Carter become public policy in the South. It is nevertheless significant that neither man criticized segregation per se, and the result was that the segregationist attorneys were able to quote such relatively enlightened men as Graham and Carter in defending racial segregation.

The facility with which segregationists could use the rhetoric of Southern moderates was strikingly illustrated by an address which Howard W. Odum delivered to the Southern Sociological Congress in April, 1951, and from which appellees quoted at length. Dr. Odum, who was Kenan Professor of Sociology at the University of North Carolina and one of the nation's most renowned and respected social scientists, was widely recognized as one of the South's most enlightened spokesmen on racial matters.

He had for a long time promoted interracial cooperation and had actively sought to improve the status and opportunities of Negroes in the South. But for whatever reason, either from expediency or conviction, Odum defended racial segregation in much the same tone as Graham and Carter had done. The appellees' attorneys were much impressed not only with Odum's academic and professional stature but with his racial views as well. They referred to his "acknowledged freedom from anything which could even remotely be suggested as prejudice or preconceived approach to racial questions," and described him as "the best informed authority in the country on southern racial matters."

In the address from which the attorneys quoted, Odum urged a four-point program concerning education and race relations in the South: (1) "remedy the inexcusable situation with reference to brutalities, injustices, inequalities and discrimination"; (2) adopt "Operation Equal Opportunity" to equalize white and Negro schools; (3) "provide immediately for non-segregation in all university education on the graduate and professional level"; and

(4) "move judiciously but speedily toward agenda for negotiations and specifications for future achievement on the total front." But lest Negroes and integrationists read too much into his program, Odum cautioned them to recognize the South's "cumulative racial and conflict heritage," and remember Nehru's admonition that "no solution which is not acceptable to the large masses of the people can have any possible enduring quality." It was such passages as these which segregationists found most appealing in Odum's address. To those who urged militancy upon Southern Negroes or demanded that the Supreme Court outlaw racial segregation, Odum addressed this warning:

> If there are those who hold that the South, having too many people of both races, would profit by a certain amount of violent revolution and slaughter of the people, as I have heard prominent metropolitan leaders say, that might be a democratic prerequisite; but to urge the Supreme Court to set the incidence of such a conflict is something else. . . .
>
> Anyone who is not naive enough to try to repeal the laws of individuation, of personality, of freedom, of opportunity, of classification, knows that the major construct [in Southern race policy] is not segregation *or* non-segregation but non-segregation *and* segregation, developed through total processes of interaction and growth, of means and ends, of moral imperatives and administrative reality.

But despite its strong roots in the past, the South, Odum continued, is undergoing a profound though gradual change, and the Southerner's task is to accommodate himself and his section to the change with the least difficulty. The "Southern compound bi-racial culture," he said, is slowly giving way to the "American complex integrated multicultured society," but this is being accomplished without a radical upheaval and does not prevent Southerners from salvaging the best elements in their traditional way of life. "Such a conversion," Odum declared, "brings with it no more compulsion or specifications for negating the facets of race and ethnic minorities, supreme in whatever personality and cultural loyalties they may wish. Such a conversion automatically, as in any organic structure or process, carries with it the inevitable continuity of separateness, autonomy, and segregation inherent in not only the American ideal but in all the differential-groups to have a say in how they shall integrate themselves in the new world society." In plain language this means that racial segregation and white supremacy will continue in the South, even though modifications in traditional practices will occur.

As this résumé indicates, the appellees' effort to refute the social science testimony in the Briggs case was uneven and incomplete. Whatever the limitations of the testimony of Clark and his collaborators, it was vastly more authoritative than the effort made by segregationists to refute it. In fact, the appellees' attorneys made poor use of the social science materials which favored their own position. At the time of the Briggs hearing there were a number of academic social scientists who believed racial segregation preferable to integration and who perhaps would have testified in behalf of this belief. The failure to call them was a gross error of judgment and can be explained in only one way—the state and local officials who handled the case considered the social science testimony less important than legal precedents. They proceeded on the assumption that the law narrowly construed was on their side. They miscalculated, and the eventual disposition of the case by the Supreme Court illustrates the magnitude of their miscalculation. (But perhaps the Supreme Court also miscalculated, for the public schools of Clarendon County are for all practical purposes still segregated today.)

3

THE DAVIS CASE AND THE APPEAL

The case of *Davis v. County School Board of Prince Edward County, Virginia*,[1] illustrates other features of the assault upon school segregation through the use of social science. Like Clarendon County, Prince Edward County was a part of the black belt, and the racial attitudes there were those of the deep South. In Prince Edward and surrounding counties "massive resistance" to racial integration was always more than a slogan; it was a way of life and

[1] *Davis v. Country School Board of Prince Edward County*, 103 F. Supp. 337 (E.D. Va. 1951).

a policy literally employed. According to the census of 1950, 45 percent of the population of Prince Edward County were Negroes, and the percentage of Negro children in the public schools was even higher. Like everything else in the county, the schools were rigidly segregated, and Negroes were relegated to an inferior status. Negro schools were grossly inferior to those of whites, and interracial tensions had recently increased because of white intransigence in the face of Negro demands for better schools. On one occasion Negro students had undertaken a short-lived boycott of their schools, and the immediate occasion for filing the Davis suit was the decision not to construct a new Negro high school in the county.

There were, however, important differences between the Briggs and Davis cases. The former involved segregation in elementary school, whereas the latter concerned segregation at the secondary level. More important for present purposes, attorneys for Virginia and Prince Edward County took the social science testimony much more seriously than had the South Carolinians. From the beginning they seem to have sensed that the NAACP was mounting a meaningful assault upon the legal and constitutional bases of segregation, and not the least of the reasons for their concern was the social science testimony in the case. As a result, they made a much greater effort to refute the testimony, first by rigorous cross-examination of each of the witnesses, and then by calling witnesses of their own. To a greater extent than any of the other cases covered by the Brown decision, the Davis case involved a systematic presentation of social science evidence by both sides. After the Brown decision was issued, segregationists charged repeatedly that the Supreme Court decided the cases without considering the evidence supporting segregation. The charge is only partially true. It is true that the segregationists' case was not presented as carefully or as thoroughly as was the integrationists', but their case was presented in the Davis testimony, and by witnesses of their own choosing.

Brewster Smith, chairman of the psychology department at Vassar, was one of the principal NAACP witnesses in the Davis case. He testified concerning racial intelligence and the relationship between race and learning ability.[2] This relationship was especially im-

2 *Davis v. County School Board of Prince Edward County,* transcript of testimony, 180ff.

portant to segregationists because of their conviction that Negroes are inferior to whites in intelligence and have less ability to learn in school. Smith disputed the idea, declaring that race and color are irrelevant to learning ability. He pointed out that there is complete overlap in the distribution of intelligence and aptitude among races and emphasized that individual differences within each race are vastly larger than differences in racial averages. Nevertheless, racial differences as measured by intelligence tests do exist, but Smith accounted for them by the "environmental handicap to which the Negro group has been subjected as a result of segregation, discrimination, and prejudice." This handicap, he suggested, comes not from school segregation alone, but from the total social environment, which impairs the Negro's intellectual and educational development. "The society in which we live, with its values, with its sources of recognition and prestige, is predominantly a white society," Smith explained. "Any pattern of human relationships that involves cutting off a segment of the group, the Negro, from full participation in this predominantly white culture that we live in, with its historical continuity of values, is, in itself bound to be impoverishing as far as the intellectual and educational development of the individual is concerned." As a result of the isolation of the Negro child from the general community, his cultural horizons are restricted, and his incentive to learn and his intellectual curiosity are less well developed than those of the white child. He has less reason to discipline himself, to sacrifice today for rewards tomorrow. He concludes that the rewards go to the white man, and in so doing surrenders to the system and becomes the kind of individual described in the racist stereotype—"stupid, illiterate, apathetic, [and] happy-go-lucky."

Smith was cross-examined at length. Attorneys for the state made much of the fact that IQ tests almost invariably show significant average differences between whites and Negroes. They also attempted to invert Smith's statement that segregation results in personality distortions among Negroes and use it for their own purposes. Forced integration, they suggested, might be just as much an insult to the integrity and self-respect of white children as forced segregation is to Negroes. This suggestion, which Smith rejected, was raised on many occasions by segregationists, but they offered no evidence other than personal surmises to substantiate it. (It would probably be even more difficult to prove objectively than the contention that segregation is psychologically harmful to Negroes.) It was a point segregationists reached by deduction, but through faulty logic, for they ignored the fact that segregation means one thing to whites and something entirely different to Negroes. Ironically, the point was premised upon a fact which Smith had gone to great lengths to prove—that segregation is an expression of the white man's contempt for Negroes. More significantly, it indicated that segregationists and integrationists had basically different views of the issues in the Davis case. The NAACP obviously considered the case as part of a general attack upon racial segregation in American society and upon the legal props which support it. The state of Virginia, however, like the state of South Carolina in the Briggs case, regarded the issue as no more than whether racial segregation should continue in the public schools of one school district in the state. The NAACP expected that victory in the Brown cases would signal the beginning of the end of segregation as a way of life; attorneys for Virginia and South Carolina clearly expected segregation to continue as the general policy in the South regardless of the outcome of the Davis and Briggs cases. This difference explains, in part at least, why the issues which the social scientists raised were not discussed or debated more effectively, why no real dialogue ever developed between the two sides in either of the cases. There was no agreement on fundamental issues, and, without this, attorneys for the two sides could do no more than argue at each other. The statement that enforced segregation would be injurious to the personalities of white children was meaningless from the integrationists' view of the issues in the case, but it was full of meaning for segregationists.

In cross-examining Smith, the attorneys raised another of the segregationists' major arguments, that court-ordered integration would be no more effective than national prohibition had been in the 1920's. They declared that an overwhelming majority of the people of Virginia were opposed to integrating the public schools, and would simply but massively refuse to obey a court order to that effect. And this, they warned, would bring the courts and the law itself into disrepute. Smith was unimpressed by this reasoning. The research of social scientists upon this point, he said, tends to show that peaceful integration can be accomplished, and in fact has been accomplished, even where a high degree of prejudice exists, provided there is a willingness on the part of state and local authorities to enforce the law firmly and impartially.[3] Even among prejudiced persons, there "is a tendency to accept directions of authority, to accept the convictions imposed by those who are regarded as superior." If, therefore, "with full authority of the court, with full and sincere backing of the state authorities, segregation were ruled . . . unconstitutional," Smith concluded, "I would say that the more highly prejudiced individual would be likely to fall in line and comply." [4]

Isidor Chein of the American Jewish Congress and co-author with Max Deutscher of the major study of the attitudes of social scientists toward racial segregation, followed Smith to the witness stand. Dr. Chein (a Ph.D. in psychology from Columbia) testified concerning the study he and Max Deutscher had made of the attitudes of social scientists toward racial segregation.[5] He discussed the ill effects of segregation upon personality, emphasizing its effects upon whites as well as Negroes. In his view segregation inflicted as much personality damage upon whites as upon Negroes, though of a different sort. The treatment accorded Negroes in a segregated society, he suggested, generates in many whites an exaggerated, unreal feeling of their own superiority and makes then contemptuous of Negroes. At the same time, it produces in them a sense of guilt and uneasiness. The result is a "dissociation of moral values," a compartmentalization of values which enables an individual committed to the democratic, egalitarian rhetoric of American life and the humanitarianism of New Testament Christianity to act and feel toward Negroes as a segregated society demands. This weakens the moral system not merely in an ethical sense but "in terms of the control which the individual has which sustains his relationship to

[3] The most convenient of these studies is by Kenneth Clark and others and is Part III of "Desegregation: An Appraisal of the Evidence," 13–68.

[4] It is perhaps appropriate to note here that events since 1954 have generally borne Smith out. The processes of integration have almost invariably worked smoothly where there has been a determination by state and local officials to uphold law and order, as in Louisville, Atlanta, Charlotte, and Miami. Violence has tended to develop only where officials themselves overtly or covertly condoned defiance, as in Little Rock, New Orleans, Oxford, and Birmingham. The analogy between prohibition and integration, which seemed at first so valid, has proven less and less accurate in recent years. Integration as the law of the land is today winning increasing acceptance among the American people, including white Southerners. Time and events are proving Smith's assessment more valid than that of the Virginia attorneys.

[5] *Davis v. County School Board of Prince Edward County,* transcript of testimony, 209ff.

authority." As a child he is told by the authority of the state that segregation is desirable and necessary, and therefore morally right, and if he has a basic respect for and loyalty to the state he must incorporate this "fact" into his value system. At this point the distortion of moral and ethical values crystallizes.

The last NAACP witness was Kenneth Clark who repeated much of his testimony from the Briggs case, but he also discussed interviews which he had with fourteen of the plaintiffs' children.[6] The purpose of his interviews was to assess the effects of segregation upon the Negro children of Prince Edward County, especially in terms of attitudes toward their schools. He found that the children had negative, critical attitudes toward their own schools, which contrasted sharply with their positive impressions of white schools in the county. "Not one of these children seemed to have thought of the possibility that the white school could have something wrong with it," Clark stated, and he concluded that school segregation creates conditions "which leads to completely distorted concepts of reality." He noted among all the children "an excessive preoccupation with matters of race [and] racial struggle." Their experiences had oriented them to consider themselves, their schools, family, and society primarily in racial terms, and invidious racial terms at that. "The most important thing to them," Clark observed, "is racial."

The attorneys for Virginia and Prince Edward County presented their rebuttal through a series of witnesses which included political and civic leaders of the state, educators, and social scientists. One of the most significant of their witnesses was Dr. Lindley Stiles, dean of education at the University of Virginia. A native of New Mexico and educated (doctorate in education) at the University of Colorado, Dean Stiles testified on a wide range of subjects, and his testimony is one of the most instructive statements of the segregationist position in the voluminous transcript of the Brown cases.[7] This is itself remarkable, for Stiles had a curiously ambivalent attitude toward segregation. He was convinced that public school segregation had many advantages for Negroes, which he enumerated at the beginning of his testimony. Segregated schools provide employ-

6 *Davis v. County School Board of Prince Edward County,* transcript of testimony, 254ff.

7 *Davis v. County School Board of Prince Edward County,* transcript of testimony, 493ff.

ment for educated Negroes, he declared, employment which they could not hope for in integrated schools, and give the race a voice in running its own school system. They shield Negro children from the taunts of white children, remove them from competition with children of a more advanced race, and protect them from the indifference or even hostility of white teachers. "Those of us who study this question," Stiles testified, "are convinced that the relationship between the teacher and the child, and between the child and the group in school, is of utmost importance in terms of how much and how well he learns in school. The teacher's acceptance of a child, her understanding of him and his background . . . her ability to teach him, or the child's being accepted in a group, or being emotionally a part of a group, is [sic] a vital factor in how well he learns."

To illustrate his point Stiles related the case of two Negro children who, he said, had enrolled in an otherwise all-white school in New Jersey. In the new school, they encountered so much difficulty that within "a very short time, the doctor ordered that [they] be taken out of the white school, because the emotional and psychological impact on their personalities was so great that they simply could not make the adjustment." Such incidents, Stiles continued, are products of race prejudice and can be prevented only by segregated schools, for prejudice exists without regard to law. In fact, he said, segregation laws tend to restrain the growth of prejudice. "Where segregation prevails by law, people seem to depend upon the law and certain customs to maintain a division between the races that is acceptable, to the white people particularly. Where the law does not exist, prejudice is substituted for the law, and many people depend much more heavily upon developing prejudices in order to defend the kind of segregation they want, than they do here in Virginia." The effects of integration might therefore be the opposite of what integrationists anticipate.

Stiles then turned his attention to the immediate issue in the Davis case, the specific problems relating to integration in secondary schools. Curiously, he thought the problems of integrating elementary schools were not insurmountable, and he foresaw "very little problem" in admitting Negroes to white graduate and professional schools. "I have seen Negro children and white children go to school . . . at the early elementary stages with very little difficulty," he testified. "But as they approach adolescence . . . where Negro and white children attend the same schools, resistance develops because of home teaching on the part of both races." And the schools, despite Stiles's faith in them as instruments of social reform, were unable to overcome this "resistance."

Stiles's testimony on this point indicates one of the most significant anomalies in the segregationists' testimony—a tendency to interpret evidence to meet an immediate need. Integration at the high school level was the immediate issue in the Davis case, and Stiles testified in effect that this was the level at which integration was most likely to prove unworkable. One wonders what the South Carolinians, who were simultaneously involved in the Briggs case which sought to integrate the elementary schools of Clarendon County, thought of Stiles's statement that integration at the elementary level could be achieved "with very little difficulty." Such inconsistencies in the segregationists' case resulted from the equivocal nature of the convictions of moderates like Stiles, and illustrated the difficulties in reconciling the moderate and more extreme defenses of segregation.

This difficulty was further reflected in other parts of Stiles's testimony. Like other moderate segregationists, Stiles was committed in his own mind to the principles of democracy and New Testament Christianity, and he felt impelled to speak in terms compatible with those principles. "In theory," he said, "I feel that Negroes are entitled to every opportunity that anyone else has, that they show the potentiality of earning." But he added, "I do not think that we have rights that come automatically"; rather, "we earn certain benefits in a society by the way we develop as a race or as individuals." Such statements are both internally contradictory (does one "earn" benefits as an individual or as a member of a race?) and implicitly discriminatory (they would require individual Negroes to "earn" rights which all whites receive automatically), but no one who accepts them can defend segregation unless he is convinced that segregation is not discriminatory.

Yet Stiles was apparently unconvinced on this point. "Obviously, a person in education who holds my convictions is deeply concerned about how we move and feel toward the abolition of segregation," he stated, "and in terms of my theory of democracy and belief in Christianity, I simply don't accept segregation as a social practice." So, immediately after testifying that segregation was beneficial to Negroes and compatible with equality of opportunity, he declared that he himself was not a segregationist. He overcame this apparent contradiction by embracing a view widely held by Southern moderates: that integration, though theoretically desirable, is impossible in the South at this time because the mores and prejudices of Southern whites will not tolerate it. Like other racial moderates, Stiles was optimistic. "It seems to me," he told the court, "that education is the intellectual and moral penicillin by which the bacteria of segregation [a curious phrase for a witness *for* segregation] are being destroyed, and the degree that Negro children are given equal opportunities to learn, and to the extent that all children in Virginia are provided better schools, segregation, in my opinion, is in fact in the process of being abolished."

Here then is the final paradox. The segregation system contains the seeds of its own destruction. The ultimate product of segregated schools in the South will be an integrated society. The process by which this is to be achieved is slow and difficult, and Stiles's argument with the NAACP witnesses was due to their desire to speed it up artificially. "The debate that goes on in this court," he declared, "is not over whether or not this patient (our society) can or should be cured of the ailment of segregation, but rather, it is a debate as to how to treat the disease; and I favor the administration of the antidote education in ever increasing dosages, rather than surgery at a time when the patient may not yet have strength enough to withstand the shock, or when the risk of spreading the infection would be too great." [8]

Stiles's equivocation stemmed from the perennial dilemma of racial moderates in the South—how best to reconcile the reality of segregation with their hopes for interracial progress and Negro improvement. Here was a man, a democrat and a Christian, who admitted that segregation violated the precepts of democracy and Christianity, and yet he testified in court in favor of an indefinite

[8] The transcript of the Davis testimony does not record that the attorneys for Virginia and Prince Edward County were discomforted or chagrined by Stiles's endorsement of integration, or by his statement that the educational system of the state was really a gigantic effort to achieve an integrated society. Stiles's optimism, though superficially plausible, was naive and contrary to the South's racial experience. There is nothing in the history of that section to indicate that integration or any improvement in the status of Negroes comes voluntarily or spontaneously; on the contrary, every advancement in the past has been a direct result of "outside" pressure and Negro protest.

continuation of segregation. By reading his testimony carefully one sees clearly that he was aware of the inequities in the dual school system of Virginia and was troubled by the injustices the system perpetrated. Moreover, his faith in the efficacy of education as a social cathartic indicated a belief in environmentalism and a view of social progress which are anomalous in a segregationist. He had, however, no corresponding faith in law and public policy as instruments of social change, and he was blind to the fact that changes in race relations in the past, whether emancipation, disfranchisement, segregation, or even various instances of integration, had invariably been forced upon the Negro or the Southern white or both. It would be possible, perhaps, to dismiss Stiles as a naive idealist or even an unctuous hypocrite, but to do so would be to miss an important point. By his ability to compartmentalize his ideas and values, he avoided conscious hypocrisy, and, more than that, had the best of both worlds: an intellectual conviction in favor of integration (and thus presumably an easy conscience) and at the same time a willingness to condone (even support) segregation as necessary and desirable for the time being.

Dr. William H. Kelley, a neurologist and psychiatrist of wide experience, followed Stiles to the witness stand. Dr. Kelley was director of the Memorial Foundation and Memorial Guidance Clinic of Richmond, a treatment center for children with behavior problems. Some form of segregation, he declared, was an integral part of all societies and cultures; and without saying so outrightly, he implied it was an inherent part of human nature.[9] Racial integration always produces racial problems, he explained, but at the secondary school level the difficulties are expecially great, for there "sex problems begin to come into the picture." The truth is that integration and not segregation is the problem, Kelley insisted, because the incessant propaganda of integrationists has an unsettling effect upon Negro children. They are told repeatedly that segregation is an evil, that they are victims of racial discrimination, and as a result they become dissatisfied with themselves and their lot in life and express their dissatisfaction in antisocial behavior.

The most significant phases of Kelley's testimony dealt with Kenneth Clark's doll tests and the relevancy of those tests to Prince

9 *Davis v. County School Board of Prince Edward County*, transcript of testimony, 519ff.

Edward County. The tests, Kelley thought, were interesting but of dubious value. They were projective tests, that is, tests in which psychologists attempt to externalize or objectify feelings which are internal and subjective. The results of such tests are too variable and too easily manipulated to be relied upon completely, Kelley stated. The sex or race or skin color of the person administering them, to say nothing of his attitudes and prejudices, might significantly influence the results. In addition, Clark's tests were not sufficiently standardized. Before their value can be determined, they should be administered by whites to Negroes, by Negroes to whites, and to other minority groups, and the results of the various combinations compared. In any case, Kelley warned, all such experiments should be used cautiously. The social sciences are still young, their techniques imperfect, their data inexact and subject to conflicting interpretations. Clark's interpretations are nothing more than his own conclusions from his particular point of view, and acceptable only to those who share his point of view. His interviews with Prince Edward County school children are similarly suspect, for more often than not such interviews only confirm the prejudices of the interviewer. The interviews and doll tests are ingenious but questionable devices through which Clark collected ostensibly objective data to buttress his personal prejudices, but they are hardly sufficient authority for a court order upsetting the Southern way of life.

Under cross-examination Kelley admitted that his observations were not based on his own professional experience, that he had in fact never conducted integrated therapy groups and had himself never studied the effects of integration on personality development or behavior patterns. These admissions, of course, reflected seriously upon his stature as an authority on the effects of integration, and undermined the effectiveness of his testimony. His views on the limited value of projective tests, however, are widely shared by psychologists.

The state climaxed its case by calling Professor Henry E. Garrett, then chairman of the psychology department at Columbia University, and a past president of the American Psychological Association. Garrett was one of the nation's most prominent psychologists, and his appearance was a major *coup* by the Virginia attorneys. Born in Virginia in 1894, he received his undergraduate education at Richmond University, and after a brief interlude as a high school teacher in Virginia, entered Columbia as a graduate student in psychology. This Southern background is quite important to an understanding of Garrett's racial views. In spite of his education at Columbia and his distinguished career as a psychologist, he never overcame many of the racial attitudes which his early life in the black belt ingrained in him. On the subjects of race, Negroes, and segregation, he is even today a proponent of ideas which an earlier generation of Americans imbibed from such books as Madison Grant's *The Passing of the Great Race* (1916) and Earnest Sevier Cox's *White America* (1923). His views are essentially the same as those of the Mississippi Citizens' Councils and other outspoken segregationists of the deep South.

In 1923 Garrett completed his graduate studies, received his Ph.D., and with it an appointment in the psychology department at Columbia, where he remained until retiring in 1956. Among his students at Columbia were Kenneth Clark, Mamie Clark, and Isidor Chein, and his attitude toward them in the Davis case was that of a learned mentor, wise with years and experience, chiding his students for their naivete and overenthusiasm. Garrett's career has been distinguished and full of recognition. During his last fifteen years at Columbia he was chairman of the psychology department. His fellow psychologists elected him president of the Psychometric Society in 1943, the Eastern Psychological Association in 1944, and the American Psychological Association in 1946. He is the author of a number of authoritative works, among them *Statistics in Psychology and Education* (1926), now in its fifth edition, *General Psychology* (1955), now in its second edition, and *Great Experiments in Psychology* (1957), a history of significant experiments in differential experimental psychology. He has, in addition, written dozens of articles and reports, and is a general editor of the *American Psychological Series*. Since his retirement from Columbia he has been visiting professor of psychology at the University of Virginia.

With this distinguished background, Garrett spoke with considerable authority on psychological subjects, especially testing and psychometrics. And inasmuch as he accepted in its entirety the segregationist position in civil rights controversies, he was a godsend for segregationists in the Davis case; he was especially useful to the Virginia attorneys, a man whose credentials matched those of any witness for the NAACP. Garrett's attitude toward segregation bore little resemblance to that of Dean Stiles. He showed none of Stiles's ambivalence, repeated none of Stiles's homilies about the future of interracial progress in the South. He endorsed segregation openly and directly, and his testimony in the Davis case was only the first of a long list of services he has performed for segregationists and scientific racists. Since 1954 he has played a leading role in the history of scientific racism, and his name will appear frequently in the course of this study.

Wasting no time on preliminaries, the Virginia attorneys at once asked Garrett if psychologists had yet reached the point "where true measurement can be made by objective tests, or any other tests, as to the impact on personality of such a factor as segregation." [10] Garrett replied simply, "I think it is very doubtful," and he proceeded to challenge the major points made by NAACP witnesses. Racially segregated schools, he declared, are no more discriminatory than parochial schools for Catholics or Jews. "Provided you have equal facilities," he stated, "it seems to me that in the State of Virginia today, taking into account the temper of its people, its mores and its customs and background, that the Negro student at the high school level will get a better education in a separate school than he will in mixed schools."

If a Negro child goes to a school as well equipped as that of his white neighbor, [he added later] if he had teachers of his own race and friends of his own race, it seems to me that he is much less likely to develop tensions, animosities, and hostilities, than if you put him into a mixed school where, in Virginia, inevitably he will be a minority group. . . . They are marked off, immediately, and I think, as I have said before, that at the adolescent level, children, being what they are, are stratifying themselves with respect to social and economic status, reflect the opinions of their parents, and the Negro would be much more likely to develop tensions, animosities, and hostilities. . . .

I think, in the high schools of Virginia, if the Negro child had equal facilities, his own teachers, his own friends, and a good feeling, he would be more likely to develop pride in himself as a Negro, which I think we would all like to see him do—to develop his own potentialities, his sense of duty, his sense of art, his sense of histrionics; and my prediction would be that if you conducted separate schools at the high school level for Negroes and whites, one of two things might happen: that the Negroes might develop their schools up to the level where they would not mix,

10 *Davis v. County School Board of Prince Edward County,* transcript of testimony, 548ff.

themselves; and I would like to see it happen. I think it would be poetic justice. They would develop their sense of domestic art, and music, which they seem to have a talent for—athletics—and they would say, "We prefer to remain as a Negro group." The other would be in a mixed school where, as I said, a great many animosities, disturbances, resentments, and hostilities, and inferiorities would develop.

Here are the contrasts between Garrett and Stiles. Garrett's attitude toward the Negro is that of the Southern white traditionalist and paternalist. He assumes, implicitly, that Negroes are intellectually inferior to whites, and that their genius lies in areas which require little intelligence. His static, hereditarian view of society was much more characteristic of segregationists than was Stiles's view.

Garrett attempted to rebut the major facets of the testimony presented by the NAACP witnesses, but he did this by speaking as a learned and experienced psychologist instead of offering specific empirical data. Asked about Brewster Smith's statement that racial segregation is an insult to the integrity of the individual, he replied, "The term 'insult' to an individual's personality . . . is fairly strong language. . . . I think an idealistic person, who is likely to let his sympathies go beyond his judgment may be so strongly prejudiced on the side of abstract goodness that he does not temper the application of the general principle with a certain amount of what might be called common sense." In similar fashion he dismissed the study of social science opinion by Isidor Chein and Max Deutscher. Their questionnaire, he said, consisted of "shotgun" or "blunderbuss" questions which are subject to varying interpretations. "I would not like to make a bet," he added, "but I would wager that I could send a questionnaire and phrase it rightly and get almost any answer I wanted."

The testimony by Garrett was doubly effective because of his professional stature. His appearance marked a significant break in academic opinion concerning integration. Moreover, he emphasized what was probably the segregationists' most effective argument— that psychology and the social sciences are infant disciplines, inexact and easily manipulated. To the data, experiments, and opinions offered by NAACP witnesses, he replied that the issues are still unresolved, that sufficient data have not yet been collected to enable one to speak with assurance. From a psychologist of Garrett's reputation, such statements were not without authority. Interestingly, much of his effectiveness came from the restraint with which he asserted the authority of psychology and the social sciences, and from the respect he paid to open-mindedness. His restraint and open-mindedness here, however, are in marked contrast to his later pronouncements on the subject. In his writings since 1954 he has often stated that the social science evidence concerning segregation and racial differences *is* conclusive, and that it demonstrates both the inferiority of Negroes and the necessity for racial segregation.

The social scientists who testified for the NAACP made virtually no impression upon the special three-judge court which heard the Davis case. In their unanimous decision the three judges, Albert V. Bryan, Armistead M. Dobie, and Sterling Hutcheson, endorsed the segregationist position in its entirety.[11] "Maintenance of the separated [school] systems in Virginia," they wrote, "has not been social despotism. . . . Whatever its demerits in theory, in practice it has gotten greater opportunity for the Negro. . . . We have found no hurt or harm to either race."

The task of Clark and his associates did not end with their appearance as expert witnesses in the Briggs, Davis, and other cases. The NAACP appealed each of the cases to the Supreme Court, and sought the assistance of social scientists in making the appeal. The NAACP attorneys asked Clark and his associates to prepare a social science appendix to their brief to the Supreme Court and in other ways assist them in making the most effective presentation of social science material to the high tribunal. Prepared by Gerhart Saenger, Isidor Chein, Stuart Cook, and Clark, the appendix to appellants' brief was a succinct and forceful statement of psychological, sociological, and educational arguments against racial discrimination, and was endorsed by thirty-five leading social scientists, among them Gordon Allport, Allison Davis, Otto Klineberg, Alfred McClung Lee, Robert M. MacIver, Gardner Murphy, Robert Redfield, Ira De A. Reid, Arnold Rose, Brewster Smith, and others of similar stature.[12]

The appendix consisted of two parts, the most important of

[11] Opinion of the Court, No. 4 *(Davis v. County School Board of Prince Edward County)*, 621, in transcript of *Brown v. Board of Education*, 347 U.S. 483 (1954).

[12] The appendix is reprinted in "The Effects of Segregation and the Consequences of Desegregation: A Social Science Statement," *Minnesota Law Review*, XXXVII (May, 1953), 427–38; and also as Appendix III in Clark, *Prejudice and Your Child*, 166–84.

which summarized the kind of material presented in the Briggs and Davis testimony, and need not be repeated here. The appendix, however, went much further than the testimony, especially in dealing with two questions frequently raised by segregationists and likely to be of concern to the Supreme Court: (1) Will widespread integration of schools adversely affect educational standards? and (2) Is school integration in the South likely to be accompanied by violence? The first question rests heavily upon the assumption that Negroes as a race are intellectually inferior, and the authors of the appendix answered it with an emphatic "no." Relying upon the pioneering works of Otto Klineberg, they noted that "the available scientific evidence indicates that much, perhaps all, of the observable differences among various racial and national groups may be adequately explained in terms of environmental differences." It had been found, they continued, that "the differences between the average intelligence test scores of Negro and white children decrease, and the overlap of the distribution increases proportionately to the number of years that the Negro children have lived in the North." Other studies, also by Klineberg, had shown that this change could not be explained by the hypothesis of selective migration. "It seems clear," they concluded, "that fears based on the assumption of innate racial differences in intelligence are not well founded." Arguments concerning the intellectual abilities of Negroes and whites are, therefore, arguments for homogeneous or ability groupings, not racial segregation.

The question whether school integration would be accompanied by violence was a vitally important one, not only for segregationists who raised it repeatedly but for social scientists trying to make a case for integration. In stressing the possibility, indeed the likelihood, of violence, segregationists insisted that laws cannot alter fundamental human convictions, and warned that the average Southern white man was so thoroughly committed to school segregation that he would use violence to prevent integration. Attorneys for South Carolina and Virginia freely predicted violence would accompany any effort to desegregate the public schools of their states, and if their predictions were accurate, a court order outlawing school segregation would indeed be unwise.

To answer such predictions the authors of the appendix studied the history of specific instances of racial integration and found numerous examples of successful integration in areas where violence had been commonly predicted. Integration in the armed forces, already virtually complete, had occurred without major incident despite the involvement of Southern men and installations on a substantial scale. Successful integration had also occurred in such sensitive areas as housing, employment, recreation facilities, and general community life. Under the right circumstances, the appendix stated, "desegregation not only proceeds without major difficulties, but has been observed to lead to the emergence of more favorable attitudes and friendlier relations between races."

The social scientists' final task was to assist NAACP attorneys in answering a series of questions which the Supreme Court asked appellants and appellees to discuss in a reargument of the Brown cases. Their assistance was especially important in answering question IV: "Assuming it is decided that segregation in public schools violates the Fourteenth Amendment, (a) Would a decree necessarily follow providing that, within the limits set by normal geographic school districting, Negro children should forthwith be admitted to schools of their choice, or (b) May this court, in the exercise of its equity powers, permit an effective gradual adjustment to be brought about from existing segregated systems to a system not based on color distinctions?"

The significance of the question is apparent, for it suggests that the justices were already considering a decision permitting gradual integration, or, in their own words, integration "with all deliberate speed." The question reflected the Court's concern that a ruling directing immediate massive integration might disrupt the public school system in the South and lead to widespread disorder and violence. It also indicated that the justices thought gradual integration would be less likely to provoke violent reactions among segregationists. The implications of the question were profound, and Clark and his associates at once set about studying those implications in light of available social science data.[13]

What they did was greatly to expand their study of the history of actual instances of integration. They studied integration in Northern, Southern, and Border states, examining each episode in as much detail as the evidence permitted. They found a surprisingly large number of instances of successful integration in such diverse areas as churches, the armed forces, housing, interstate

13 For the results of their efforts see Clark, "Desegregation: An Appraisal of the Evidence."

transportation, public accommodations, organized sports, employment, voting, government service, higher education, and even in public elementary and secondary schools. In some cases integration had been voluntary; in others the result of court orders, political pressure, administrative action, population changes, threats of adverse publicity, interracial negotiation, or a combination of these. Sometimes it had been gradual and piecemeal, at other times immediate and largescale. Rarely, however, had there been "overt violent resistance." The most significant and perhaps the most surprising result of the study was the evidence that immediate desegregation was no more likely to produce violence than was gradual desegregation. Indeed, wrote Clark summarizing the study, "there is some suggestive evidence that the larger the scale of the desegregation the greater the likelihood of general acceptance or the lack of overt resistance."

On the basis of this study Clark and his colleagues asked the Supreme Court for a decision ordering substantial desegregation of public schools within a brief period of time. The Court, of course, rejected this advice, a point which is never mentioned by segregationists who allege that the Court was "duped" by the social scientists, and chose instead to permit school integration to be dragged out interminably. On two crucial points—the speed with which integration must be achieved and the amount of integration necessary to satisfy the letter of the law—the Court ignored the best available social science data and followed instead a course which the social scientists warned against.[14]

14 When viewed from the hindsight afforded by the history of integration over the last dozen years, the evidence offered by the social scientists on these points seems astonishingly valid. Despite some conspicuous exceptions, e.g., abandonment of the public school system in Prince Edward County, the evidence has stood the test of time well. If the Supreme Court had not been so lenient in interpreting the phrase "with all deliberate speed," and had not so readily accepted pupil placement laws, which from the beginning were transparent devices to limit school integration to tokenism, the transition from a segregated to a desegregated society in the South might have been more rapid and less agonizing. Despite vehement denunciations from Southern segregationists, the Brown decision as modified by "all deliberate speed" and pupil placement laws is a tokenism decision rather than an integration decision. Its effectiveness depends almost completely upon the willingness of local officials to abide by it, and there has accordingly been much school integration in border areas and very little in the deep South. Moreover, most of the integration in the deep South since 1954 has occurred in areas outside the classroom and has come from sit-ins, picketing, and voter registration

Despite the limitations which the Court has accepted in implementing the Brown decision, the decision was itself substantially influenced by the work of Clark and his collaborators. They did an impressive job summarizing a massive amount of scientific evidence and presenting it to the courts. The measure of their performance is the Brown decision itself which recognized as a fact that racial segregation in the public schools is psychologically damaging to Negroes and that this fact "is amply supported by modern [social science] authority."

---

drives rather than the Brown decision itself. Even the speed-up in school integration since 1964 has been a result of the Civil Rights Act of 1964 and, in turn, of the Birmingham riots of 1963 and only indirectly from the decision.

4

SCIENTIFIC RACISM AND PSYCHOLOGY

The Brown decision caught segregationists by surprise. They expected the Court to uphold the separate-but-equal principle on condition that the facilities and curricula of Negro schools be brought up to white standards at once. Such a decision would be acceptable to them for it would follow the recommendations of Professor Garrett and others who testified for segregation in the Davis case. The Court, however, rejected both Garrett's testimony and the separate-but-equal doctrine, and to whatever extent the Brown decision rested upon science it was the science of equalitarians and environmentalists. To segregationists, however, "equalitarian" science was pseudoscience, a nefarious mixture of calculated misrepresentation, artful pleading, and wishful thinking—and patently invalid. It is not surprising, then, that in attempting to discredit the Brown decision they turned to science. They sought not only to refute the social science incorporated in the decision, but more importantly, they endeavored to develop a systematic scientific defense of segregation, especially segregation in the public schools of the South.

The success of this endeavor would depend upon their ability to enlist the services of at least a few reputable social scientists, whose task would be to systematize the ideas of scientific racism and marshal scientific data in the manner most useful to segregationists. Nor were they entirely unsuccessful. They attracted to their ranks a small cadre of academic social scientists, who over the last decade have produced a substantial body of ostensibly scientific literature, some of which has achieved a wide circulation and a certain notoriety. In concert with these social scientists, segregationists have sponsored an effort, informally coordinated, to "educate" the American people on the subject of race and challenge the Brown decision in the federal courts on grounds that it rests upon false science. The result has been not to reverse the decision—this the courts have refused to do—but to stimulate a series of bitter controversies between racists and hereditarians on one side and equalitarians and environmentalists on the other. Another result has been the publication of a large body of literature which many racists today accept as scientific proof of Negro inferiority, and which they often cite as justification for segregation. The purpose of this and succeeding chapters is to discuss the major works and ideas of these social scientists who have served the cause of segregation and to demonstrate the close ties between them and Southern segregationists.

The immediate objective of segregationists has been to prevent the integration of public schools in the South. As a result, the most pressing task of scientific racists has been to formulate a scientific defense for segregated education, and no social science discipline has been more important in that task than psychology. Scientific racists are especially concerned with comparative racial intelligence, psychological test results, and the relative educational capacity of whites and Negroes. They are similarly concerned with the psychic traits and personality characteristics of both races, especially Negroes, and the extent to which these are transmitted by heredity and influenced by environment. To psychologists who serve their cause, segregationists posed several crucial questions: Are Negroes inferior to whites in intelligence? Do psychological test results prove this inferiority? Will integration lower educational standards in "white" schools? Are Negroes by nature more immoral and socially irresponsible than whites? Are such traits transmitted by heredity? Will racial amalgamation lower the quality of the American people? Racists answer these questions in the affirmative, but they seek from psychologists a scientific basis for their answer.

In exploiting psychology racists enjoyed several advantages. Negroes *do,* on the average, make consistently lower scores than whites on intelligence, aptitude, and achievement tests. Negro schools *are,* on the whole, inferior to white schools. The level of achievement of Negro students *is,* in general, significantly below that of whites, especially in the South and the ghettoes of Northern cities. Negroes *do,* on the average, commit more crimes of violence and have higher rates of illegitimacy and venereal disease. They *do* have more broken homes and more rundown neighborhoods. They *do* deviate further from middle class standards of conduct.[1] The point of controversy between racists and equalitarians is not whether these conditions exist, but rather the cause and cure of them. To blame them on race is easy and convenient, and, to racists at least, obviously correct. That explanation suits their purposes and they find it easy to defend. One need only look around, they insist, to see the importance of race and the differences it produces between whites and Negroes. These differences, whether of physical features, intelligence test scores, or personal and moral traits, are, in the eyes of racists, the meaning and manifestation of race.

The exploitation of psychology by racists had no specific beginning. Among psychologists in this country there has always been a group, of varying numbers and influence, committed to the idea of innate racial inequality. After World War I, however, as investigative techniques improved and social scientists became more careful and objective in studying race, psychologists found the idea of

[1] For a brilliant summary of these facts see Daniel Patrick Moynihan, *The Negro Family: The Case for National Action* (U.S. Department of Labor, 1965) .

innate inequality less and less acceptable. By the 1930's and 1940's they had discarded it altogether, or virtually so. But it left a legacy, in the form of a voluminous literature ostensibly proving racial inequality and Negro inferiority, which latter-day racists have searched out, dusted off, and used liberally.

Other psychologists who have contributed substantially to the literature of scientific racism in recent years, in addition to Henry E. Garrett, are Frank C. J. McGurk, Audrey Shuey, and Robert T. Osborne.[2] Professor McGurk, in an article published in *U.S. News and World Report* in 1956, made what was apparently the first systematic effort by a social scientist to dispute the social science incorporated in the Brown decision.[3] Born in Philadelphia in 1910, McGurk received his undergraduate education at the Catholic University of America, where he also earned a Ph.D. in psychology in 1951. He has had several teaching appointments, at the University of Pennsylvania, the Catholic University, Lehigh, and from 1956 to 1964 at Villanova University, where he was an associate professor of psychology. He is now a professor of psychology at Alabama College. He has had several years' experience as a staff psychologist, including two years at the United States Military Academy. An academic, a psychologist, and an apologist for racial segregation, McGurk has been sometimes rebuked and often challenged by his fellow psychologists, few of whom find much merit in his work on comparative racial intelligence. Because of their criticisms he and other scientific racists have come to look upon himself as a martyr to academic freedom.[4]

As a social scientist, McGurk is chiefly interested in psychological testing, especially comparative testing of white and Negro intelligence and the influence of socioeconomic factors on test results,

[2] Since Professor Garrett's contributions easily outweigh those of the others, and since his services as a protagonist for segregation transcend psychology, he is treated in a later chapter.

[3] Frank C. J. McGurk, "A Scientist's Report on Race Differences," *U.S. News and World Report,* September 21, 1956, pp. 92–96.

[4] McGurk has been especially concerned by the fact that most of his fellow social scientists are "liberals." He feels that this has resulted in the creation of an orthodoxy in the social sciences which is intolerant of dissenting opinion and has virtually destroyed academic freedom. For one of his discussions of this subject see his paper, "The Law, Social Science, and Academic Freedom," *Villanova Law Review,* V (Winter, 1959–60), 247–54. This paper was read at a symposium on law and social science at the annual meeting in 1959 of the American Psychological Association.

and his interest long antedated the Brown decision.[5] His research had convinced him well before 1954 that whites and Negroes are so different in intelligence or scholastic aptitude that they cannot be effectively educated together. In 1951 he offered as his doctoral thesis a study entitled "Comparison of the Performance of Negro and White High School Seniors on Cultural and Non-cultural Test Questions," [6] the purpose of which was to determine whether socioeconomic factors account for the consistently lower scores of Negroes on intelligence tests. In accomplishing this study, which is frequently cited by scientific racists, McGurk administered tests consisting of 103 "least cultural" and 81 "most cultural" questions to 213 white and 213 Negro high school students in New Jersey and Pennsylvania. Matching the two groups in age, sex, educational background, socioeconomic status, and other environmental factors which affect test results, he believed that he was enabled thereby to eliminate or neutralize environmental factors and thus measure innate racial intelligence. His results, however, were substantially the same as those obtained by other psychologists in studies in which environmental factors were not controlled. Negroes made significantly lower scores than whites, overlapping the white average by approximately 28 percent.[7] But, surprisingly, they did better on the "most cultural" than on the "least cultural" items, a fact which McGurk took as additional evidence that the low scores of Negroes cannot be explained by environment. As a further check, he divided the students into groups according to socioeconomic status and compared the results of each status group by race. He found "high-status" Negroes well below "high-status" whites, though Negroes did relatively much better in lower status groups. In fact, the higher the status of the groups the poorer the Negroes' relative performance. "There is no evidence," McGurk wrote in a later study, "that as the socioeconomic status of the Negro increases, racial test-score differences decrease." [8]

[5] Frank C. J. McGurk, "Comparative Test Scores of Negro and White School Children in Richmond, Virginia," *Journal of Educational Psychology,* XXXIV (November, 1943), 473–84.

[6] (Washington: Catholic University of America Press, 1951, microcard).

[7] "Overlap" refers to the percentage of Negroes who equal or exceed the average score made by whites. An overlap of 50 percent represents equality.

[8] Frank C. J. McGurk, "On White and Negro Test Performance and Socioeconomic Factors," *Journal of Abnormal and Social Psychology,* XLVIII (July, 1953), 450.

It was from this background that McGurk published his article in *U.S. News and World Report* in September, 1956. In that article he refined and reiterated the basic ideas of his 1951 study. "Are Negroes really equal to whites in their capacity for education?" he asked again. Can they compete on even terms in mixed schools, or do they drag down educational levels? His answers were substantially the same as they had been in his earlier study: Negroes are significantly below whites in educational capacity, and their incapacity is not removed by improving their socioeconomic conditions.

To substantiate these answers, McGurk examined the results of several experimental studies in comparative racial intelligence. Specifically, he compared the results of tests given to Army inductees in World War I with those of several studies made between 1935 and 1950, in which the examiners attempted to control environmental variables. The technique was ingenious. McGurk reasoned that the socioeconomic status of Negroes had improved markedly since World War I, and, if the environmental hypothesis were valid, Negroes should score significantly higher in 1935–50 than they had in 1917–18. The first of these assumptions is no doubt valid, but to transpose it into the conclusion that Negroes should therefore score higher on psychological tests is fallacious. The transpositions ignores environmental improvements which whites have also undergone, as well as changes in the test themselves. Though Negroes did not improve their scores relative to whites, there is evidence that both races had substantially improved their performance on psychological tests since World War I. In one study, for example, in which a group of white enlisted men in World War II were given the much simpler tests used in World War I, 83 percent exceeded the average score made by enlisted men in the earlier war.[9]

In addition to these weaknesses, McGurk also failed to specify the environmental improvements among Negroes which he thought should improve their relative test scores. In 1935 and 1950 Negroes were still generally segregated, still discriminated against, still told by society that theirs was a second-class race and they were second-rate human beings. In a thousand subtle and unsubtle ways they were still made to feel inferior and despised. Despite such factors as

[9] See Thomas F. Pettigrew, *A Profile of the Negro American* (Princeton, 1964), 121–22.

these, McGurk found that the Negroes' performance had not significantly changed between 1917–18 and 1935–50, and their overlap of white averages was only 20 to 30 percent in each period. The significant improvement in socioeconomic status, he concluded, had not materially affected their performance on psychological tests.

Delving further into the relationship between environment, socioeconomic status, and intelligence, McGurk reported the results of a study of his own in which he had attempted to control environmental factors. He found that high-status Negroes overlapped high-status whites by only 18 percent, while low-status Negroes overlapped low-status whites by 41 percent. "What we have found is, again, a strange kind of reversal of what most writers say about the efficacy of socio-economic factors," he wrote. "If social and economic factors were so important, there should have been no differences between Negroes and whites in any of these comparisons." However, the reverse was the case. "An improvement in the socioeconomic positions of the Negro made him *less* able to compete with whites on psychological tests." He concluded therefore that "the factual evidence *completely* denies the theory that improving the social and economic status of the Negro improves his capacity for education." [10]

Having drawn this conclusion McGurk related his findings to the integration controversy. But he did so indirectly, for he always insisted that he was a disinterested scientist following wherever his research led. "As far as psychological differences between Negroes and whites are concerned, we have wished—and dreamed—that there were no such differences," he declared. "We have identified this wish with reality, and on it we have established a race relations policy that was so clearly a failure that we had to appeal to distorting propaganda for support. When that, too, failed, we appealed to the legal machinery to do what nature was not content to do." Clearly the Brown decision was unwise, for school integration placed whites and Negroes in an unnatural relationship. The social order, McGurk wrote elsewhere, must recognize that "biogenetic factors play a major role in causing psychic differences between races." [11]

10 McGurk, "A Scientist's Report on Race Difference," 96, 95. Emphasis added.
11 Frank C. J. McGurk, "Introduction" to Nathaniel Weyl, *The Negro in American Civilization* (Washington, 1960), v. See also Frank C. J. McGurk, "Fact and Prejudice," *Contemporary Psychology*, III (September, 1958), 280.

The significance of McGurk's article in *U.S. News and World Report* in the developing controversy between racists and equalitarians is indicated by the response it evoked from both groups. Segregationists hailed it as definitive proof that school integration violates the laws of science and nature, and cited it repeatedly in their controversy with integrationists. *The Citizens' Council* described it as a "severe jolt" to integrationists, and another outspoken segregationist considered it "thorough and well-documented" proof "that the White race has a greater innate capacity to respond to favorable environment." [12]

Social scientists were less impressed. Eighteen of them issued a statement challenging McGurk's premises and method and denying the validity of his conclusions.[13] Citing the 1950 UNESCO "Statement on Race," a 1952 statement by physical anthropologists and geneticists, and the appendix to appellants' brief in the Brown cases, they dismissed McGurk's article as misleading to laymen and a misuse of science. "The scientific material available to us," they wrote, quoting the 1952 statement of physical anthropologists and geneticists, "does not justify the conclusion that inherited genetic differences are a major factor in producing the differences between the cultures and cultural achievements of different people." And they added, "we know of no new research which would reverse [this 1952 conclusion]."

In more specific terms they rejected McGurk's claim that he (or anyone else) had adequately controlled or neutralized environmental factors which affect the results of psychological tests. They insisted that such a task was impossible, at least at present, and that anyone who presumed otherwise was deceiving himself and, more

12 *The Citizens' Council,* II (October, 1956), 4; and Richard W. Edmonds, *Segregation, Is It Justified?* (Columbus, Georgia, 1957), 29, 34.

13 "Does Race Really Make a Difference in Intelligence?" *U.S. News and World Report,* October 26, 1956, pp. 74–76. The signers of the statement were Otto Klineberg of Columbia University; Theodore Newcomb and Daniel Katz of the University of Michigan; Gardner Murphy of the Menninger Foundation; David Krech of the University of California; Allison Davis of the University of Chicago; Anne Anastasi of Fordham University; Stuart Cook, Isidor Chein, and Marie Jahoda of New York University; Kenneth Clark of City College of New York; Nevitt Sanford of Vassar; Robin Williams, Jr., of Cornell University; Jerome Brunner of Harvard University; Bingham Dai of Duke University; Irving Lorge of Teachers College, Columbia; Solomon Asch of Swarthmore College; and David Rapaport of the Austen Riggs Foundation. The statement is also printed in "No Scientific Evidence of Race Differences," *Science News Letter,* October 27, 1956, p. 265.

importantly in McGurk's case, was misleading laymen. Segregation and discrimination, which exist in some form or another throughout this nation, make it impossible to equate environmental factors for whites and Negroes, or to devise a valid "non-cultural" test as McGurk claimed he had done. As two of his critics pointed out, the indices of socioeconomic status which McGurk used in formulating "noncultural" tests were designed to measure the differences between social *classes,* but the differences between social *castes* cannot be reduced to a neat index. "Not only in the South but [in the] North as well," wrote psychologists Ralph M. Dreger and Kent S. Miller, "whites and Negroes comprise separate castes; they are not merely representative of different classes." [14]

According to McGurk's critics, then, both his methodology and his conclusions were unscientific. His tests did not do what he claimed for them. He read far too much into his data, while at the same time ignoring evidence of his own which pointed to a direct relationship between environment and intelligence. His high-status subjects, whether whites or Negroes, scored substantially above his low-status subjects, but he apparently saw no significance in this. In his considerable research on racial intelligence, McGurk found that Negroes as a group score significantly below whites as a group, a fact which is universally acknowledged. But that, substantially, was all he found. He *inferred* that the lower Negro performance was due to factors connected with race, and not environment, but it was only an inference. He gave it the appearance of an empirically demonstrated fact by discussing several other studies which made, but did not prove, the same inference. In his writings, however, he gave the inference the coloration of fact, and it thereby became the basis for his views on social and educational policy.

McGurk's critics insisted that "any decision to use differences in average achievement of the two racial groups for classifying in advance *any individual child,* Negro or white, is scientifically unjustified." [15] And therein lies a major difference between equalitarians and scientific racists. Racists categorize people as members of a race, and define their civil rights and social status in racial

14 See Ralph M. Dreger and Kent S. Miller, "Comparative Psychological Studies of Negroes and Whites in the United States," *Psychological Bulletin,* LVII (No. 5, 1960), 361–402.
15 "Does Race Really Make a Difference in Intelligence?" 76.

terms. Equalitarians, on the other hand, insist that innate differences in intelligence have not been proved and cannot be assumed, and that in any event racial intelligence is irrelevant to political and social policy. Constitutional and civil rights are rights of the individual as a citizen and are his without regard to race or intelligence, they assert. A citizen is an individual, not a racial abstraction, and must be treated as such by his government. If Negroes score *on the average* below whites on intelligence tests, racists accept this as sufficient cause to segregate public schools. Equalitarians draw no such conclusion, reasoning instead that if IQ is an appropriate criterion for assigning children to a particular school, it should be applied without regard to race. To them, McGurk's evidence, insofar as it was relevant to educational policy, argued not for racial segregation but for segregation by ability or intelligence. Racists reject this reasoning, and their rejection indicates that their real concern is not educational standards but racial segregation.

In a reply to two of his critics McGurk contended that he had no interest in trying to prove that Negroes are less intelligent than whites.[16] He was not even sure, he said, that IQ tests measure innate intelligence, though he was convinced that they accurately predict scholastic achievement. In integrated schools, he reasoned, whites will be held back by Negroes, and in the process the nation's intellectual resources will be wasted. The same objection, however, applies to Negro schools. Slow students impede bright ones without regard to race. If, as scientific racists insisted repeatedly, intelligence is the best guarantee of the survival of America and of Western civilization, it behooves the nation not to squander its intellectual resources, whether those resources are white or Negro.

Scientific racists do not claim that *all* Negroes make lower test scores than *all* whites. There is always an overlap, but this, they insist, should not obscure the more significant differences in racial averages. Typically, Negroes overlap whites by 20 to 30 percent. In his 1951 study, for example, McGurk found an overlap of 28

---

16 Frank C. J. McGurk, "Negro vs. White Intelligence—An Answer," *Harvard Educational Review*, XXIX (Winter, 1959), 54–62. He was answering William M. McCord and Nicholas J. Demerath III, "Negro Versus White Intelligence: A Continuing Controversy," *ibid.*, XXVII (Spring, 1958), 120–35. McCord and Demerath offered evidence from a study of their own that IQ test scores are closely related to environmental factors.

percent. Such figures, however, are sometimes deceiving, especially to laymen. Technically, "overlap" means the percentage of Negroes who score higher than the *average* score made by whites. Thus, an overlap of 50 percent, not 100 percent, means equality. Perhaps a more meaningful way to express test results to laymen is to point out the *range* of scores made by each racial group. In the tests in which McGurk found a 28-percent overlap, *91 percent* of the Negroes scored between the highest and lowest scores made by whites who took the test.[17] By expressing results in this fashion it becomes apparent that the differences *within* each race are much larger than the differences *between* the races. But here as elsewhere racists insist that racial *differences,* however minute, are the crucial factor.

McGurk's study is not the racists' most important work on Negro intelligence. That distinction belongs to a lengthy and detailed study, *The Testing of Negro Intelligence,* published in 1958 and reissued in a second edition in 1966, by Professor Audrey M. Shuey, chairman of the department of psychology at Randolph-Macon Woman's College, Lynchburg, Virginia. Dr. Shuey was born in 1900 in Illinois, and received her undergraduate education at the University of Illinois. She earned graduate degrees at Wellesley and Columbia, receiving a Ph.D. in psychology from the latter in 1931. At Columbia she studied under Professor Henry E. Garrett, and he contributed a laudatory foreword to both editions of her study of Negro intelligence. She has held various academic appointments, at Barnard, Washington Square College of New York University, and since 1943 at Randolph-Macon. In *American Men of Science* she lists her specializations as "after images; learning behavior of kittens; [and] race differences."

The Testing of Negro Intelligence is, in briefest terms, a cataloging of the statistical results of some 240 studies of the performance of Negroes (and, in some instances, of whites) on psychological and intelligence tests from 1913 to 1958. The studies included results from approximately sixty different tests and 80,000 Negro subjects, not including those who took the armed forces psychological tests in the two world wars. Professor Shuey's intention was to collect the results of all the studies of Negro intelligence ever made in

17 See Howard Hale Long, "The Relative Learning Capacities of Negroes and Whites," *Journal of Negro Education,* XXVI (Spring, 1957), 121–34.

this country and to understand the meaning of the accumulated results. This was a worthy objective, and also a colossal task. It involved not only a prodigious amount of research but also a detachment which only the most careful students possess, and a full awareness of the limitations and pitfalls of psychological testing. Miss Shuey's research was remarkable despite the fact that she omitted "numerous and important publications . . . which run counter to [her] conclusion." [18] Her lack of detachment, however, led her to make questionable use of the data she had so painstakingly collected.

She divided the studies into seven groups, according to the age or condition of the Negro subjects: preschool children, elementary school children, high school and college students, armed forces inductees in the two world wars, "deviates" of exceptionally high or low intelligence, delinquents and criminals, and "racial hybrids." In virtually every study she used in each of the categories, Negroes scored on the average significantly below whites. Several of her findings are noteworthy:

1. Among preschool children the average IQ for Negroes is 96.3, for whites 105.9. This was the highest average reported for any age group of Negroes and the best relative performance. After this age Negro IQ scores *decrease* both relatively and absolutely.

2. Among elementary school children, Southern urban Negroes score four to six points higher than Southern rural Negroes, and six to nine points below Northern and border state urban Negroes. The average IQ of Southern Negro children is 79, of Northern Negro children 87.

3. Among high school students the average IQ of Southern Negroes is approximately 82, of Northern Negroes 91. In both groups the Negro averages are significantly below those of whites, despite the fact that Negroes in high school are much more highly selected than whites in high school. "About half or possibly two-thirds" of the difference between the test scores of Northern and Southern Negroes, Miss Shuey concluded, are due to environmental factores, the remainder to selective migration of superior Negroes from South to North.

4. Negro college students, who are still more highly selected than whites, do poorest of all in relation to whites. The explana-

18 Pettigrew, *A Profile of the Negro American,* 102.

tion for this "may lie in the abstract nature of the test material used on the college group," for Negroes do consistently better on tests of "common-sense concrete material than on tests involving abstract concepts." The results of the college tests left "serious doubt" in Miss Shuey's mind "that the obtained differences are completely or primarily due to the cumulative effect of an inferior environment." [19]

5. Negro soldiers in World War II did as poorly as those of World War I, and in both wars Negroes scored well below whites. "This holds true in comparisons between the northern Negro and the southern white draft, although the difference between these groups is less marked than between the northern Negro and the northern white or between the southern Negro and the southern white." [20] This was Miss Shuey's description of what were for racists the most embarrassing results of the World War I tests, namely, that Negroes in four Northern states made higher scores than whites in four Southern states. Otto Klineberg reported these results as follows:[21]

Whites	Median Score	Negroes	Median Score
Mississippi	41.25	Pennsylvania	42.00
Kentucky	41.50	New York	45.02
Arkansas	41.55	Illinois	47.35
Georgia	42.12	Ohio	49.50

Racists countered Klineberg's listing by pointing out that whites in Pennsylvania, New York, Illinois, and Ohio scored much higher than Negroes in those states, just as whites in Mississippi, Kentucky, Arkansas, and Georgia scored substantially above Negroes in those states.

6. In most instances there is a direct correlation between the skin color of "racial hybrids" and their performance on the tests: the lighter the skin color, the higher the score. Professor Shuey, however, did not place great weight upon this.[22]

[19] Audrey Shuey, *The Testing of Negro Intelligence* (Lynchburg, Va., 1958), 177–78. The second edition of this work was published in 1966 by the Social Science Press of New York.

[20] Shuey, *The Testing of Negro Intelligence*, 219.

[21] Otto Klineberg, *Race Differences* (New York, 1935), 182.

[22] Cf. the statement of Harvard psychologist Thomas F. Pettigrew: "A further embarrassment to racist theories is created by the fact that the degree of white ancestry does not relate to Negro I.Q. scores." Pettigrew, *A Profile of the Negro American*, 130.

On the basis of such findings Miss Shuey reached the following general conclusion:

> The remarkable consistency in test results . . . the fact that the colored-white differences are present not only in the rural South and urban South, but in the border and northern areas; the fact that relatively small average differences are found between the IQ's of northern-born and southern-born Negro children in northern cities; the evidence that the tested differences appear to be greater for abstract than for practical or concrete problems; the evidence that the differences obtained are not due primarily to a lack of language skills, the colored averaging no better on non-verbal tests than on verbal tests; the fact that differences are reported in all studies in which the cultural environment of the whites appeared to be no more complex, rich, or stimulating than the environment of the Negroes; the fact that in many comparisons (including those in which the colored appeared to best advantage) the Negro subjects have been either more representative of their racial group, or more highly selected than have the comparable white subjects; all point to the presence of some native differences between Negroes and whites as determined by intelligence tests.[23]

This conclusion is remarkably cautious in view of the massive evidence Miss Shuey offered to substantiate it. In fact, if her evidence is as valid as she claims it is, she understated her conclusion. In her compilation of test results, she heaped study upon study in which Negroes scored significantly below whites, but in drawing her general conclusion, she backed away from the obvious implications of her evidence—assuming the evidence is valid. If it is valid and her handling of it sound, if the tests she summarized do measure innate intelligence, and if psychologists are able to control or neutralize environmental factors as she believed, then she has proven that Negroes are innately inferior to whites. She has also proven that their inferiority is sufficiently large to justify public school segregation. Ironically, her restrained conclusion and dispassionate language have enhanced the book's usefulness to scientific racists, for they are enabled thereby to point to it as cautious and restrained and to Miss Shuey as a disinterested scientist who refused to read more into her data than was actually there. *The Testing of Negro Intelligence* is not written in the impassioned tones characteristic of most of the literature of scientific racism. It is not full of loaded phrases, nor does it take the usual side swipes at integrationists. It is scientific racism in its most effective form.

[23] Shuey, *The Testing of Negro Intelligence,* 318.

"The scientist, to be of any value to society, must avoid wishful thinking and report the truth as far as he has discovered it, without pretending to know more than he actually does," wrote Miss Shuey in her Introduction, and in this spirit, ostensibly, she offered her study. In his Foreword, Professor Garrett remarked that the *"honest* psychologist, like any true scientist, has no preconceived racial bias," and he welcomed "every *honest* effort to aid Negroes in improving their status as American citizens." [24] Miss Shuey, however, sometimes ignored Garrett's admonition, just as she sometimes forgot her own stated principles. Invariably, she interpreted her data in the manner most favorable to Negro inferiority and white superiority. She accepted at face value all studies which indicated Negro inferiority, but sought to explain away the results of those in any way favorable to Negroes. On the point in which the evidence supporting environmentalism was strongest, the effects of selective migration upon the performance of Northern Negroes, she included an entire chapter, though she did this for no other such topic. Northern Negroes made significantly higher test scores than Southern Negroes (some investigators have even found a positive correlation between IQ and length of time individual Negroes had lived outside the South), and equalitarians accepted this as an indication of the influence of environment upon IQ.

Miss Shuey's method is suspect in several important instances. She was interested only in the statistical results of the studies she cited, which she lumped together without regard to the limitations of individual studies or the comments or warnings of the authors. She accepted all the studies as equally valid, whether made in 1913 or 1957. In quantifying the results, she failed to distinguish adequately between studies which made no effort to control environmental factors, and those which, with varying degrees of success, did make such an effort. Even more seriously, she was uncritical of the tests themselves. She made insufficient allowance for such questions as whether the tests had been standardized upon

---

24 "We are forced to conclude that the regularity and consistency of [psychological] test results strongly suggest a genetic basis for the differences [between test scores of whites and Negroes]," Garrett wrote in his Foreword to the second edition. "I believe that the weight of evidence (biological, historical, and social) supports this judgment." *Ibid.,* 2nd ed., vii. Emphasis added.

white, middle-class Americans; whether or to what extent Negroes in various parts of the United States are handicapped by socio-economic status, caste, motivation, educational discrimination, and a multitude of other factors; and whether the rapport between examiner and subject was satisfactory. The doubts she might have had about such questions she overcame by noting the "remarkable consistency" in the test results, which indicates that she thought the questions were of limited significance. What she did, then, was to lump together an odd assortment of experiments, the sum of which she took to be proof of "some native differences" between the races. But the sum depended upon the validity of its parts, and Professor Shuey totaled up not only the statistical results of the tests but also their limitations, biases, and other deficiencies.

Consider, for example, her treatment of a 1913 study in which Howard Odum compared the results of tests he administered to white and Negro school children in Philadelphia. Odum reported that white children scored substantially higher than the Negroes, but concluded that "environment alone seems sufficient to account for [the] majority of results." Miss Shuey duly noted this comment, but then added Odum's results to her totals, where they became part of the evidence for "some native differences" between the races. Or consider her treatment of Carl C. Brigham's study of the tests administered to Army inductees in World War I. Brigham found marked Negro inferiority and concluded that "the average negro child cannot advance through an educational curriculum adapted to the Anglo-Saxon child in step with that child." [25] A few years later, however, Brigham had second thoughts about the matter and repudiated his earlier findings on the grounds that environmental factors were such that the tests were not true indicators of racial intelligence.[26] Miss Shuey used Brigham's results as part of her evidence, but dismissed his repudiation of his own study as unimportant. Her authority for doing so was a statement by Professor Garrett that the repudiation was of no merit.[27]

The use of Garrett in this manner indicates a significant charac-

[25] Carl C. Brigham, *A Study of American Intelligence* (Princeton, 1923), 194.

[26] See Carl C. Brigham, "Intelligence Tests of Immigrant Groups," *Psychological Review*, CXXXVII (1930), 158–65.

[27] Shuey, *The Testing of Negro Intelligence*, 196–97, 206–07.

teristic of the literature of scientific racism: it is heavily inbred. Since there are few social scientists who lend their authority to racism, those who do must cite each other frequently. In this instance Miss Shuey cited Garrett, who wrote the Foreword to her study, to prove an important point. On another occasion she cited McGurk to explain the decline in Negro test scores from elementary school through college, declaring that "there remains the possibility that we have here a real and normal decline in the IQ's which may be expected of children of dull-normal intelligence." [28] These examples are typical, and if a scientific work depends in part upon the strength of its authorities, they are germane to an evaluation of the literature of scientific racism.

It is obvious, then, that Miss Shuey did not approach her study completely free of the "preconceived racial bias" Garrett warned against.[29] Her study was widely applauded by segregationists and racists of various persuasions. *The Citizens' Council* printed a highly favorable review, quoting a statement by Garrett that the study "should be a standard scientific reference work in every well-informed person's library." Nathaniel Weyl, himself a disseminator of ultraconservative and racist views, likewise accepted it as "a definitive summary." [30]

Social scientists, however, are generally less impressed, and are in fact almost invariably critical of Miss Shuey's assumptions, methods, and conclusions. A reviewer in *Eugenics Review,* journal of the British Eugenics Society, did describe her work as "a valuable and scholarly survey," "as impartial a study as any that have been made in the racial field, [and] an important corrective to extremist views on both sides." [31] But this was an exceptional view. More typical were the responses to a questionnaire conducted by Princeton sociologist Melvin M. Tumin under sponsorship of the

28 *Ibid.,* 156.

29 Long before 1958 she published a study in which she reached conclusions similar to those of *The Testing of Negro Intelligence*. See Shuey, "A Comparison of Negro and White College Students by Means of the American Council Psychological Examination," *Journal of Psychology,* XIV (July, 1942), 35–52.

30 *The Citizens' Council,* III (May, 1958), 4; and Weyl, *The Negro in American Civilization,* 181.

31 P. E. Vernon, "Negro Intelligence," *Eugenics Review,* LII (October, 1960), 174. For a favorable review by Italian sociologist Corrado Gini, see "The Testing of Negro Intelligence: A Review," *Mankind Quarterly,* I (October, 1961), 120–25.

Anti-Defamation League of B'nai B'rith. Tumin asked four social scientists, each a student of race or psychological testing, the following question: "In your judgment, is there sufficient evidence in the Shuey volume to justify Dr. Shuey's conclusion regarding the presence of native differences between Negroes and whites . . .?" He posed the question to Henry C. Dyer, vice-president of the Educational Testing Service and an authority on intelligence and ability testing; psychologist Silvan S. Tomkins of Princeton, an authority on personality testing; sociologist Ralph H. Turner of UCLA, an authority on social and cultural patterns among Negroes; and anthropologist Sherwood L. Washburn of the University of California, formerly president of the American Anthropological Association, and one of the country's most distinguished anthropologists.

These authorities dismissed Dr. Shuey's conclusions as unfounded and unsubstantiated by her evidence. The studies she used did not measure native or innate racial intelligence, they stated. The tests used in the studies were not "adequate tests of native intelligence and other mental and psychological capacities, with proven reliability and validity." Such tests, they added, are impossible to devise, at least at present, and racial intelligence cannot therefore be measured with any degree of accuracy. "Even the most avid defender of intelligence tests today will acknowledge that the tests measure the effects of opportunity to learn the kinds of items included in the tests, motivation, and meaningfulness of the items to the test-takers as well as innate capacity," stated Professor Turner. Dr. Dyer was equally emphatic. "The nature of intelligence tests," he added, "is such that they are incapable of identifying *native* (i.e. genetic) differences between any two groups." [32]

Racists were not impressed by such criticisms.[33] *The Testing of Negro Intelligence,* they insisted, dealt with facts. It offered empirical data to substantiate its conclusions, and it could not be refuted by questionnaires or by resolutions adopted by equalitarian-dominated social science associations. Only factual data, they declared, only the results of tests in which Negroes equal or exceed white averages, will suffice.

These responses to critics of Dr. Shuey are good illustrations of

[32] Melvin M. Tumin (ed.), *Race and Intelligence* (New York, 1963), 14, 15.
[33] See for example Ernest van den Haag, "Intelligence or Prejudice?" *National Review,* December 1, 1964, pp. 1059–63.

TABLE I

PERFORMANCE OF SOUTHERN WHITES ON INTELLIGENCE TESTS COMPARED TO PERFORMANCE OF NORTHERN WHITES

(From Shuey, *The Testing of Negro Intelligence*)

Test Used in Study	Reference (Shuey's page)	Location Of Study — North	Location Of Study — South	Number Tested — North	Number Tested — South	(Score or I.Q.) — North	(Score or I.Q.) — South
Stanford Binet, Forms L & M	10–11	Minneapolis (1944)		341		107.1 (IQ)	
		Philadelphia (1945)		113		103.9 (IQ)	
			Arlington, Va. (1954)		49		95.8 (IQ)
Stanford Binet, 1916 Form	32–33	Lawrence, Kansas (1920)		58		103.9 (IQ)	
	28–29		New Orleans (1925)		947		91.2 (IQ)
	30–31		Nashville, Tenn (1933)		30		96.4 (IQ)
Pintner-Patterson Scale of Performance Test	34–35	Kent Co., Ont.	West Virginia (1928)	211	100	109.59 (IQ)	99.0 (IQ)
Arthur Point Scale	36–37	*Nat'l Norms*	Rural Co. in Virginia (1940)		25	100.0 (IQ)	94.2 (IQ)
Haggerty Delta I	62–63	*Nat'l Norms* Median Scores Age 7–59	Elizabeth City, N. Ca. (1923)		71	59.0 (Score)	42.0 (Score)
		Age 8–68				68.0 (Score)	30.0 (Score)
Otis Quick Scoring Mental Ability, Alpha	68–69	*Nat'l Norms* 100.00	Rural Co. in Va. (1952)		53	100.0 (IQ)	90.0 (IQ)

TABLE II

PERFORMANCE OF SOUTHERN WHITES ON INTELLIGENCE TESTS COMPARED TO PERFORMANCE OF NORTHERN WHITES

(From Shuey, *The Testing of Negro Intelligence*)

Test Used in Study	Reference (Shuey's Page)	Location Of Study North	Location Of Study South	Number Tested North	Number Tested South	(Score or I.Q.) North	(Score or I.Q.) South
Kuhlman-Anderson	90–91	*Nat'l Norms* 100.0	N. Ca. Co. (1923)		438	100.00 (IQ)	93.0 (IQ)
	90–91		Nashville, Tenn. (1939)		112		98.5 (IQ)
							96.6 (IQ)
	90–91		Rural Co. in Va. (1940)		521		88.1 (IQ)
	90–91		Williamson Co., Tenn. (1945)		3,501		86.6 (IQ)
National Intelligence Test	94–95	Los Angeles (1923)		4,326		106.0 (IQ)	
	96–97	New York City (1924)		194		102.0 (IQ)	
	96–97	New York City (1937)		5,007		97.8 (IQ)	
	96–97	Kent Co., Ont.		386		103.59 (IQ)	
	94–95		Mississippi 1926; 3rd and 4th Grades		9,500		89.64 (IQ)
							95.98 (IQ)
Pintner General Ability Verbal Series	108–109	*Nat'l Norms* 100.0 (IQ)	County in N. Ca. (1947)		1,980		91.4 (IQ)
California Test of Mental Ability	110–111	*Nat'l Norms* 100.0 (IQ)	Rural Co., Va. (1952)		53		Lang.–87.0 (IQ)
							Non-L.–95.2 (IQ)
Detroit Primary Test	112–113	*Nat'l Norms* 100.0 (IQ)	West Va. (1928)		3,567		3rd Gr.–88.0 (IQ)
							4th Gr.–84.0 (IQ)
Army Tests—World War I	190–191	Draftees from North (1918)	Draftees from 300,000 South (1918)		100,000	*Sample of State Scores*	
	196–197				Ohio	–66.7	Miss. –41.25
					Ill.	–63.0	Ky. –41.50
					Penna.	–64.6	Ark. –41.55
					N. Y.	–64.0	Ga. –42.12

the racist mind at work. In their controversy with equalitarians, racists invariably do one of two things. They assume racial inequality and Negro inferiority as first premises, or accept studies such as Miss Shuey's as proof of such inequality and inferiority. They take as proof of their case all evidence from which it is possible to infer that Negroes are inferior, and concede to equalitarians only the evidence from which it is impossible to infer Negro inferiority.

Among the criticisms of Miss Shuey's study none was more telling than that of educator Horace Mann Bond, himself the author of one of the studies she used in proving "some native differences" between whites and Negroes. Reviewing *The Testing of Negro Intelligence* for the *Journal of Negro Education,* Bond took her method and with it sought to determine the relative intelligence of Southern and Northern whites. Extracting from her charts all the information on that subject, he constructed a chart of his own (see Tables I and II), and found a "remarkable consistency" in the test results. On the basis of Miss Shuey's own evidence, he concluded, with tongue in cheek, that there are "some native differences" between the intelligence of the two groups, and that the differences all indicate that Southern whites are inferior. If her charts are valid, so also are Bond's, for his rest upon the same logic and data as hers.[34]

Robert Travis Osborne, professor of psychology and director of the student guidance center at the University of Georgia is a third academic psychologist who has made significant contributions to the literature of scientific racism. Born in Florida in 1913, Professor Osborne was educated in Florida and Georgia and received his Ph.D. from the University of Georgia. Since 1937 he has been on the faculty at Georgia.

Osborne is especially valuable to scientific racists because his work complements that of McGurk and Miss Shuey. McGurk and Miss Shuey have not themselves tested the intelligence or educational achievement of significant numbers of Negroes in the deep South, those Negroes, that is, who would attend integrated schools if the Brown decision were fully implemented. Osborne has made such a study.

[34] Horace Mann Bond, "Cat on a Hot Tin Roof," *Journal of Negro Education,* XXVII (Fall, 1958), 519–23.

In Savannah and Chatham County, Georgia, between 1954 and 1960 Osborne conducted "a comprehensive longitudinal study of ethnic differences in mental growth in school achievement," during which he studied the comparative mental maturation of more than eight hundred white and Negro students as they progressed from the sixth through the twelfth grades. The students were tested four times, in the sixth, eighth, tenth, and twelfth grades, and Osborne compared the progress of white and Negro pupils in school achievement and mental maturity. He hoped in this way to be able "to point out some of the practical problems for educators who are forced to balance their schools in terms of factors other than knowledge of and skills in the fundamental subjects." [35] As this indicates, Osborne is avowedly a segregationist. He is convinced that psychological test scores prove that segregated schools are necessary for quality education.

Osborne reported the results of his study in the form of comparative abilities of whites and Negroes in basic school subjects. In the sixth grade, he found, the reading level of white pupils is two full years above that of Negroes, and by the twelfth grade more than three years. In arithmetic skills the differences are even more pronounced. The white advantage is only one year in the sixth grade, but increases to almost four years by the twelfth grade. He found, in fact, that white eighth graders do slightly better in arithmetic skills than Negro twelfth graders. Concerning the comparative rates of mental growth, he found that both races improve at first, but Negroes improve more slowly than whites and their rate of improvement "appears to slow down and level off in the 14 to 16 year age range." Thus, the mental age of Negroes is about two years below that of whites in the sixth grade and about three years below in the tenth, after which their mental growth ceases altogether.

Osborne was careful to point out that these results could not be explained by environment. In his opinion the fact that Negro pupils did relatively better in arithmetic than reading corroborated "the careful work of McGurk and others who consistently report that it is not the cultural but the non-cultural items which are

[35] Robert T. Osborne, "Racial Differences in School Achievement," *Mankind Monographs*, III (November, 1962), 3. See also Osborne, "Racial Differences in Mental Growth and School Achievement: A Longitudinal Study," *Psychological Reports*, VII (October, 1960), 233–39.

[most] difficult for Negro pupils to learn." [36] Nor, he added, could the sorry performance of Negroes be blamed upon poor teaching, for Negro teachers in Savannah and Chatham County have more years of college training and more master's degrees from "the better" Northern and Eastern universities than white teachers, and they receive higher average salaries. He apparently intended these facts to mean that the Negro schools of Savannah and Chatham County are equal to those of whites.

Osborne's study was valuable to segregationists because of its implications for school policy. "What the [public school] administrator needs to know is how to assimilate into white school systems Negro children who in spite of better-trained and higher paid teachers still learn at a rate only one-half to three-fourths that of the white children in the same school district," he wrote. In integrated schools administrators can do one of three things. They can lower academic standards to the Negro's level, thereby reducing white pupils to boredom; maintain standards at white levels, thereby inviting a failure rate among Negro pupils of 40 to 60 percent in intermediate grades and 80 to 90 percent in high school; or group children according to ability, thereby restoring *de facto* segregation, especially in upper grades. "An education system artificially balanced in terms of some factor other than academic performance," Osborne wrote elsewhere, "can do nothing more than polish a dull mediocrity," [37] This is not the place to go into the effects which ability grouping would have upon racial balance in the classroom, or whether such groupings are educationally desirable. It should be noted, however, that nothing in the Brown decision prevents the schools from segregating pupils on the basis of their ability.

Osborne concluded from his study that the schools must be segregated, for only in this way can the schools meet the needs and develop the potentialities of every student. By the twelfth grade, Negro performance is so poor that virtually all white stu-

[36] On this point see Osborne, "Cultural Bias of Psychological Test Items," *Mankind Quarterly*, IV (January–March, 1964), 134–37.

[37] Osborne, "School Achievement of White and Negro Children of the Same Mental and Chronological Ages," *Mankind Quarterly*, II (July–September, 1961), 29.

dents perform at a higher level than the best Negroes. Even those Negroes who equalled or exceeded the performance of some white students in the sixth grade were one or two years behind the same white student by the twelfth grade. Regardless of the perspective from which he viewed his study, Osborne reached the same conclusion: Negroes are so inferior to whites in mental growth and educational capacity that for their own good, and the good of society as well, they must be educated in segregated schools.

Despite Osborne's confidence in his study, the conclusions he drew from it are as questionable as those reached by Shuey and McGurk. Their validity rests almost entirely upon the implicit though unstated assumption that Negro schools in Savannah are equal to white schools and are therefore sufficient to neutralize the environmental disadvantages which Negroes experience in the deep South. Osborne's statement that Negro teachers have more years of college and more masters degrees from non-Southern universities and receive more pay than white teachers is insufficient evidence for so sweeping an assumption. To validate his study he must demonstrate, not merely assume, that the schools of the two races were equal. This, of course, would be a difficult if not impossible task. Perhaps nowhere in the South were Negro schools in 1954 equal to those of whites, and, though in many instances remarkable improvements were made after that date, it is questionable whether equal physical facilities could in a few years overcome the effects of earlier inequalities. In virtually every relevant category of measurement, whether expenditure per pupil, physical facilities, teacher-pupil ratio, or number of library books per pupil, to say nothing of intangibles such as the Supreme Court took cognizance of in the Brown decision, Negro schools were inferior to white schools in 1954, and more often than not continued to be of inferior quality in 1960.

Osborne's case would have been stronger had he admitted that the inferiority of Negro schools accounted for a substantial part of the poor performance of Negroes in his tests. In explaining his test results, however, he gave no weight to environment. It is a striking fact, however, that students in the best school system in Savannah—the white system—achieved the best scores on Osborne's tests, and the longer they attended the superior schools the better their relative performance. And the opposite is true of Negroes. The longer they attended the inferior schools, the poorer their performance.

In fairness to Osborne it should be remarked that he never discussed the subject of innate racial inequality or claimed that Negroes are genetically inferior to whites in intelligence. That he believed this was the case, however, is indicated in his writings. He referred to his Savannah study as a "genetic longitudinal approach" to racial intelligence, and his failure to give weight to environmental factors suggests that he believed the results of his tests were genetically determined. Finally, his endorsement of segregated schools indicates that to him racial differences are permanent and largely immune to environmental influences.

Osborne, McGurk, and Shuey have each made major contributions to scientific racism since 1954. Their works are vitally important to segregationists who seek to reverse the Brown decision or prevent school integration in the South. But despite their appeal among racists and segregationists, they and their works are not widely accepted among psychologists. A few older psychologists endorse the racist position in varying degrees, but such exceptions only prove the generalization. Henry E. Garrett and Clairette P. Armstrong accept the views of Osborne, McGurk, and Shuey, and Stanley D. Porteus accepts portions of it, but their acceptance is atypical. Best known for the Porteus Maze Test, which he developed in 1914, Porteus is an emeritus professor of clinical psychology at the University of Hawaii. Born in Australia in 1883, he is chiefly interested in the psychology of primitive peoples, and it was this interest which led him to develop his maze test. He does not agree with racists that innate racial inequalities have been demonstrated, and he insists that his only interest is the study of racial and ethnic differences. Some of his views, however, are appealing to racists. He has, for example, criticized "missionaries, educators, social workers, reformers and extreme environmentalists" for creating the "beautifully consoling illusion" that all men are "born with equal individual potentialities." [38] He has also served as advisory editor of *Mankind Quarterly,* the chief publication outlet for scientific racists in recent years, and his article, "Ethnic Group Differences," is circulated by the Mississippi Citizens' Councils.

Dr. Clairette P. Armstrong of New York City is even more pronounced than McGurk, Osborne, and Shuey in her views concerning racial inequality. Born in Memphis, Tennessee, and educated at Columbia and New York University, she holds a Ph.D. in psychology from the latter. She has had wide experience as a clinical psychologist and is chiefly interested in the psychology of juvenile delinquents. For a time in the mid-1920's, she was a staff psychologist at Bellevue Hospital in New York City, and later served in a similar capacity in Boston Psychopathic Hospital and in the Childrens' Court and Domestic Relations Court in New York City.

In a critique of the social science testimony in the Brown cases [39] Miss Armstrong went much further than McGurk, Osborne, or Shuey in attacking school integration on the basis of psychological evidence. The idea that segregation is a basic cause of personality disturbance among Negroes is completely false, she stated. In fact the opposite is more likely the case. "Mass integration," she declared, "will create many unhappy misfit Negro school children—today's incipient truants and juvenile court cases, and often tomorrow's criminals." Therefore, the integration movement is "an extremely cruel, inhuman hoax." It instills exaggerated hopes in Negroes, only to shatter those hopes abruptly when "over-age, dull Negroes" find themselves in class with "younger, brighter White classmates." The Negroes are "embarrassed and chagrined by their scholastic disabilities and all that accompanies low mental age," and the result is rage, resentment, frustration. Integration thus denies the Negro child an opportunity for success. Yet, she warned, everything psychologists know about personality adjustment indicates that reasonable prospects for success in life are vital to men-

[38] Stanley D. Porteus, "Ethnic Group Differences," *Mankind Quarterly,* I (January, 1961).

[39] Clairette P. Armstrong, "Psychodiagnosis, Prognosis, School Desegregation and Delinquency," *Mankind Quarterly,* V (October–December, 1964), 63–80.

tal health. For their own mental well-being, Negroes should be segregated and offered "more manual training and trade schools" and other educational experiences suited to their capabilities. "There is no evidence of 'pathogenicity' to Negro children from segregated schools," Dr. Armstrong concluded, "but rather of 'pathogenicity' from desegregated schools as shown by truancy, nervous habits, home deserting and juvenile delinquency." Integrated schools "worsen the plight of most Negro children causing maladjustment, lasting trauma, unhappiness, and delinquency."

Miss Armstrong was convinced that much of the integrationists' concern about the emotional stresses of Negro children is misplaced. "Self-control under stress is one differential between stability and instability, between normal and abnormal," she declared, and everyone, including Negro children, must accept this fact. "Resistance to the temptation to lament unpleasant realities builds good mental health. Restraint of the segregated southern Negro, if under strain, does credit to parents, perhaps to teachers too. Children can be toughened psychologically as well as physically. Character is built by discipline. Repressions in many ways make for good mental health."

The failure of racists to impress more than a handful of American psychologists is explained by the fact that they have been unable to prove their case scientifically. They have therefore failed to convince psychologists that racial segregation is in the public interest. Psychologist Thomas F. Pettigrew of Harvard has demonstrated with great effectiveness the limitations and fallacies in the studies of a number of scientific racists, and has amassed an impressive collection of evidence from a multitude of sources which point to nonracist conclusions.[40]

In *A Profile of the Negro American* Pettigrew summarized much of the recent research of psychologists on the subject of intelligence, and reported the results of dozens of recent studies which seem to indicate that the influence of environment upon intelligence is

[40] Pettigrew, "Negro American Intelligence: A New Look at an Old Controversy," *Journal of Negro Education*, XXXIII (Winter, 1964), 6–25; and Pettigrew, *A Profile of the Negro American*, 100–35.

much greater than racists believe. Intelligence, Pettigrew suggested, is influenced by both heredity and environment. Heredity sets the generally wide limits of individual, but not racial, capacity, and environment determines the extent to which that capacity is realized. According to studies he cited, intelligence is affected by such diverse environmental factors as the diet of the mother during pregnancy, home life, cultural opportunities, especially during early childhood, personality, personal ambition, racial discrimination, and "role-playing" by Negroes. Other scholars have offered similar evidence, equally damaging to the racists' case.[41] It must be admitted that the evidence of the equalitarians is not yet definitive, that is, they have not been able to prove that the races are equal in intelligence or educational capacity. They have, however, clearly demonstrated that environment plays a major role in both IQ test results and intellectual achievement.

The extent to which social scientists reject racist ideas is indicated by a series of resolutions adopted in recent years by several professional groups. The Society for the Psychological Study of Social Issues, a division of the American Psychological Association, and the Society for the Study of Social Problems, a division of the American Sociological Association, have both denounced scientific racism. The latter group declared in 1961 that "the great preponderance of scientific opinion has favored the conclusion that there is little or no ground on which to assume that [whites and Negroes] are innately different in any important human capacity. . . . The conclusion of scientists is that the differences in test performance by members of so-called racial groups are due not to racial but to environmental factors. This is the operating assumption today of the vast majority of the competent scientists in the field." [42] Similarly, the American Anthropological Association, also in 1961, repudiated "statements now appearing in the United

41 See for example Otto Klineberg, "Negro-White Differences in Intelligence Test Performance: A New Look at an Old Problem," *American Psychologist,* XVIII (April, 1963) , 198–203; and Dreger and Miller, "Comparative Psychological Studies of Negroes and Whites in the United States." See also such important works as Otto Klineberg, *Race Differences;* J. McV. Hunt, *Intelligence and Experience* (New York, 1961) , and Anne Anastasi, *Differential Psychology* (New York, 1958.)

42 Quoted in Pettigrew, *A Profile of the Negro American,* 133.

States that Negroes are biologically and in innate mental ability inferior to whites, and reaffirm[ed] the fact that there is no scientifically established evidence to justify the exclusion of any race from the rights guaranteed by the Constitution of the United States. . . . All races possess the abilities needed to participate fully in the democratic way of life and in modern technological civilization." [43]

[43] Quoted in "Science and Segregation: The American Anthropological Association Dips into Politics," *Science*, CXXXIV, December 8, 1961, p. 1869.

5

THE FIELD MARSHALS
OF SCIENTIFIC RACISM

Despite the significance of Osborne, McGurk, and Shuey, theirs was not the most important role in the racists' exploitation of psychology. Individually and collectively their contributions were overshadowed by those of Professor Henry E. Garrett, one of the nation's leading authorities on psychometrics and psychological testing.[1] Because he is the most distinguished social scientist who joined the racists, Garrett's significance transcends that of other psychologists. By and large, McGurk, Osborne, and Shuey did little

---

[1] See above p. 53–57.

more than undertake individual studies and publish their findings. Garrett, however, has alternately played the role of oracle and field marshal for scientific racists of all sorts, whether academic social scientists or outspoken white supremacists. He challenges the data and conclusions of anyone who questions the racist-hereditarian point of view; acts as a general propagandist for racial inequality, and school segregation; issues jeremiads against social integration and racial amalgamation; and cooperates with such zealous segregationists as those who join the Citizens' Councils of America. In each of these tasks he assumes the stance of a purveyor of ideas from the scientific community to the general public, and many laymen accept him as just that.

Garrett's role in the story of scientific racism is best approached within the framework of his social and racial philosophy. He endorses the major ideas of McGurk, Osborne, and Shuey,[2] though he is even readier than they are to translate those ideas into propaganda for racial segregation and political and social reaction. Perhaps the most instructive statement of his social and racial views is his article, "The Equalitarian Dogma," which first appeared in *Perspectives in Biology and Medicine,* was reprinted in *U.S. News and World Report,* and reissued in revised form as a pamphlet, *The South and the Second Reconstruction.*[3] In its various forms the article illustrates the facility with which Garrett combines science and racism, and the extent to which he uses science to buttress reactionary social and political convictions.

"The equalitarian dogma" of which Garrett wrote is nothing more than the ideas of racial equality and environmentalism, ideas which he accused equalitaritarians of accepting on faith and in the face of absolutely convincing data to the contrary.[4] The dogma

2 See for example Henry E. Garrett's "Foreword" to Shuey, *The Testing of Negro Intelligence,* vii–viii; Garrett, "Genetics and Intelligence," *Mankind Quarterly,* IV (April-June, 1964) , 202–04; Garrett, "Klineberg's 'Negro-White Differences in Intelligence Test Performance,'" *ibid.,* 221–22; and *Race, 11 Questions and 11 Answers* (Washington, n. d.) , 3–12.

3 Henry E. Garrett, "The Equalitarian Dogma," *Perspectives in Biology and Medicine,* IV (Summer, 1961) , 480–84; Garrett, "One Psychologist's View of 'Equality of the Races,'" *U.S. News and World Report,* August 14, 1961, pp. 72–74; and Garrett, *The South and the Second Reconstruction* (no imprint) .

4 My summary of Garrett's ideas about "the equalitarian dogma" follow his pamphlet *The South and the Second Reconstruction.* Garrett recently repeated many of these same ideas in his *Desegregation: Fact and Hokum* (Richmond, 1965) , published and distributed by "the Patrick Henry Group."

appeals to intellectuals, humanitarians, social reformers, crusaders, sentimentalists, politicians, ministers, liberals and communists, he declared, and has infiltrated the social sciences, the education establishment, the press, and other communications media. This situation is the reverse of what it was two generations ago— when Garrett grew up and was educated and the racist-hereditarian viewpoint dominated American social science—and one of his major concerns was to explain the change.

It all began with "modern" anthropology, which he traced to the influences of his one-time colleague at Columbia, Franz Boas. Through Boas, Garrett charged, equalitarianism infiltrated the social science departments of colleges and universities, and eventually became a major premise of most social scientists. On another occasion, Garrett described his personal observation of this process. At Columbia, "[I] was able to observe the influence of Boas as founder of the so-called subject of cultural anthropology in America," he wrote in a letter to the New York *Times*,[5] "and to witness the extent to which Boas' socialistic ideology dominated his thinking and permeated the teaching of his disciples, first at Columbia and later at other universities fed from the Boas cult." As a result of Boas' influence, equalitarian orthodoxy replaced freedom of inquiry in the social sciences. College classes became indoctrination sessions in which students were taught to "parrot the equalitarian arguments without competent familiarity with the evidence" and to shift "from the scientific to the moral position as the occasion requires." The "evidence" to which Garrett referred was Professor Shuey's study of Negro intelligence, and it does not, he declared emphatically, favor the equalitarian dogma; in fact, it discredits that dogma.

A second factor which contributed to the success of equalitarianism in social science circles was the racist excesses of Hitler and the Nazis. "Hitler was a true 'racist,' " declared Garrett, "as is anyone who believes in the general superiority in intelligence and character of some group (usually his own). Racism uses such terms as 'nordic supremacy' and 'Chosen People.' " Hitler's extremism was unfortunate in many ways. It made the study of race suspect at best and odious at worst, and subjected anyone who speaks of

[5] Garrett and Wesley C. George to editor, New York *Times*, October 24, 1962, p. 38.

racial differences to charges of racism and fascism. It made many Americans, including Jews, overly sensitive to "anything that smacks of racial exclusion." As a result, many well-meaning people have lost all perspective concerning race, and in overcompensating for Hitlerism they indiscriminately support any movement, however radical or irresponsible, which claims to foster brotherhood, racial integration, or civil rights. "Ironically enough," Garrett added, "the Jews who usually draw the racial line at the marriage altar stand to lose very little by so-called integration."

A third reason for the triumph of equalitarianism was the rise of African nationalism and the emergence of independent pseudo-nations in Negro Africa. Equalitarians blame colonialism for the backwardness and savagery of black Africans, Garrett charged, but it is the Africans themselves who are to blame. The white colonial powers rescued the continent from witch doctors, cannibals, and slave traders, and in their stead brought civilization, Christianity, and the rule of law. Expelling white colonialists is thus an effectual example of misdirected do-goodism and an illustration of the blind faith equalitarians have in their dogma. There is little evidence that Africans can govern themselves, Garrett declared, but overwhelming evidence, as events in the Congo recently demonstrated, that without the supervision of white men they turn naturally to murder, mutilation, slavery, and cannibalism.

The fourth factor which Garrett offered to explain the success of equalitarianism was the Brown decision, a decision which not only rested upon false social science but was patently unconstitutional. He also pointed out that Barry Goldwater had ably demonstrated this weakness in *The Conscience of a Conservative*. As a matter of fact, Garrett charged, it was the absence of valid constitutional precedents which led the Court to turn to social science. The justices, however, knew even less about psychology and sociology than they did about law, and allowed themselves to be deceived by equalitarian witnesses. Of the eight social scientists they cited in footnote eleven, "none had a national reputation; one had 18 citations of membership in communist front organizations, [and] another 10. Two were Negroes. Obviously the Court's authorities did not come before the American people without bias and with clean hands." [6]

[6] Garrett's reference to the fact that two of the authorities were Negroes

A final reason for the spread of equalitarianism was the influence of communism. "It is certain that the Communists have aided in the acceptance and spread of equalitarianism," Garrett wrote, "although the extent and method of their help is difficult to assess. Equalitarianism is good Marxist doctrine not likely to change with gyrations of the Kremlin 'line.' Moreover, the forceful application of the dogma foments tensions and bitterness on which the Communists thrive."

According to Garrett, these five factors account for the spread of the equalitarian virus and explain the success of environmentalists in deceiving the American people and leading them away from truths which an earlier generation knew and accepted. The truth had not changed, only the willingness to accept it and use it in formulating social policies. "The weight of the evidence strongly favors the view that racial differences in mental ability are real and are probably genetic," Garrett wrote, and the nation can ignore this fact only at great peril. This does not mean that Negroes must be exploited and deprived of their basic rights, as has sometimes happened in the past. "No effort should be spared to give the Negro better training, to upgrade him in his job, to provide technical and professional education," continued Garrett. "But unless the equalitarian dogma is discredited and abandoned, it will lead inevitably to social integration, inter-marriage, amalgamation of white and Negro, and to a general deterioration in American standards of culture and intelligence."

These remarks, from *The South and the Second Reconstruction,* are typical of the views which Garrett expressed, somewhat more circumspectly, in an article in *Perspectives in Biology and Medicine,* a journal published chiefly for physiologists and medical researchers. "The equalitarian dogma, at best, represents a sincere if misguided effort to help the Negro by ignoring or even suppressing evidence of his mental and social immaturity," he wrote

---

is typical of an inference frequently made by segregationists. He rejected Negroes as authorities on racial matters because of their obvious grounds for bias, though it apparently never occurred to him that a white man might have a bias of his own. Perhaps he agreed with the traditional view of Southern segregationists: living among Negroes in the South does not make the white man biased or prejudiced; on the contrary, it is the only way a white man can ever understand and appreciate Negroes.

in the scientific journal. "At worst, the equalitarian dogma is the scientific hoax of the century."

For a scientific journal to print such an article is unusual, and its appearance brought down a torrent of criticism upon the journal and its editor, physiologist Dwight J. Ingle of the University of Chicago, himself no racist. At its annual meeting in September, 1961, the Society for the Psychological Study of Social Issues (SPSSI), a division of the American Psychological Association, adopted a resolution describing Garrett's article as unscientific and denouncing it as a misuse of science for undemocratic purposes. There is "no evidence" that racial differences in intelligence test scores are innate, the psychologists declared. "Quite to the contrary, the evidence points overwhemingly to the fact that when one compares Negroes and whites of comparable cultural and educational background, differences in intelligence diminish markedly; the more comparable the background, the less the difference." [7] In fact, they pointed out Garrett was himself unwilling to state flatly that innate differences in intelligence have been proved. He only suggested that such differences as exist may be or appear to be innate. For purposes of social and educational policy, however, he assumes—and this is the crucial point—that the differences are innate. He thus made a major unproven assumption in translating "scientific" data into social policy.

Garrett did not take the SPSSI resolution in silence. In a reply published in *American Psychologist*,[8] he took vigorous exception to it. To the statement that there is no evidence that racial differences in intelligence are innate, he replied that psychologists have clearly demonstrated that such differences exist and that they persist even when environmental factors are neutralized. As proof he cited the studies of McGurk, Shuey, H. A. Tanser,[9] and others. He noted

[7] "Statement on Race and Intelligence from the Society for the Psychological Study of Social Issues," *Perspectives in Biology and Medicine*, V (Autumn, 1961) , 129.

[8] Henry E. Garrett, "The SPSSI and Racial Differences," *American Psychologist*, XVII (May, 1962) , 260–63.

[9] H. A. Tanser, *The Settlement of Negroes in Kent County, Ontario, and A Study of the Mental Capacity of Their Descendants* (Chatham, Ontario, 1939) . The premise of Tanser's study was that Negroes in Kent County, located opposite Detroit, were not discriminated against and had all the advantages enjoyed by white Canadians. Tanser thus reasoned that they offered an opportunity for the study of innate racial differences. He found significant differences between the races in favor of whites. For criticism of this study see Pettigrew, *A Profile of the Negro American*, 102–03.

the results of several studies which tended to support the view that the performance of Negroes improves when environmental factors are controlled, and found the results "dubious at best." He concluded: "Instead of the evidence for diminished differences between Negroes and whites of comparable status being 'over-whelming' as the SPSSI statement asserts, it is, in fact, nonexistent."

Like other racists Garrett accepts the plot theory of history. In his writings in recent years there is an implicit assumption that the civil rights movement, like "the equalitarian dogma," is in part the result of a gigantic conspiracy to stifle scientific inquiry and conceal the truth from the American people. Convinced that equalitarians are engaged in a concerted effort to abuse, ridicule, censure, and impugn the motives of nonequalitarians, he came to regard any social scientist who questioned equalitarian orthodoxy as a hero in the perennial struggle for academic freedom and the pursuit of truth. Following the appearance of McGurk's article in *U.S. News and World Report* in 1956, Garrett declared, McGurk "was castigated by rabid equalitarians, resolutions were passed condemning his study, the newspapers were bombarded with denunciatory letters . . . he and his wife were beseiged with anonymous telephone calls, he was 'silenced' by his university for a year, and it was demanded that he be expelled from the American Psychological Association." [10] And this because "he had published what he found." Similarly, several major publishers turned down Professor Shuey's study of Negro intelligence solely because they objected to its point of view and its conclusions.

To Garrett and Dr. Wesley C. George, who expressed these views in a letter to the editor of *Science,* this censorship was a real threat to academic freedom. "Frequently we have been told by young scientists that they would not dare to 'come out' for hereditary differences between Negroes and whites," wrote Garrett and George, for "their promotions, even their jobs would be in jeopardy. Even in the South, young scientists find that school officials have the attitude that it is better to keep quiet and play it safe; reprisals are not unknown." It was these convictions which led Garrett (and George) to conclude that equalitarians had organized a cabal against freedom of inquiry. "Attacks on those who support racial differences are too persistent, too regular, and too

[10] Henry E. Garrett and Wesley C. George, letter to the editor, *Science,* February 28, 1964, p. 913.

emotional to be unplanned and accidental. And so is the name calling."

Garrett is influential among scientific racists because he embodies so many of their opinions. His criticisms of intellectuals are representative of the anti-intellectualism endemic in scientific racism. His denunciations of Jewish integrationists and the new African nations are typical too, as are his endorsement of right-wing political and constitutional views and his prophecies of gloom and doom. He insists that the integration movement is no mere effort to secure rights for Negroes. It is instead an assault upon the American way of life and the United States Constitution, and a threat to the fabric of western civilization. The South, he believes, is fighting to preserve America, to uphold the Constitution, to perpetuate the grandest civilization in man's history. This explains "why the South is refusing again to be reconstructed," and why the agitation for "so-called integration" will not induce Southerners to abandon social segregation. "Like most white Americans whose contact with the Negro is direct and personal," he wrote, white Southerners "realize . . . the great gulf between the two races. They know intuitively that we can ill afford any retrogression in the world today. And racial amalgamation might just be the difference between survival and destruction." [11] This is the great concern of segregationists, of Citizens' Councils, of Southern politicians. Their motive is not callous self-interest, not prejudice and bigotry. They are selfless fighters for freedom, for law and order, for human progress. And their efforts are rooted in scientific truth.

Unfortunately, Garrett and other racists never systematically developed the political implications of these claims. Scientific racists, or at least those in academic circles, seek to avoid the appearance of overt racial bigotry, and they disclaim any intention or desire to deprive the Negro of his civil rights, including the right to vote and equality before the law. But this involves a paradox, which scientific racists have never satisfactorily resolved. "Civil rights as legally defined, include the right to vote, to hold public office, and to have free access to the courts," wrote Garrett and George in their letter to the editor of *Science*. Upon occasion, they admitted, these rights have been denied to Negroes, as well as to other underprivileged Americans. "But no responsible scientist

---

[11] Garrett, *The South and the Second Reconstruction,* 9th page. (This pamphlet has no pagination.)

who believes in native differences between Negroes and whites has advocated the withdrawal of civil rights for *anyone*." Of course, they added, "the *facts* of racial differences must be faced by those in power," who must recognize that "the demand for social privileges and associations, based on the no-difference assumption, will lead to continuing strife and could lead to national disaster." There are "no moral imperatives which demand social acceptance of Negroes by whites, and the Constitution does not guarantee social 'rights' to anyone—Negro or white." Despite this, "extreme champions of 'rights' for Negroes often include in their demands forms of legal compulsion which cannot be tolerated in a free society."

These generalities are, of course, open to interpretation and are therefore too imprecise to serve as a practical guide for public affairs. If Negroes can vote freely, for example, there is the possibility, indeed the likelihood, that they will vote for integrated schools. But integrated schools violate Garrett's scientific and constitutional principles as well as his admonitions against social integration. May, then, Negroes vote freely for everything—except integrated schools? In recent years Negroes and their political allies have demanded the integration of public accommodations, and their voting strength and political pressure have been sufficient to accomplish their objective. This, too, however, violates Garrett's scientific and constitutional principles, but is a logical consequence of Negro voting. Would Garrett again interpose his scientific principles to prevent integration of public accommodations? To do so would circumscribe the Negro's right to vote in a way in which the white man's is not circumscribed. Garrett would allow the white man to use government, which rests upon the right to vote, to preserve segregation, but he would deny Negroes the use of government to achieve integration.

The truth is that Garrett's distinction between political and social rights is, as a practical matter, an artificial one. If Negroes vote they will be courted—no pun intended—by white politicians. More importantly they will be wooed by Negro politicians, and might, as Garrett himself foresees, elect Negroes to office. When this occurs can social integration be avoided? Elected officials have social as well as official responsibilities, and so also do appointed officials and party politicians. Apparently Garrett would permit Negroes to be elected to public office but would require them to preserve social segregation when dealing with their white col-

leagues and constituents. The success of the civil rights movement is due to the Negro's ability to bring democratic political
pressure. It is a direct result of the right to vote. Anyone who
endorses the Negro's unconditional right to vote must, it would
seem, reconcile himself to the "so-called" integration movement.

Garrett's political philosophy, like that of other segregationists,
is intensely conservative, not to say reactionary. To him racial
integration, when forced by the federal government, is a form of
"legal compulsion which cannot be tolerated in a free society."
Yet it might just as easily be maintained that segregation is itself
a form of legal compulsion which is incompatible with free society. To Garrett compulsory segregation is tolerable for Negroes,
but compulsory integration is intolerable for whites. Whenever any
part of the citizenry objects to integration or segregation there is
of course an element of compulsion in each, but there are meaningful distinctions between the two forms of compulsion that would
seem to have constitutional significance. Compulsory segregation of
Negroes implies a stigma of inferiority and a denial of equality
before the law, whereas compulsory integration carries no similar
implications. In his preoccupation with compulsions which produce social and educational integration and in his solicitude for the
white man, Garrett forgot those compulsions which inhere in segregation.

His oversight, however, is consistent with the attitude he has
toward Negroes. "Observers here and abroad generally agree that
the Negro is usually cheerful, frequently childish, often slovenly
and irresponsible," Garrett wrote in one instance. "Many Negroes, of course, do not possess these traits to a greater degree than
does the White man. But the conviction that most Negroes do is
widespread and strong and it holds more than a kernel of truth."
On other occasions, he described Negroes as equal or superior to
white men in physical strength and agility, in sports, and in "certain forms of entertainment and music," but inferior in "abstract
intelligence" and "the sort of ability that creates a modern technical society," including the ability "to think in terms of symbols—
words, numbers, formulas, diagrams." [12] Perversely, Garrett's de-

[12] See Garrett, *Race, 11 Questions and 11 Answers*, 10; Garrett, "The Scientific Racism of Juan Comas," *Mankind Quarterly*, II (October–December, 1961),
100–06; and Garrett, "Race Mixing Could be Catastrophic," *U.S. News and
World Report*, November 18, 1963, pp. 92–93.

scriptions do have a certain accuracy. He acknowledged, perhaps unwittingly, the fact that Negroes excel in those areas where they meet the least amount of prejudice and discrimination, in sports, entertainment and hard physical labor. But even this needs further refining. In certain sports, for example, boxing, football, and baseball, Negroes encounter little or no discrimination outside the South, and in these their accomplishments equal or perhaps exceed those of whites. In socially oriented sports, however, such as tennis and golf, racial discriminations are more meaningful and the accomplishments of Negroes much less impressive. Racists usually recognize certain activities as appropriate for Negroes and acknowledge—and applaud—their accomplishments in those areas. Elsewhere, however, they belittle Negro achievement while failing to take sufficient account of the prejudice and discrimination which handicap the race in those areas.

Garrett's conviction that the racial traits and capacities of Negroes are inferior to those of whites is the basis of his opposition to racial amalgamation, for he believes that those traits and capacities are perpetuated by heredity. But though he spoke as a scientist on this point, his opposition seems largely social. "When you come to a race mixture, I don't see that there would be any evil effects as far as the physical structure of the hybrid is concerned," he told an interviewer in *U.S. News and World Report*. "The difficulty, it seems to me, comes in mass mixing, which is the goal of the Negro pressure groups." Apparently he never discussed the specific genetic factors which make mixing undesirable. He seems to believe something like this: first, Negroes are inferior to whites in important capabilities which are necessary to preserve and expand the complex, technological civilization of today; second, inferior racial characteristics tend to predominate over superior ones in inheritance; and third, mass racial intermixture will therefore lower the quality of the American people.

To substantiate these views, Garrett pointed not to scientific studies of race crossings but to history. "I don't believe that, historically, amalgamation with the Negro has ever done anything except lower the general level of the national life of those people who have been willing to mix," he declared, and as proof cited the history of Latin America. Latin Americans, he believed, had failed to match the achievements of North Americans because the Europeans who settled in South America failed to keep their race pure, and he saw in the failure an object lesson for the United States. "My concern was—and is—that American whites, under the prodding of equalitarians and moralistic social reformers will become convinced that it is their duty to absorb the eighteen million or so Negroes and Negroids in this country," he wrote, warning that nothing has ever so imperiled the nation. "No matter how low (in a socioeconomic sense) an American white may be," Garrett stated, "his ancestors built the civilizations of Europe; and no matter how high (again in a socioeconomic sense) a Negro may be, his ancestors were (and his kinsmen still are) savages in an African jungle." The mass mixture of races of such uneven accomplishments is "not only dysgenic but socially disastrous." [13]

Garrett's views on this subject help explain his attitudes toward civil rights and voting. Here as elsewhere he tended to look upon Negroes as members of a stereotyped racial group. He sometimes gives the impression that individual Negroes, whatever their personal merit, are to be judged by the worst features of their racial past, and he gives each a share of guilt for the misdeeds and failures of every other Negro. Individual whites, on the other hand, he judges by the best accomplishments of their race. To give a specific example, Garrett believes that the recent atrocities in the Congo are to be explained by the racial shortcomings of Negroes, but he sees no racial significance in the atrocities committed by Germans in World War II.

"It is idle," Garrett once stated, "to argue that all members of *homo sapiens* should be treated as individuals regardless of race." [14] Yet to judge an individual on his personal merits is an elemental feature of democracy. Democracy, however, was another subject Garrett never discussed. His writings imply that he views democracy in terms of a nineteenth-century *laissez faire* liberal, which is to say he has a fear of centralized government and is in mid-twentieth century terms a political reactionary. To him, the best way to preserve American democracy is to interpret the Constitution as strictly as possible and to limit government to the fewest possible responsibilities (at least in the realm of race relations and social welfare). In this way he reconciled his endorsement of

[13] Henry E. Garrett, "Racial Differences and Witch Hunting," *Science*, March 16, 1962, pp. 982–84.

[14] Garrett, "The Scientific Racism of Juan Comas," 106.

Negro suffrage with his support of legalized segregation. Negroes should be able to vote, he felt, but the value of their vote will be circumscribed by rigid limits placed on the powers of government, especially the federal government. The latter, he insisted, must not be used to serve the whims of pressure groups or special interest blocs. It must not, in other words, promote the civil rights movement. It could be argued, however, that the government's *failure* to act might serve the interests of one pressure group (segregationists) just as its actions might serve another (Negroes). Historically, segregation has been perpetuated by the widespread use of government power, including the power of the federal government. Since this is the case, Garrett is vulnerable to the charge that he is not so much fearful of governmental power per se as he is of the use of power for ends he disapproves.

Garrett is convinced that segregation and democracy are compatible. Public policy, he insists, must benefit the maximum number of people, and segregation does just that. It benefits Negroes as well as whites. "Maintain separate schools," he advised equalitarians who sought ways to improve Negro education. "Set up the Negro curriculum to accommodate their [sic] lesser degree of abstract intelligence, stop excusing the Negro's lag as being wholly 'environmental,' and stop misleading him by urging goals he cannot attain." [15] The "alleged horrors" of segregated schools exist only in the minds of adult white do-gooders, who feel that the Negro child *should be* frustrated by segregation because they would themselves be frustrated. Actually, wrote Garrett, integrated schools benefit no one, least of all the Negro child, who suffers "real emotional harm" when forced into a hostile white school by court order.[16]

Thus it was that Henry E. Garrett, after a long and distinguished career as a psychologist, emerged as the most significant exponent of racism in social science circles. Even his contributions to the journal of the Citizens' Councils of America[17] and his active co-

[15] Garrett's review of Wallace A. Kennedy, et al, *A Normative Sample of Intelligence. . . ,* in *Mankind Quarterly,* V (July–September 1964), 58–59.

[16] Henry E. Garrett, " 'Benefits' of Integrated Schools Are a Myth!" *The Citizen,* XI (January, 1965), 4–6.

[17] See for example Henry E. Garrett, "Facts vs. Opinions on 'Race and Reason,' " *The Citizen,* VII (February, 1963), 7–12; Garrett, "Professor Cites Fallacies of Integration Arguments," *The Citizens' Council,* II (October, 1956), 1, 4; and Garrett, " 'Benefits' of Integrated Schools Are a Myth!"

operation with the Councils did not lessen his appeal among social scientists who are also racists. Not even his favorable reviews of unscientific work by racists, white supremacists, or political reactionaries dim their ardor for him.[18] Garrett has not accomplished what he set out to accomplish—to provide a scientifically valid rationale for racial segregation—but he has reinforced the impression among laymen that there are valid scientific reasons for segregation and white supremacy.

Scientific racists needed a broader base for their ideology than psychology alone could provide. With the assistance of such cooperative psychologists as McGurk and Osborne, they demonstrated, to their own satisfaction, that racial differences in intelligence and educability are so great as to justify school segregation. But this was only one facet of a larger task. They needed also to demonstrate that white-Negro differences in IQ test scores are matched by equally significant differences in physiology and morphology, and that all racial differences, whether psychological or physiological, are perpetuated by an unerring process of heredity. Thus, biology, physiology, and genetics are also important to racists, and from these disciplines they seek evidence to buttress their case against school integration and racial amalgamation. Their success in these disciplines, however, has been less substantial than in psychology. A miniscule number of racists have appeared in these disciplines, but they have exerted no influence among the generality of their colleagues. They have, however, significantly enhanced the appeal of scientific racism among segregationists.

The most notable result of their efforts and perhaps the most important item in the literature of scientific racism is Wesley Critz George's *The Biology of the Race Problem* (1962). George is one of not more than three or four biological scientists who have endorsed the ideas of scientific racism. His value to racists therefore far exceeds the scientific merits of anything he has written. Born in North Carolina in 1888 and educated in his native state

18 See for example his review of James J. Kilpatrick, *The Southern Case for School Segregation, Mankind Quarterly*, III (April–June 1963), 264–65; his comments on Carleton Putnam's *Race and Reason, The Citizen*, VII (February 1963), 7–12; and his castigation of liberals in his laudatory review of James Burnham's *Suicide of the West, Mankind Quarterly*, V (July–September 1964), 53–54.

(he received a Ph.D. in zoology from the University of North Carolina in 1918), he has held teaching positions at several Southern universities in zoology, biology, histology, embryology, and anatomy. From 1924 until his retirement a few years ago he was professor of anatomy at the University of North Carolina Medical School, serving as chairman of the department from 1940 to 1949.

George's contributions to the literature of scientific racism are not as voluminous as Professor Garrett's, but he shares with Garrett the role of field marshal of scientific racists. His writings and public utterances are as authoritative among racists as Garrett's, and the contributions of the two men admirably complement each other. Garrett's special preserve is racial psychology, George's the physiology of race, and both would use "science" as the basis for formulating social, educational, and racial policies.

In 1961 Governor John Patterson of Alabama invited George to undertake a brief study of science and race, in which he would spell out the scientific facts about race and explain their implications for race relations and school integration. The governor gave George $3,000 of state funds to finance the study. The product of his endeavor was *The Biology of the Race Problem,* an 87-page booklet published by commission of Governor Patterson and now in its fifth printing. Since its publication in 1962, it has been cited and endorsed by racists of all shades of opinion, and is today distributed by such groups as the Citizens' Councils, the National Putnam Letters Committee, and the American Eugenics Party, the last a tiny fringe group which urges, among other things, such "eugenic reforms" as absolute prohibition of interracial marriage, sterilization of defectives, and immediate "return" of all Negroes and mulattoes to Africa. An official of the Citizens' Council praised George's work as "a major scientific report" which "shattered the equalitarian myth" and deserves "careful study by all serious students of racial problems." Garrett described it as "the best single reference" on the physiology of the Negro brain.[19]

Because of its authority among scientific racists, *The Biology of the Race Problem* deserves examination in detail. Written in sim-

[19] W. J. Simmons, "The Truth About Racial Differences!" *The Citizen,* VII (October, 1962), 7–8; and Garrett, "Facts vs. Opinions on 'Race and Reason,' " 12.

ple, straightforward language, it was obviously aimed at laymen, who are perhaps overawed by the paraphernalia of scholarship and the multitude of scientific authorities quoted, footnoted, or otherwise alluded to. It is filled with citations of and quotations from many of the nation's most respected scientists and social scientists. At first glance it is an impressive work, especially to laymen seeking scientific justification for racial segregation.

George had several purposes in writing *The Biology of the Race Problem*. He sought to prove that whites and Negroes are psychologically as well as physiologically different, that psychological differences between whites and Negroes are of such a nature and magnitude as to constitute white superiority and Negro inferiority. He hoped also to demonstrate that racial amalgamation would destroy the small but vital margin of white superiority, a margin which, in his opinion, is the genetic basis of American civilization. On the basis of his evidence on these points, he warned the American people that integration of the public schools will inevitably lead to social equality, racial amalgamation—and national deterioration.

George devoted the first four pages of his work to listing and identifying most of the scientists he later cited, and an impression results that his study rests upon massive scientific authority. Though uneven, the list is imposing. It includes several prominent scientific racists, Garrett, McGurk, Shuey, and the late British geneticist R. Ruggles Gates; several anti-equalitarian scientists whom racists are fond of quoting, among them Roger J. Williams of the University of Texas, author of *Free and Unequal* (1953), a denunciation of environmentalism;[20] and a number of older scientists who accepted in varying degrees the ideas of racial inequality and Negro inferiority, such as Sir Francis Galton, Robert M. Yerkes, Henry Pratt Fairchild, and Robert Bennett Bean. More significantly, George's list also contains a number of contemporary authorities on race and related subjects, including Ward C. Hal-

[20] "The uniformity doctrine is in accord with Communistic thinking and is basically completely out of line with liberty-loving democracy and its emphasis on individual worth," wrote Williams in a typical passage. "The acceptance of the uniformity idea, which has often been done vaguely without facing the implications, has undoubtedly much to do with the fear mentioned earlier, namely that to understand Communism might lead to its acceptance." *Free and Unequal* (Austin, Texas, 1953), 142.

stead, professor of experimental psychology, Department of Medicine, University of Chicago; Charles J. Herrick, late professor of neurology, University of Chicago and editor of the *Journal of Comparative Neurology*; Wilder Penfield, professor of neurology and neurosurgery at McGill University and director of the Montreal Neurological Institute; Curt Stern, professor of genetics, University of California, Berkeley; anthropologist Carleton S. Coon, and others of similar stature. Altogether George listed forty-one authorities and in addition cited perhaps two dozen others in the body of his work.

The list gives the impression that *The Biology of the Race Problem* rests upon the authority of the scientists in the list. Now, if the research of those scientists did in fact support George's conclusions, his work would indeed be authoritative. This, however, is not the case, as George himself indirectly admits. "The views of these and other scientists will follow," he wrote at the end of the list. But then he added, *"I do not ascribe any particular opinion to any of these people regarding the school integration problem,* but as to the specific points on which they are cited, their testimony is authoritative." [21] The whole purpose of *The Biology of the Race Problem* was to prove the necessity for public school segregation, and for George to disassociate his authorities from his purpose is a revealing confession. The disclaimer was his way of saying that most of the scientists in the list disagreed with his use of their works and the conclusions he reached.

There are numerous indications that *The Biology of the Race Problem* is more concerned with racist propaganda than scientific truth. "One of the most important problems facing Americans today," wrote George in the introduction, "is, Shall we pursue programs that would result in mixing the genes of the Negro race with those of the White race and so convert the population of the United States into a mixed-blooded people?" This question is really George's chief concern. "Before saying yes to that question, before making any revolutionary decisions relative to so important and irreversible a matter, the information we have that bears on the issue should be carefully and critically evaluated." A mixed-blooded people, he warned, will be the logical result of educa-

21 Emphasis added.

tional (and thus social) integration. *The Biology of the Race Problem* was his effort to demonstrate the folly of such a policy.

The appeal of George's work is enhanced by his failure to inform his readers on two critical points: the relative stature of the scientists he quotes and their attitudes toward Negroes, segregation, and racial equality. He treated each of his authorities as equally valid and ignored their racial views altogether. He thus told only a part of the story, and as a result created the erroneous impression that his conclusions are supported by massive scientific authority.

To illustrate the magnitude of the deception, consider, for example, the first entry in George's list of authorities: "Robert Bennett Bean, M.D.; anthropologist; Professor of Anatomy, University of Virginia." Bean's usefulness to George rested upon a study of the size and morphology of Negro brains made in 1906 and which few authorities today consider of any value whatever.[22] George accepts Bean's study at face value and treats Bean himself as a scientist whose studies are as valid as those of the most recent and disinterested scholars. He fails to mention that Bean was a racist of the most patronizing sort whose racial attitudes were typical of Southern segregationists of the post-Reconstruction era. Bean's racial views pervade everything he wrote about race, including the 1906 study which George cited. One of the tasks Bean set for himself in that study was to explain the social and psychological implications of his findings that the Negro brain is inferior to the white brain. "The Caucasian—more particularly the Anglo-Saxon, which was derived from the Primitives of Europe, is dominant and domineering, and possessed primarily with determination, will power, self-control, self-government, and all the attributes of the subjective self, with a high development of the ethical and aesthetic faculties," Bean wrote. "The Negro [on the other hand] is primarily affectionate, immensely emotional, then sensual and under stimulation passionate. There is [among Negroes] love of ostentation, of outward show, of approbation; there is love of music, and capacity for melodious articulation; there is undeveloped artistic power and taste—Negroes make good artisans, handicraftsmen—and there is instability of character incident to lack of self-control,

22 See for example the review of Bean's study in Dwight J. Ingle, "Comments on the Teachings of Carleton Putnam," *Mankind Quarterly,* IV (1963), 30–36.

especially in connection with the sexual relation." [23] These qualities, Bean explained, are due to the differences in size and morphology of the brains of the two races. Despite such pseudoscience
as this, George offered Bean as one of his authorities, and few
laymen feel able to challenge the work of a man identified only
as an M.D., an anthropologist, and a professor of anatomy at the
University of Virginia.

Numerous other instances, involving contemporary authorities,
are equally damaging to George's case. On two occasions he cited
geneticist Curt Stern, once to summarize the contributions of
Gregor Mendel (p. 8), and again to state that *men* (Stern does
not say or imply *races*) differ and are genetically unequal (p.
54). On this basis George lists Stern as one of the authorities
whose "views . . . will follow." Again, however, he omits vital parts
of the story. He fails to note that Stern is an outspoken equalitarian who on at least one occasion predicted the complete amalgamation of whites and Negroes in America and foresaw no ill
consequences as a result. In Stern's view, neither Negroes nor
mulattoes have any biological or mental deficiencies which make
them, as a group, inferior to Caucasians.[24] Stern's view, then, was
the opposite of what George was trying to prove, namely, that
racial amalgamation is scientifically unwise and will bring genetic
deterioration and national disaster. Stern is one of the nation's
foremost geneticists, and George, himself a member of the American Society of Human Geneticists, presumably felt Stern's name
would add luster to his work, even though Stern's research adds
nothing to the case he was attempting to prove.

Several of the men George included in his list have themelves
denounced his misuse of their works. He quoted statements by
biopsychologist Ward C. Halstead to the effect that frontal lobes
of the human brain control the higher forms of intelligence, and
underdevelopment of the frontal lobes adversely affects intelligence.
Halstead did indeed say these things, but in no wise implied that
they had any racial significance. Instead, he has disavowed the

---

[23] Robert Bennett Bean, "Some Racial Peculiarities of the Negro Brain,"
American Journal of Anatomy, V (September, 1906), 379. For similar views
see Bean, "The Training of the Negro," *Century Magazine,* LXXII (October,
1906), 947–53.

[24] Curt Stern, "The Biology of the Negro," *Scientific American,* CXCI (October, 1954), 81–85.

use of his works by racists such as George and Carleton Putnam. "Both authors quote my work . . . indicating that the frontal lobes of the brain are of particular significance to the advance of civilization," Halstead has written. "This is my view, and I am quoted correctly by both of them—but I am quoted in a context which has in some, if not many readers, generated the impression that I subscribe to the views on racism set forth by George and Putnam. I wish to make it clear that this is not the case. It is probably a sound perspective in biology to be extremely wary of the *non-sequitur* involved in generalizing from our limited science of *human-organisms* to value judgments about people. . . . In my opinion the ghost of racist dogma must be laid to rest before any comprehensive investigation of the important scientific problem posed by race can be undertaken." [25]

Neurologist Wilder Penfield, whose research on the morphology of the human brain George cited, similarly repudiated the abuse of his work by racists. "In my clinical and pathological work I know of no good evidence of superiority in structure or function of the brain of White or Black, either way," Penfield declared. "Variations in human capacity have not been directly correlated to differences in brain structure by any clear scientific work as yet. . . . My own belief is that the innate intellectual capacity of White, Mulatto and Negro is probably the same." [26] Another of George's authorities, geographer George F. Carter of Johns Hopkins, wrote of *The Biology of the Race Problem* that its "arguments . . . are Swiss cheese—full of holes." [27]

It seems fair to say that an overwhelming majority of the scientists cited by George, at least of those whose major works were published within the last generation, regard his use of their works as spurious, and consider *The Biology of the Race Problem* pseudoscience. But in spite of his shortcomings as a scientist, George is an effective propagandist, and the fact that most of the authorities he cites are equalitarians has worked to his advantage. He and the racists to whom he appeals are enabled thereby to present his study to unsuspecting laymen as a genuine work of science and scholarship.

George begins his study by first erecting and then demolishing

[25] Quoted in Ingle, "Comments on the Teachings of Carleton Putnam," 38.
[26] Quoted in *ibid.*, 38–39.
[27] Quoted in Carleton Putnam, "These Are the Guilty," *The Citizen,* VII (March, 1963) , 40.

an equalitarian straw man. He will prove, he states at the outset, that equalitarians (who are unnamed) are incorrect in contending that "all babies [are] approximately uniform and equal in endowments when they are born." These nameless equalitarians, he continues, have foisted upon the American public the erroneous idea that "all men are equal biologically"; and as a result the "doctrine of the essential uniformity of human infants" is now "held by a great body of social psychologists, sociologists, social anthropologists and many men in public life." This is a misrepresentation of environmentalist views concerning the significance of individual differences. No reputable scientist or social scientist has ever accepted such notions as the biological equality of all men or the "essential uniformity of human infants." [28] But by alleging that equalitarians, i.e., integrationists, do accept such ideas, and then refuting those ideas, George perhaps enhanced the plausibility of his own views, at least to uncritical readers.

The first significant issue George dealt with was "non-morphological racial differences." His purpose was to describe the psychological and personality traits of Negroes and, more significantly, to relate them to the physiology of the race. To a considerable extent the validity of his entire work depended upon his ability to accomplish the latter task.

To illustrate the psychological and personality traits of Negroes, George cited four authorities, the first of them Sir Francis Galton, who in discussing African Negroes in 1869 had referred to them as "savages" and spoken of their "incapacity . . . for civilization" and their unwillingness to work steadily for a sustained period of time. The second authority was Francis B. Stevens, an American diplomat whose knowledge of the characteristics of Negroes came from his diplomatic services in Africa. African Negroes, Stevens remarked in an interview in *U.S. News and World Report,* are "highly emotional," "readily goaded by irresponsible leaders into violence against blacks or whites alike," and "normally content if they have the security of food, shelter and police protection." Dr. J. C. Carothers, an Englishman who spent much of his adult life in Africa and for a time was a medical officer in the British colonial government in Kenya, was George's third authority on the characteristics of Negroes. In 1953, under auspices of

[28] See for example Theodosius Dobzhansky, *The Biological Basis of Human Freedom* (New York, 1956).

the World Health Organization for which he was then a consultant, Carothers published *The African Mind in Health and Disease,* a work which racists are fond of quoting. To a considerable extent, Carothers' view of the African reflected his experiences as a colonial official, though he was rather cautious in most of his conclusions. He did, however, describe Africans as typically lacking in foresight, perseverance, and power of concentration, as "governed more by emotion than by intellect," as dominated by "momentary and explosive thinking," and so enamored of their own conversation and discussion that they lose sight of "the essential triviality, inconsequence, or even falsity of [their] themes." George's final authority was Dr. Simon Biesheuvel, Director of the South African National Institute for Personnel Research in Johannesburg, who described Negroes in much the same language as Carothers, Stevens, and Galton.

None of George's authorities offered any empirical evidence to substantiate his description of Negroes. Each reported his personal observations, and each described African Negroes, though George was elsewhere preoccupied with American Negroes. The apparent reason for this sudden shift to African Negroes is twofold. First, American Negroes do not always conform to the stereotyped description he sought to convey, and Africans are too far away for his readers to observe personally; and second, American Negroes are so racially mixed that, as racists frequently point out, they are no longer "pure." In making the shift George was assuming that there are behavioral and personality characteristics which "pure" Negroes everywhere have, whether in Africa or America.

Having decided that Negroes behave substantially as Galton and the other authorities indicated, George turned his attention to more specific aspects of racial behavior such as IQ test scores and crime rates, but this time of American Negroes. His authorities here are McGurk, Garrett, H. A. Tanser, H. M. Roland (a county school superintendent in North Carolina), a statement made in 1929 by sociologist Pitirim Sorokin, FBI crime reports, and the United States census bureau. Noting the high crime rates among Negroes as reflected in FBI crime statistics, he concluded that the race has a special propensity for crime.[29] Throughout his discussion

[29] George ignored the vast literature which disputes his conclusions on this point. See for example Marvin E. Wolfgang, *Crime and Race, Conceptions and Misconceptions* (New York, 1964). Wolfgang is a sociologist at the University of Pennsylvania.

of this and related subjects, George's lack of scientific detatchment is especially obvious. He had a double standard in discussing whites and Negroes, always interpreting his material in the most derogatory manner possible for Negroes.

The lack of objectivity is especially apparent in George's effort to prove that personality traits, IQ test scores, and crime rates are "attributable to inherent morphological rather than environmental causes." Are there, he asked, "hereditary structural and other biological differences between individuals and races that might serve to explain the observed differences in intelligence and in behavior in those areas of activity that make western civilization?" His answer was an emphatic "yes." The cerebral cortex and frontal lobes of the brain, he explained, control the higher mental processes, and cited Wilder Penfield, Theodore Rasmussen, Ward C. Halstead, and C. Judson Herrick to substantiate the point.[30]

Having demonstrated the significance of the cerebral cortex and frontal lobes of the brain, George then pointed to several studies concerning the morphological differences between white and Negro brains, emphasizing their conclusions that the frontal lobes and cerebral cortex in Negro brains are underdeveloped. He cited four studies, by Robert Bennett Bean in 1906, Franklin P. Mall in 1909, F. W. Vint in 1934, and C. J. Connolly in 1950. George considered the study by Vint, who in 1934 was director of the Medical Research Laboratory in Kenya, especially valuable because of the various differences Vint reported in his measurement of white and Negro brains. He had found, for example, that the supragranular layer of the cortex of the average Negro brain was about 14 percent thinner than that of the average Caucasian brain, and on the basis of this and other differences equally significant, had concluded that the brain of an average Negro is morphologically inferior to that of an average Caucasian.

Endorsing Vint's conclusion, George now linked the studies of Penfield, Rasmussen, Halstead, and Herrick—who said that the frontal lobes of the brain control the higher mental processes—with those of Vint, Bean, Mall, and Connolly—who said the frontal lobes in the Negro brain are underdeveloped—and claimed the authority of all eight men for his statement that the behavioral

[30] These men were eminent authorities on this subject, but unfortunately for George's case, three of them have publicly repudiated the implications he drew from their studies, and the fourth, Herrick, is dead. See Ingle, "Comments on the Teachings of Carleton Putnam," 38–39.

and personality traits of Negroes are explained by the morphology of the Negro brain. Penfield, Rasmussen, Halstead, and Herrick, however, had made no such claim, and as for the studies of Vint, Bean, Mall, and Connolly, there is little of scientific value in them. According to physiologist Dwight J. Ingle of the University of Chicago, who has carefully reviewed and compared these four latter studies, none of them has any real scientific merit. There is no scientific evidence, Ingle declared, that the Negro brain is in any respect inferior to that of the Caucasian. On this point, the most vital in his study, George's authorities failed him. They simply did not substantiate the conclusions he based upon them.

But he was not yet ready to leave the subject. To further buttress his conclusion he offered statements from J. C. Carothers, Audrey Shuey, and psychologist Robert M. Yerkes [31] that Negroes do well enough on tests which measure lower forms of mental ability but quite poorly on those which measure higher forms, those forms, that is, which are controlled by the frontal lobes. Again George links the works of bona fide scientists with those of scientific racists. The line that separates the works of Penfield, Halstead, Rasmussen, and Herrick from those of Bean and Vint, Shuey and Yerkes is the line that separates science from pseudoscience and scientism. The similarity between the two groups of authorities consists largely of the fact that both were interested in brains and intelligence.

George's next important task was to demonstrate that the physiological basis of the Negro's intelligence, social behavior, and personality traits is inherited. Again he quoted Sir Francis Galton, this time citing Galton's observation that a few families in Britain had in the last few generations contributed a disproportionate number of British leaders in public service, religion, society, and the arts. Galton concluded from this fact, and George did, too, that superior ability runs in certain families, and both men accepted it as evidence that heredity predominates over environment. Neither Galton nor George felt it necessary to inquire into the extent to which equality of opportunity actually existed in Victorian Britain or the degree to which "establishment" families offered their members built-in advantages. George was convinced

---

[31] Yerkes, a Yale psychologist, was director of psychological testing for the United States Army in World War I. After the war he published several studies drawing racist conclusions from the test results he obtained during the war.

that ability rises to the top regardless of environmental conditions.

It was the latter fact which led him to place so much weight upon several studies of criminality and mental abnormality among identical twins. The studies showed unmistakably that if one twin is a criminal or is mentally abnormal the incidence of the same thing in the second twin is higher than in the population as a whole. The studies, however, deal with individual, not racial, inheritance, and their implications for race are unclear—rather the implications depend upon one's concept of race and the extent to which individual traits are racially determined. George concludes from the studies that the Negro's alleged propensity to crime is inherited. His reasoning here is best illustrated syllogistically: Studies of identical twins indicate that "genetical influences are probably important in criminal behavior"; crime rates are higher among Negroes than whites; therefore, Negroes inherit a greater propensity to crime than do whites. "When one sees at one end of the scale that genius runs in families," George wrote, "and at the other end of the scale that microcephaly and amaurotic idiocy run in families, and remembers that crime does also, one can hardly avoid the conclusion that heredity is an important factor in determining the character of a population." The validity of this conclusion would seem to depend in large part upon whether it refers to individual or to racial inheritance. Leaving aside altogether the question of its validity, the evidence which George presents suggests only that some *individuals* inherit a propensity toward certain behavior traits. He does not prove that the inheritance is related to the individual's race.

Like other scientific racists, George readily made the transition from scientist to social critic. He warned that racial amalgamation would produce a nation of mulattoes intermediate in ability between whites and Negroes and would thus destroy that vital margin of difference between whites and Negroes, the margin which represents the white man's capacity to create and advance civilization and the Negro's incapacity for either. To George, this margin explained the difference between European and African civilizations. Civilization is dependent upon "the presence or absence in the population of the pool of genes necessary to produce the minds and the personalities that will find and make use of . . . ideas," he wrote. It was their "pool of genes" which made Europeans a creative people, and they retained their creativity wherever they preserved their genetic purity, in North America, Australia, New Zealand, South Africa. In Latin America, however, where they amalgamated with Indians or Negroes, they stagnated. "The facts of history throughout the world provide no justification for any faith that a mulatto population would advance our civilization in this country or would even maintain it," George declared. "No where in the world have [mulattoes] demonstrated that they have the creative capacities (the intelligence, the industry, the drive, and the persistence) to make a civilization; nor is there an advanced civilization in any area where there has been a high degree of absorption of Negro genes into a white population." [32]

The supreme danger, then, was racial amalgamation, and George urged the American people to look upon "civil rights" and school integration from the vantage point of genetics. Americans must "avoid those actions and programs that seem destined to bring about deterioration in the quality of [their] genetic pool," he warned. They must shun "compulsory programs that would tend to bring about the mating of well-endowed, potentially creative people with poorly endowed, uncreative people." They must "adopt programs that have good promise of raising the quality of [their] pool of genes." White Americans might "assist Negroes in providing as good an environment for their children as they are capable of creating; but for the federal government to compel White parents to send their children to school in as bad an environment as Negroes can and do create is neither social justice nor wise national policy." [33]

This means, of course, that the individual is less important than the race, and here as elsewhere George's views paralleled those of Garrett. "During recent months we have often heard the appealing argument that we should treat every one according to his worth as an individual regardless of his race," he observed. "To be sure, we should value every man according to his merit—within his own race. It does not follow that virtue would be served by admitting every man or woman that we value, regardless of his race, into those areas of Caucasian social life where mates are chosen. If we open those doors to select Negroes of high merit, we also open them in the end to millions of inferior individuals." [34]

Except for a handful of racists, scientists have either condemned

[32] George, *The Biology of the Race Problem*, 73–74.
[33] *Ibid.*, 75–76.
[34] *Ibid.*, 78.

or ignored *The Biology of the Race Problem*. A writer in *Science* described it as "hokum," [35] and that term seems aptly to summarize the attitudes of most scientists. Scientific journals did not review it, for which George blamed the alleged conspiracy of equalitarians to suppress everything which challenged their prejudices. It is more likely, however, that scientific journals ignored *The Biology of the Race Problem* because their editors did not consider it a work of science. One might as well condemn astronomers for ignoring the latest work of astrology or horoscope reading as criticize scientists for ignoring George's work.

Many scientists, in fact, did not ignore it, though their interest in it was due solely to their determination to prevent racists from misusing science. A committee of the American Association for the Advancement of Science denounced George's study, along with other items of scientific racism, as reactionary racist propaganda and scientifically worthless.[36] The committee repudiated George's contention that science is a proper basis for determining the civil rights and constitutional rights of Negro citizens. "To criticize a judicial decision by means of scientific evidence which is wholly irrelevant to the issue is to conceal a fallacy in the cloak of scientific precision," the committee stated. There is no evidence, they continued, that Negroes are in any way racially inferior to whites, nor is there any valid evidence to support the assertion that scientists have "conspired to mislead the public about the scientific evidence regarding racial differences." On the contrary, the committee concluded, George and his fellow racists have no real understanding of race or, indeed, of the scientific process itself.[37]

[35] "Science and Segregation: The American Anthropological Association Dips into Politics," 1868.

[36] "Science and the Race Problem: A Report of the AAAS Committee on Science in the Promotion of Human Welfare," *Science*, November 1, 1963, pp. 558–61.

[37] George is author of several other items in the literature of scientific racism, among them, "Brains, Intelligence, and Race," in Garrett, *Race, 11 Questions and 11 Answers*, 21–34, which he prepared to present to a Senate committee hearing testimony on the Civil Rights Act of 1964; and a booklet, *Race, Heredity, and Civilization* (New York, 1963), the introduction to which was by Archibald Roosevelt of the Veritas Foundation, a prominent spokesman for some of the ultraconservative elements in American politics. Roosevelt's letter of introduction is printed in "Why Won't They Teach the Truth About Race?," *The Citizen*, VII (July–August 1963), 4–6.

6

SCIENTIFIC RACISTS ORGANIZE

The history of scientific racism since 1954 is not exclusively a story of individual scientists. The role of certain individuals was vital to the development of scientific racism, especially in the cases of Garrett, who was already an established authority in his discipline, and George, who proved to be an effective propagandist. A propaganda or "educational" movement, however, needs organization and central direction, and for scientific racists this was especially true. For maximum effectiveness, it was essential that they have an organization to oversee and coordinate their efforts, a central agency to encourage and publish their research, circulate their

118

literature, act as a clearing house for their ideas, and serve as a liaison between social scientists and Southern segregationists. To a considerable extent, their achievements in recent years were due to their success in organizing such an agency.

The agency is a little-known organization with an imposing title, the International Association for the Advancement of Ethnology and Eugenics (IAAEE). Chartered in 1959 in Baltimore, the IAAEE is a nonprofit educational corporation "dedicated to the further-ance of the sciences of ethnology and eugenics, including the re-lated disciplines of physical and cultural anthropology, sociology, psychology, raciology, archaeology, linguistics, physiology, genetics, ecology, and demography." According to a statement appended to all its publications, it is also interested in "encouraging a free flow of information between scholars in the above disciplines in the United States and in the other countries of the Western World and in restoring freedom of inquiry to those areas (particularly the study of race and race relations) where extraneous political and philosophical predispositions have frequently terminated dis-cussions to the general detriment of the social and biological sciences."

The key to this statement and to the real objectives of the or-ganization is the reference to *restoring* freedom of inquiry to the study of race and race relations and to eliminating "extraneous political and philosophical predispositions" which allegedly in-terfere with that freedom. The Association promises to study racial topics unfettered by the biases and prejudices which so often in-trude therein and make those topics touchy and controversial. Un-fortunately, however, the Association has consistently ignored its own admonitions. Far from promoting the unbiased and unpreju-diced study of race, it has done more than any other "scientific" body in the country to facilitate the use of science and scientific literature by segregationists and anti-Negro racists. This fact is made abundantly clear by an examination of the racial views of the officers and governing body of the Association and of the litera-ture it endorses and circulates.

The president of the IAAEE is Robert Kuttner, a biologist at Creighton University Medical School, Omaha, Nebraska. Dr. Kutt-ner, who holds a Ph.D. in zoology from the University of Con-necticut, detailed his racial views before a congressional committee hearing testimony on the civil rights legislation President Kennedy submitted to Congress in the aftermath of the race riots in Birmingham, Alabama, in 1963.[1] He appeared before the committee not as an official representative of the IAAEE but as spokesman for the ultraconservative Liberty Lobby.

Kuttner opposed the pending legislation (it eventually became the Civil Rights Act of 1964) on several grounds, not all of them scientific. He objected to the coercive features of the legislation, which he thought would intensify rather than ameliorate racial antipathies, infringe upon property rights, and violate the basic precepts of free enterprise. The increasing regulation of private property by the federal government, he told the committee, encourages emerging nations in Africa and Asia to believe that capitalism and free enterprise have inherent limitations in coping with the complexities of the twentieth century. "And this," he added, "encourages Marxism."

The purpose of Kuttner's testimony, however, was not to repeat the reactionary economic and political views of the Liberty Lobby, but to provide a scientific rationale for the Lobby's opposition to the civil rights bill. Kuttner warned the congressmen that the pending legislation would encourage racial intermixture, a consequence which he thought even more abhorrent than violating the Constitution or threatening free enterprise. "Doubtless, this is merely the first of a series of cumulative measures aimed at complete social blending," he testified. "This bill caters to the motivations underlying much of the drive for social blending. Association with whites has become for some segments of the Negro population a sort of status symbol. This is abnormal and destructive of the development of a mature and stable Negro society."

Kuttner had other objections to the legislation on scientific grounds. "Psychological, biological, sociological facts cannot be ignored in making good laws," he reminded the congressmen, and the "facts" indicate that the proposed bill is unwise. The "facts," which he then brought to the committee's attention, consisted largely of the high rates of immorality and illegitimacy among Negroes and the poor performance of the race on intelligence tests, which are not, he suggested, due to environment alone. "I would seriously question whether or not the element of heredity

---

[1] U.S. House of Representatives, Committee on the Judiciary. *Hearings on Civil Rights,* May 8 to August 2, 1963, pp. 1963–80.

does not enter into some areas of performance in society," he said ambiguously. "I do not believe in a doctrine of race superiority, but I do recognize race differences, and this might mean that one race might perform better in one task than another." He did not believe, he added later, "that there is [racial] equality on the great majority of items one could measure."

But aside from this, Kuttner continued, civil rights legislation "often loses sight of existing psychological, biological, and sociological realities." In some instances the white majority suffers from integration. "Integrationists believe that [it is good] educational experience for white children to attend school with illegitimate Negro children. Yet few white parents would regard this as a desired broadening for the purpose of schools."

Kuttner's remarks sometimes went far beyond the legislation then pending before the committee. He repeatedly criticized the civil rights and school integration movements, charging that both are products of a "dangerous idealism" and are led by "misguided individuals who have misjudged the extent of damage that some of their actions may produce." He also hinted that the two movements have been substantially influenced by communists. "I recognize," he said, "that [communists] are very strong environmentalists."

There was nothing distinctive in Kuttner's views. Nor was he an effective spokesman even for his own point of view. In testifying before the committee he had great difficulty articulating his views. He frequently rambled off the subject and made vague, ambiguous statements which members of the committee often challenged. It is for this reason, perhaps, that Kuttner is not the most important spokesman for the IAAEE. That distinction belongs to A. James Gregor, secretary of the Association. Gregor, who was born in New York City in 1929, is the youngest and in many respects most distinctive of the prominent scientific racists. Perhaps it is accurate to say that he is unique among them. Certainly his intellectual orientation is vastly different from that of other social scientists whose names have appeared in this study. Educated at Purdue and Columbia, he earned a B.A. (history), M.A. (philosophy), and Ph.D. (social and political philosophy) from the latter institution. He has held several academic appointments, in the philosophy departments of Washington College in Maryland, the University of Hawaii, and, since 1964, the University of Kentucky.

Gregor's distinctiveness is the result of several factors. He is younger than other prominent scientific racists by a generation or more—Garrett, Miss Armstrong, Miss Shuey, McGurk, Osborne, van den Haag, and Kuttner were each born between 1888 and 1914—and he does not have the intimate ties with the South which some of them have. The intellectual orientation of these older scholars was originally molded, directly or indirectly, by the intellectual and racial milieu in this country between 1890 and 1925. During those years most social scientists were hereditarians, and they accepted the ideas of racial inequality and Negro inferiority. But they also shared the patronizing and paternal attitude toward Negroes which was typical of that generation and which was also, in a perverse way, not unsympathetic to individual members of the race. Those attitudes, often reshaped and reinforced by life among Negroes in the South, are the source of the racial views of George, Garrett, and many other scientific racists today. The Southern white man, with orthodox segregationist views, especially of George and Garrett's generation, *knows* the Negro and is oblivious to anyone who questions his racial convictions. It is important to remember, however, that this attitude incorporates an element of paternalism and patronizing good will which prevents Southern segregationists from "disliking" Negroes— at least those Negroes who remain in their "place." One result of this is that the most extreme ideas of anti-Negro racism (e.g., deportation of Negroes to Africa) have never appealed to such men as George and Garrett. Another is that they regard themselves as men of goodwill who "like" Negroes and who use science as merely one more prop for traditional Southern race policies.

Gregor's racism is of an entirely different sort. He has read widely in older authorities; indeed, he is perhaps more knowledgeable in the literature of scientific racism than any other social scientist previously discussed in this study. But he has none of the paternalism of the older generation. His writings give the impression that he is a racist not because he *knows* Negroes as do Southern paternalists or European colonialists, or because of the influence of an older scholar such as Garrett or George, but because of sheer intellectual conviction, a conviction that is at once austere, scientific, and logical and immune to emotion or humaneness. Where George and Garrett are racists by emotional commitment and, one might say by force of circumstance, Gregor is a racist because his intellect has propelled him to that conclusion. The difference is illustrated by the fact that George and Garrett are concerned only with immediate issues—race relations and school integration in this country—whereas Gregor has given much more attention to formulating a scientific concept of race applicable to the entire spectrum of interracial and interethnic relations.

Gregor developed his racial views in a series of articles published during the last several years. A primary ingredient of his views is the conviction that "race prejudice," as equalitarians call it, is really a deep-rooted, instinctive preference for one's own kind. This "instinctive" explanation of race prejudice, which most racists accept without bothering to articulate, is especially important to Gregor. He uses it to elevate his racial views from the level of bigotry and intolerance to the more satisfying one of human instinct. In the process he transforms "consciousness of kind" into an objective phenomenon which he thinks can be studied rationally and demonstrated scientifically. Race prejudice, Gregor wrote in an article circulated by the IAAEE,[2] is the surface manifestation of "a consciousness of kind, an identification of like members" which disposes the individual "to identify with an ideal physical type" of his own race, and in turn is "the psycho-social basis for *race* prejudice." In simplest terms, this means that human beings prefer the familiar and are repelled by the alien and unfamiliar. Physical differences set races and ethnic groups apart, and the extent to which their differences are obvious to the eye is the extent to which the instinct for exclusiveness operates. This is always true wherever races and ethnic groups meet, and Gregor predicted it will remain so in the future. Racial prejudices (or preferences) are therefore instinctive, and are immune to environmental influences, whether civil rights laws, Supreme Court decisions, or brotherhood weeks.

If such a view is correct, racial accommodation can at best consist of nothing more than mutually agreeable segregation. In fact, if Gregor were correct one would expect segregation to be voluntary and spontaneous. His "consciousness of kind," however, seems to work only among whites, and not even among all whites. Many Southerners have it in excess while most Northerners and Westerners apparently have less than their share. Mulattoes present a curious problem. Their "consciousness of kind" might

[2] A. James Gregor, "On the Nature of Prejudice," *Eugenics Review,* LII (January, 1961).

lead them to prefer association with either of the two races, or perhaps only with other mulattoes, thus creating a third element in the race problem. Should it lead them to prefer association with whites and whites to reject that association, it could be the source of an unresolvable racial dilemma.

Gregor never developed these aspects of his theories. In 1961, however, he did pursue his ideas concerning consciousness of kind at greater length in an article which demonstrated his intellectual debt to sociologists Franklin Henry Giddings and E. A. Ross, to Josiah Nott (whose *Types of Mankind,* 1855, was the foremost work of scientific racism published in the United States before the Civil War) and to the contemporary Italian sociologist, Corrado Gini.[3] In this article Gregor takes Giddings' concept of the consciousness of kind and makes it the central factor in the formation of races. Consciousness of kind, he explained, is not only a source of racial preference, it is also "a behavioral 'syndrome' having positive selective value in the process of race formation." Thus, racism or racist thinking should not be thought of as "an excrescence of capitalism or the rationale for an economy of exploitation," as equalitarians and communists suppose, but as a basic human instinct. As Gregor defined it, Giddings' concept of consciousness of kind goes far beyond race in its implications. He understood it to include a "self-regarding tendency to associate with [one's] own kind (religious, political, social, cultural, economic, or racial group)" and "a systematic disposition to limit contact with outgroup members and to regard that which is foreign as at best curious, at worst the target of enmity." But these factors, too, have racial implications, for they lead to genetic isolation, even of groups living side by side, and intensify what Gregor termed "the will to group identification." The relevance of this to race relations in the United States is obvious. "The high social visibility of the Negro," Gregor explained, "acts as a focal point, around which collect all the attitudes that characterize man as a social animal, as a product of microevolution, given to identifying with kind, animated by a natural disposition to conform to prevailing racial as well as cultural norms." Racial prejudice in America will therefore never disappear; racial harmony will come only when whites and Negroes agree to live together—separately.

[3] A. James Gregor, "Corrado Gini and the Theory of Race Formation," *Sociology and Sociological Research,* XLV (January, 1961), 175–81.

The most striking fact about Gregor's racism is its admitted kinship with some of the ideas of fascist race theorists. In 1958 he published an article in *The European,* the journal of British fascist leader Sir Oswald Mosley, surveying the evolution of race theories in Nazi Germany.[4] He distinguished three stages in the evolution. The first, before 1935, was characterized by an absurd Aryanism and hysterical Nordicism which were pure fantasy and of no scientific or historical validity. The second, approximately 1935 to 1940, was a period of transition in which serious Nazi scholars began to formulate sounder racial theories but in which the fantasies of the earlier period still dominated Nazi thinking. The third, from 1940 to 1945, witnessed major changes as the research of responsible Nazi scholars began to appear and to influence Nazi race theorists. This process was never completed, however, because of the military collapse of Germany. In the dislocations accompanying the German defeat and the ensuing military occupation, the scholarship of the war years was scattered or destroyed, and "the tragic-comic image" of the irresponsible Nordicism of the early 1930's remained as "the popular misconception" of Nazi racial theories. Gregor's description of the third phase of Nazi racial thought is worth quoting at length:

Actually the elements of a far more profound theory are to be discerned in a few surviving books that mark the last dynamic phase of development of a concept of race free of the encumberances of an hysterical Nordicism.

Everywhere the talk was no longer of fixed and immutable races, but of races in formation, the components for which arise out of the crucible of the past—races in formation cast over by the ideal of a living heritage—for Germany a Nordic Mythos, for Italy an animating devotion to Romanita. The talk is of races yet to be fashioned by living an ideal, united by a common destiny, nurtured in a common environment, the political expression of which is nationhood.

Here are the germs of a world view which makes of man a creator, a builder of future races; a philosophy which unites history, politics, and race, eugenics and humanism, pride in self and respect for others, a philosophy scientifically sound and emotionally satisfying.[5]

[4] A. James Gregor, "National Socialism and Race," *The European,* XI (July, 1958) , 273–91.
[5] It was in this period, the reader will recall, that the Nazis liquidated millions of Jews and Eastern Europeans in the process of implementing their racial views.

This is the promise of a world-view as yet half-formulated and ill-expressed, with which our time must contend; the Weltanshauung which bears within itself the promise of Nietzsche's Good European.

This description of Nazi race theory is important to the story of the IAAEE and scientific racism in this country because it corresponds to Gregor's own view of what "race" is. In the same year he published this description of Nazi race theories, he wrote another article detailing his own racial views.[6] The similarity between his own views and those he previously attributed to the Nazis is remarkable.

"Race" in any significant natural sense can only signify a given breeding community (a mendelian population) which displays a difference of relative frequency for specific variables. . . . Historic continuity for such a race can be established only tentatively by demonstrating the temporal persistence of an empirically ascertained genetic balance. This must always be qualified by the knowledge that balanced polymorphism is a dynamic constant, that relative frequencies can be altered by a differential birth rate, an accelerated mutation rate, successive changes in breeding practices . . . eugenic or dysgenic practices in the environment.

Such a dynamic conception of race synthesizes natural, cultural, economic, political and biological factors. All influence the evolutionary development of races. All have influenced the racial composition of our planet in the past and will continue to influence it in the future either through intelligent control or happenstance.

The importance of such a mature conception of race cannot escape the intelligent layman. It helps point up the fallacies of "Marxist biology," on the one hand and the narrow "racism" of the recent past which did so much to undermine the cultural and political vitality of Europe.[7]

In 1963 Gregor published a critique of the social science testimony in the Brown cases, in which he not only vigorously denounced that testimony but applied his racial views to the question of public school integration.[8] Like other scientific racists, he believed the Supreme Court had been grossly misled by the social scientists. His chief objection to the testimony was its failure to prove that *de jure* school segregation itself had caused the per-

---

[6] A. James Gregor, "The Logic of Race Classification," *Genus*, XIV, (1958), 150–61.

[7] The reference to "narrow 'racism'" is to the early racist views of German and Italian fascists, as opposed to those views which began to appear in the late 1930's.

[8] A. James Gregor, "The Law, Social Science, and School Segregation: An Assessment," *Western Reserve Law Review*, XIV (1963), 621–36.

sonality disturbances in Negro children which Clark and other witnesses had described. "No argument [was] offered to indicate that the 'self-hatred' and 'in-group rejection' evinced by Negroes was the consequence of school segregation per se," Gregor wrote; yet this was the issue before the Court. The witnesses should have limited their testimony to the specific effects of *de jure* school segregation upon children in the same age and circumstances as those involved in the suits. He insisted that the witnesses isolate and measure the ill effects of one facet of segregation, and charged that social scientists had been unable to do this because there were in fact no ill effects of school segregation per se. Negro school children do suffer certain "psychodynamic impairments," he admitted, but these inhere in their minority status and are substantially the same in segregated and integrated schools, though the differences which exist favor segregated schools.

As this statement indicates, Gregor assumed that a Negro child attending a technically integrated school was in a bona fide integrated situation. His assumption, however, ignores the fact that such a child almost certainly comes from an environment in which *de facto* segregation and race discrimination are the rule, not the exception. The effects of this environment cannot be put on and taken off like a cloak when the child enters or leaves an "integrated" classroom. The school is not isolated from society; on the contrary, it reflects the society it serves. If the ill effects of segregation are to be eliminated from the classroom they must be simultaneously eliminated from society at large.

Gregor did not merely dispute the testimony in the Brown cases; he asserted positively that the available data indicate that Negro children are psychologically better off in segregated schools. Perhaps the final truth is not yet in, he declared, "but where social science material is available, *it tends to support racial separation in the schools, at least through adolescence under conditions approximating equality of plant and instruction.*" This statement is the key to Gregor's view of school integration. "Minority children of high social visibility," he wrote, "enjoy positive advantages at critical periods of personality formation in a racially insulated environment." To support this view Gregor cited, among other things, Kenneth Clark's study on the comparative responses of Northern and Southern Negro children to the doll and drawings tests, and Mary Ellen Goodman's *Race Awareness in Young Chil-*

dren. The latter he took as evidence that Negro children have psychological problems in schools where "de jure segregation does not obtain and where the incidence of Negroes is considered 'optimum.' " [9]

As further justification for school segregation, Gregor took evidence that white children have "negative attitudes" toward Negroes and used it against Negroes. In integrated schools, Negro children face "systematic and regular rejection" from white classmates, he remarked, and "the result can only be serious personality defects" on the part of Negroes. "Children, *before they enter school,* evince attitudes which would only create an atmosphere of tension for minority children of high social visibility," he wrote. "There is little reason to believe that such attitudes, which antedate school attendance, can be reduced by either education, protracted contact, propaganda, or a combination of these. Minority children of distinctive appearance can only suffer serious personality disabilities as a consequence of congregation." Moreover, these disabilities would be exascerbated by the low academic achievement, for most Negro children, Gregor believed, simply do not have the mental capacity to compete with whites. The Negro child who becomes aware of this fact in an integrated classroom can not fail to conclude that his race is inferior. The result will be "gross feelings of inferiority and a deep sense of personal humiliation."

Why this result should be undesirable to Gregor is puzzling. If his comments on the Negro's intelligence and scholastic ability are correct, Negroes are in fact inferior, and it is unclear why the truth should be hidden from them. Presumably an individual's image of himself and his own racial group should be realistic. If Negroes *are* inferior it would seem to be best for them, and for whites too, if they recognized and accepted that fact and ceased their efforts to enter the white man's schools. Gregor said as much in the last pages of his article. "The Guatemalan Indians seem to suffer no personality impairments as a consequence of their inferior status," he stated. "This is because they are sustained by a

[9] Miss Goodman's study did indicate this, but a more accurate statement would be that her study demonstrates that the ill effects of *de facto* segregation and discrimination outside the schools are apparent in integrated schools. Her study was a persuasive argument for general racial integration, not for segregated public schools.

coherent sense of possessing an integral and significant culture of their own. They do not attempt to identify with the upper caste and consequently do not suffer status frustrations, self-rejection, and its attendant disabilities."

Here at last is Gregor's real view. If Negroes would only accept their assigned place in American society and halt their efforts "to identify with the upper caste" the whole issue of the psychological effects of segregation would be solved. This was to Gregor the real solution to the integration dispute.[10]

The relationship between the IAAEE and the social scientists previously discussed in this study is not limited to the similarity of their ideas concerning race. Members of the Association's executive committee in 1965 included, besides Kuttner and Gregor, Henry E. Garrett, Wesley C. George, Robert T. Osborne, Clairette P. Armstrong, Stanley D. Porteus, Frank C. J. McGurk, and sociologist Ernest van den Haag of New York University. These are, however, only the more significant Americans on the committee. There are several others whose racial views are germane to an evaluation of the IAAEE.

Philosopher Gerrit Daams of Kent State University, Kent, Ohio, is one of the lesser-known members of the IAAEE executive committee. Professor Daams detailed his racial views in an address prepared for delivery to the Portage County, Ohio, Board of Realtors and reprinted by the Mississippi Citizens' Councils.[11] He offered a number of arguments for racial segregation, among them "objective differences between the races that cause white people to prefer freedom of choice and association." These differences include, in Daam's words, "temperamental differences in mode of mental functioning," "electro-encephalogram characteristics which proceed further in the European than in the black native," and

10 Accompanying Gregor's article was a closely reasoned rebuttal by Professor Ovid C. Lewis of the Western Reserve Law School. See Lewis, "Parry and Riposte to Gregor's 'The Law, Social Science, and School Segregation: An Assessment,' " *Western Reserve Law Review*, XIV (1963) , 637–82. Lewis emphasized the fact that in concentrating on the relevancy of social science testimony Gregor lost sight of the larger issue–justice for Negroes. In perhaps his most damaging criticisms, Lewis pointed out that Gregor distorted the meaning of several of the authorities he quoted, or quoted them out of context. Many of the authorities Gregor cited in favor of segregation were actually arguing in favor of integration.

11 Gerrit Daams, "Northern Professor Summarizes Reasons for Racial Segregation," *The Citizen*, IX (May, 1965) , 12–20.

"differences in comparative anatomy," including indications of "superior development of the white brain." The evidence on all these points "is not perfect," he conceded, "but that cannot be grounds for basing a social revolution on the assumption that the opposite of the best available evidence is true."

Daams warned that school integration will have bitter consequences. "Children are suggestible and readily assimilate the experiences, conceptual beliefs, customs, and morals of others," he stated. "When the child comes into contact with secondary groups that are markedly different . . . the child's value system looses [sic] coherency and his self-conception is undermined. The child either abandons cherished values, or undergoes adjustment to conflicting customs and possibly mutually exclusive values with debilitating psychological consequences for the process of maturation."

Just why the psychological influences of integration is a one-way street Daams did not explain. He seems to say in the above passage that immoral and antisocial Negro children will exercise a pervasive and sinister influence over white children, but that the influence of white children upon Negroes will be negligible. In any event, Daams thus fails to resolve the issue of the relative significance of heredity and environment. He believes that personality and behavioral traits are racially determined and those of Negroes are immune to environment. Those of whites, however, are fragile enough to be destroyed by association with Negroes in the public schools.

Daams' most novel idea was that American Negroes, far from being victims of racial discrimination, in fact receive special benefits solely because of their race. At each socioeconomic level, he pointed out, whites score higher than Negroes on IQ tests, a fact which he took to mean that it is easier for a Negro than a white man of equal ability to advance up the socioeconomic ladder. Given the frequency distribution of intelligence among Negroes and whites, he reasoned, it is easier for a Negro than a white man to enter a profession or white collar employment. "Our society tends, on the average to demand more ability and performance from the whites than the Negroes for the same economic rewards," Daams told the realtors. "This is equivalent to the Negro having had, since a few decades prior to World War II, on the average, a better chance of attaining some desired socio-economic status level than does a white person of equal ability and performance. . . . On the average, the Negro is NOT required to be more able than a white person in order to get the same rewards. . . . White people in general are sympathetic to the underdog. Then, the skin color of the Negro aids in making him visible so as to draw the solicitous attention of white people, whereas the disadvantaged white man is more easily hidden and forgotten."

Charles C. Josey, emeritus professor of psychology at Butler University, is still another member of the IAAEE executive committee. As long ago as 1923 Professor Josey spelled out his racial views in a volume entitled *Race and National Solidarity.* In that work, he had sounded an alarm to the American people, warning them that race was the most important issue then facing the world and urging them to make race instead of nationality the primary element in international relations. In a booklet published in 1965 by the IAAEE, *An Inquiry Concerning Racial Prejudice* Josey updated and repeated many of the ideas he first expressed more than forty years ago.[12] Racial prejudice, he declared is a much misunderstood subject, because equalitarians intentionally seek to obfuscate its true nature. It may very well be that "some of the attitudes and processes lumped under the rubric prejudice are essential to man becoming a free, rational, moral person," Josey suggested. Everyone has a natural preference for others of his own kind, the healthy exercise of which produces a sense of identity and a feeling of belonging and is the basis of group dynamics and the source of much of the inspiration which spurs human progress.

The concept of race preference did not contain, at least for Josey, the pessimistic implications of Gregor's ideas on the same subject. For Josey, race preference was a bedrock upon which harmonious race relations could be made to rest, and his view of racial harmony was that of a Southern paternalist and traditionalist. "That two races can live in the same community with mutual respect and goodwill has been demonstrated by numerous communities in the South," he wrote. "There, in spite of physical proximity, psychological and social distance prevented one [race] from appearing to the other as a threat," and the result was in-

[12] Charles C. Josey, *An Inquiry Concerning Racial Prejudice* (New York, 1965). This 32-page booklet is No. 1 in the IAAEE Monograph Series.

terracial harmony.[13] To Josey, the Brown decision was "a step backwards" in race relations because it introduced an unfortunate coercive element in the relations between whites and Negroes. "Might and court decrees cannot engender love, friendship, good-will, and righteousness, or even justice," he declared, "when they ignore the rights, wishes, and ideals of larger segments of the population."

"We live in a morally confused age, one that lacks standards and definite norms," Josey continued. "This can reasonably be attributed in part to the mingling of diverse ethnic groups, for in an ethnically homogeneous group the chances are increased of developing common standards" and protecting children "from romantic attachments that can only bring unnecessary difficulties and sorrow." The incompatibility of the latter statement with his previous remarks about natural preferences for one's own kind is instructive. Josey, like other racists, sometimes used contradictory arguments, and not the least of his contradictions concerned his statement that the Brown decision did violence to the precepts of American democracy. "Democracy can only flourish when men respect the feelings and wishes of each other, and are animated by a refined and delicate sense of self-respect, forebearance, and concern for the common good," he stated. "The democratic way of life is too complex to be imposed or regulated by law. . . . To preserve a democracy, it is important to recognize that it is not always *right* to insist upon 'legal rights.' Otherwise, the law and the courts may smother both freedom and democracy." To apply these statements to segregation in the South is to reveal again the logical difficulties in Josey's position. Racial segregation, which he defended, does violence to every precept he listed as an essential feature of democracy.

George A. Lundberg, emeritus professor of sociology at the University of Washington, is another member of the IAAEE executive committee. Professor Lundberg is one of the nation's better known sociologists, having been president of the American Sociological Society and the Sociological Research Association, and from 1941 to 1947 editor of *Sociometry*. Author of a number of significant

13 Perhaps no one ever gave a more striking illustration of the tendency of racists to view race relations solely from the white man's perspective. Josey was concerned only with the extent to which Negroes "threatened" whites. It never occurred to him that whites might themselves threaten Negroes.

sociological works, his racial views are not as pronounced as those of most other members of the IAAEE. He specifically disavows the idea of racial superiority or inferiority, but his emphasis upon racial differences, his denunciations of equalitarians, and his implied criticisms of the civil rights movement are appealing to racists.

They find his essay, "Some Neglected Aspects of the 'Minorities' Problem," which the IAAEE has reprinted, especially attractive.[14] It is a résumé of standard criticisms of equalitarians, though with a few distinctions of its own. "*Some* of the hostility complained of by *some* minorities is not based on prejudice at all, but on grounds warranted by community consensus," he remarked in a revealing statement. Moreover, "the right to discriminate and to choose one's primary group associates on whatever discriminatory basis one pleases is among the most generally recognized in our culture by both common and statute law." What equalitarians are fond of calling "inalienable rights" originate in "community consensus and continue only as long as community consensus supports them. It is the privilege of those who disagree with the consensus to attempt to alter it by whatever means the mores allow. In the meantime it is the privilege of others to exercise without apology the rights which by consensus are recognized."

What Lundberg did in "Some Neglected Aspects of the 'Minorities' Problem" was to remove from the discussion of minority rights every element of justice, morality, and humanity. By so doing, he claimed to have achieved the impartiality and disinterestedness which he accused equalitarians of lacking. The question is worth asking, however, why criticizing equalitarians is less biased than criticizing racists, or why justice, morality, and humaneness are irrelevant to "the minorities problem," especially when disregarding them serves the cause of racial and ethnic intolerance. Whether Lundberg intended it or not, the banishment of justice, morality, and humaneness from his discussion of race relations played directly into the hands of racists and segregationists.

Such are the racial views of the American members of the

---

14 George A. Lundberg, "Some Neglected Aspects of the 'Minorities' Problem," *Mankind Quarterly*, III (April–June, 1963). Lundberg, in collaboration with Lenore Dickson, is also the author of the most recent publication of the IAAEE, *Selective Association of Ethnic Groups in a High School* (New York, 1965), which is IAAEE Monograph No. 2.

executive committee of the IAAEE. Despite their scholarly degrees and their stature in the academic world, these men espouse racist views themselves or are tolerant of racism in others. As a practical matter, their view of the Negro's proper place in American life is not unlike that of many Southern segregationists and white supremacists. Like segregationists and white supremacists, they, too, would make the Negro a segregated citizen, which is to say a second-class citizen whose rights and interests are subordinated to those of white men.[15]

One of the major purposes of the IAAEE is "to publish a series of books, monographs, and articles presenting the results of original research and summarizing the state of contemporary scientific opinion in the areas of its principal interest." Accordingly, the Association encourages research by social scientists with acceptable racial views and facilitates publication and distribution of their works. The effort is threefold: publication of a Monograph Series, sponsorship of a Reprint Series, and promotion of a journal, *Mankind Quarterly*.

[15] In addition to the men listed above, Clarence P. Oliver of the University of Texas, David C. Rife of Ohio State University, Ralph W. Erickson of Mississippi State College, William E. Hoy of the University of South Carolina, and Herbert Sanborn of Vanderbilt University are members of the IAAEE executive committee. Until his death in 1964, historian Charles C. Tansill of Georgetown University was also a member. Tansill is perhaps best known for his criticisms of American foreign policy of the 1930's and 1940's, and for his charge that Franklin Roosevelt maneuvered the United States into World War II by enticing the Japanese to destroy the American fleet at Pearl Harbor. In recent years Tansill had been a regular contributor to the John Birch Society magazine, *American Opinion*, of which he was a contributing editor at the time of his death. On Professor Hoy, who testified for segregationists in *Brown v. School District 20 of Charleston County*, one of several cases in which segregationists have sought to overturn the Brown decision by social science evidence of their own, see *Southern School News*, September, 1963, p. 22.

Non-Americans on the IAAEE executive committee in 1965 were John R. Baker and C. D. Darlington of Oxford University; Robert Gayre of Scotland and the University of Saugor, India; Luigi Gedda, Corrado Gini, and Michele Marotta, University of Rome; J. D. J. Hofmeyr, Pretoria University, South Africa; Bertil Lundman, University of Uppsala, Sweden; Branimiro Males, University of Tucuman, Argentina; Otto Reche, University of Vienna; Dr. Helmut Reuning, National Institute of Personnel Research, South Africa; and Pierre Vassal, University of Paris. This author has made no effort to study the writings of these non-Americans associated with the IAAEE. A cursory reading of a few items by some of them gives the impression that they are not so obviously racists as are some of the Americans associated with the IAAEE. However, if any of the non-Americans have criticized the racism of their American colleagues, it has escaped the notice of this author.

The Monograph Series was launched in 1965 with publication of Charles C. Josey's *An Inquiry Concerning Racial Prejudice*. According to an editorial statement in the Foreword of this work, the purpose of the series is "to expose the fact that the findings of many prominent natural and social scientists do not support the dogmatic assertions on the question of racial differences of the contingent of social scientists who now dominate America's institutions of higher learning." Here, spokesmen for the Association dropped their mask of impartiality and disinterest, and their statement more accurately reflects the Association's real purposes than does the list of aims and objectives appended to its publications. The Association encourages the study of race and related subjects by scientists who reject the premises and conclusions of equalitarians and who therefore, intentionally or not, promote the ideas of racial inequality and the practice of racial segregation and white supremacy. This fact is amply demonstrated by an examination of the Reprint Series, which constitutes the major part of IAAEE literature.

Several of the items in the series have already been discussed in this study,[16] and several others incorporate in varying degrees elements of racist, elitist, or hereditarian thought which racists find attractive.[17] One of them, John M. Radzinski's "The American Melting Pot" [18] merits a brief review since it indicates that the Association's interests are not restricted to Negroes and race relations in the United States. Dr. Radzinski was born in Poland in 1901,

[16] The items in the Reprint Series already discussed are Garrett, "Klineberg's Chapter on Race and Psychology"; Gregor, "On the Nature of Prejudice"; Porteus, "Ethnic Group Differences"; Lundberg, "Some Neglected Aspects of the 'Minorities' Problem"; Garrett, "The SPSSI and Racial Differences"; van den Haag, "Social Science Testimony in the Desegregation Cases—A Reply to Professor Kenneth Clark"; and Armstrong, "Psychodiagnosis, Prognosis, School Desegregation and Delinquency." These are Reprints Nos. 1, 3, 4, 8, 9, 10, and 13, respectively.

[17] E. Raymond Hall, "The Zoological Subspecies of Man," *Mankind Quarterly*, I (October, 1960), 113–19, reprinted from *Journal of Mammalogy*, XXVII (November, 1946), 358–64; R. Ruggles Gates, "The Emergence of Racial Genetics," *Mankind Quarterly*, I (June, 1960); Bertil J. Lundman, "The Racial History of Scandinavia," *ibid.*, III (October–December, 1962); C. D. Darlington, "The Control of Evolution in Man," *Eugenics Review*, L (October, 1958); and Sir Cyril Burt, "The Inheritance of Mental Ability," *American Psychologist*, XIII (January, 1958).

[18] John M. Radzinski, "The American Melting Pot: Its Meaning to Us," *American Journal of Psychiatry*, CXV (April, 1959).

but at the age of twelve migrated to this country with his parents, who settled in Chicago. Educated at the University of Chicago's Rush Medical College, he was a neurologist and psychiatrist. His foreign birth is especially interesting because "The American Melting Pot" is an attack upon American immigration policies and the melting pot concept, which in tone and content resembles the nativist writings of such men as Madison Grant and Lothrop Stoddard. The late Dr. Radzinski (he died in 1963) denounced the immigration policies of this country as too lax because, in his opinion at least, they permit the entrance of too many people whose ethnic makeup is unlike that of older Americans. He dismissed the melting pot concept as a delusion concocted by environmentalists to promote equalitarian social policies which were to him indistinguishable from those of communism.

Endorsing the ideas that civilization is the product of a creative minority of mankind and that genius for civilization is inherited and varies among ethnic groups, Radzinski believed that a too rapid change in the ethnic composition of a nation will inevitably lead to a degeneration of its culture and civilization. The probable cause of the decline of ancient Rome, he suggested by way of illustration, was "a biologic dislocation of the delicately balanced genic constellations required for creative potentialities," which in plain language means that too many prolific non-Romans entered Italy at a time when the birth rate among old Romans was too low. Similarly, the mass immigration of Europeans to this country in the last century brought together "the greatest assortment of ethnic stocks in the world and probably in history," and a serious cultural decline is even now under way. "Symptoms of the decline are already apparent in the deteriorating state of some aspects of our culture, in the irresolution and confusion of our national leaders and in the virulence of frank antisocial behavior among our people far in excess of that encountered in west European countries, Canada, and Australia," Radzinski wrote. "We face the unpalatable truth that the present American society is sick."

But this is only the general picture; the details are even worse. "In the past 40 years, America has produced few political figures comparable in clarity of wisdom and purpose to some of the great names of the preceding century. At the same time, we have suffered an alarming epidemic of traitors in high places compared to whom Benedict Arnold was a rather sympathetic figure. Foreign governments and blocs of poorly assimilated Americans," the Polish immigrant wrote, "have been able to influence and sway the American ship of state causing it to flounder in the mire of conflicting interests and indecision. American 'masses' are clamoring for bonuses, pensions, subsidies and other sinecures. . . . Today no less than 37.8 million Americans are receiving direct monthly checks from the federal government. The Revolutionary maxim that that government is best which governs least has fallen by the board."

Radzinski's article was in reality a racial-genetic explanation for all the things which racists, segregationists, and political reactionaries object to and cite as evidence of national decline. If Radzinski's analysis is correct, however, its implications are terrifying, for nothing fundamental can be done to check national degeneration. The American people today are victims of the genetic folly of their ancestors—how such superior people could commit so gigantic a blunder is puzzling—and they must wait passively upon those "centuries of incubation and biologic fusion" which will eliminate the genetic disharmonies caused by the melting pot. Prolonged breeding between these diverse races and ethnic groups will eventually result in "biologic fusion" and genetic harmony and—hopefully—a new ability to create and sustain an advanced civilization. "Much time will elapse, measurable in generations, before a biologic fusion among the White elements of our population is attained," Radzinski wrote. "Many more generations, measurable in centuries, will be required to effect a biologic integration with the non-White segments of our people, provided, of course, that the problem is not perpetuated by further infusion of large numbers of immigrants of any race."

In the meantime, the American people must learn from experience. "If there is one practical lesson to be derived from the present status of the American melting pot, it is that we should be extremely circumspect in our immigration policies," Radzinski stated, drawing the moral of his essay. "The U.S.A. can no longer afford to be the foster home for the unfortunates of the world. Biologically, there already are present here so many human types that further additions can hardly enhance the genetic end product. But such additions will tend to postpone indefinitely the salutary fusion necessary for harmonious society. Today, in excessive homicide, treason, juvenile delinquency and other crimes with their tremendous cost in suffering and treasure, we are paying the price for our reckless generosity to peoples of other lands. Politicians, who for reasons of expediency and false humanitarianism press for the relaxation of our too liberal immigration laws, are, in effect, asking for the perpetuation of this high tide of confusion and lawlessness."

Mankind Quarterly, a small journal with an imposing name, is the nearest thing scientific racists have to an official journal. Published in Edinburgh, Scotland, it has, since its first issue in 1960, played a major role in the promotion of scientific racism. In many instances the same men direct the affairs of the *Quarterly* and the IAAEE. Among the Americans who are or have been members of the honorary editorial board of the *Quarterly* are Henry E. Garrett, an honorary associate editor, Frank C. J. McGurk, Stanley D. Porteus, Audrey Shuey, Charles C. Tansill, Herbert Sanborn, Clarence P. Oliver, and anthropologist Harry Turney-High of the University of South Carolina. Robert Kuttner and A. James Gregor, the chief officials of the IAAEE, have served as assistant editors. Robert Gayre, a Scotsman, is editor. R. Ruggles Gates, a British geneticist who generally endorsed the ideas of scientific racism, was, until his death in 1962, an honorary associate editor.

According to the editors, *Mankind Quarterly* is "an international quarterly journal dealing with race and inheritance in the fields of ethnology, ethno- and human genetics, ethno-psychology, racial history, demography, and anthropo-geography." In point of fact, however, it is little more than an outlet for disseminating the ideas of scientific racism which have been discussed in this study. This conclusion is demonstrable in several ways. The journal and its editors espouse racial views which were fashionable among social scientists two generations ago but which have since largely disappeared from scientific circles. The editors regularly print articles of the kind which filled scientific journals two or three generations ago: articles describing anthropometric features of whites and Negroes; articles discussing "natives" and aboriginal peoples in condescending tones; articles attacking environmentalism, "the cultural hypothesis," and Franz Boas; and articles denouncing liberals, reformers, integrationists, intellectuals, and communists.

The editors frequently open their journal to racists, segregationists, and political reactionaries, some of whom are not scientists and make no pretense at scholarship or scientific detachment but who use science as a point of departure for denouncing the civil rights movement and racial integration.[19] A few excerpts from one such author will demonstrate this. A 1963 issue of the *Quarterly* carried William A. Massey's article, "The New Fanatics," an emotional polemic against intellectuals. The following passages typify its tone and content:

Who are the new fanatics? They are the intellectuals: those people whose interests extend beyond the people and problems in their own area. They are writers, commentators, reporters, clergymen, teachers, social scientists, and many other executive and professional groups.

. . . .

The argument that science has shown that all races are equal is not satisfactory. The scientists who claim they have proved that all races are equal are suspect because of their obvious desire that all races should be equal. This may seem strange but it can be verified by a study of the literature in sociology and related fields.

. . . .

The fog of sentimentality generated by those who believe in the brotherhood of men and nations has so befuddled America and Western Europe that we are ashamed of our superiority. And we obviously are superior, for it is the other nations that envy us and not vice versa. . . . This backwardness of certain races would seem to argue that they are not our equal. Treating them as such is, if not stupid, at least neurotic.

. . . .

The uncomfortable fact is that the Negro may never make a good American citizen. Even if he is of adequate intelligence he may be tempermentally unsuited for citizenship in a democracy. It is possible that democracy is not the natural state of mankind, in spite of our fond belief to the contrary.

The real nature of *Mankind Quarterly* is further illustrated in its book review section. Each issue includes several book reviews, a surprisingly large number of which are of works that are not scientific and make no pretense of being scientific. Most such works deal with civil rights and racial integration, though some of them are propaganda tracts by political reactionaries or out-

[19] See for example William A. Massey, "The New Fanatics," *Mankind Quarterly*, IV (October–December, 1963), 70–104; Carleton Putnam, "These Are the Guilty," *ibid.*, IV (July–September, 1963), 12–27; Nathaniel Weyl, "Ethnic and National Characteristics of the U.S. Elite," *ibid*, I (January–March 1961), 245; and Armstrong, "Psychodiagnosis, Prognosis, School Desegregation and Delinquency."

spoken anticommunists. Invariably, books with a segregationist, reactionary, or hereditarian slant receive favorable reviews, while those expressing integrationist, liberal, or environmentalist views receive unfavorable treatment. Among the books which have been reviewed favorably are T. Robert Ingram, *Essays on Segregation* (1960), a collection of articles in praise of segregation by several Protestant ministers; Lambert and Patricia Schuyler, *Close That Bedroom Door!* (1957), a polemic against racial amalgamation, the tone of which is indicated by the title; Robert Kendall, *White Teacher in a Black School* (1964), an account of the author's experiences in a Negro school, an account which segregationists and political conservatives have praised highly; and Frank L. Kluchhohn, *Lyndon's Legacy: A Candid Look at the President's Policymakers* (1964), a collection of ultraright-wing charges against President Lyndon Johnson and his administration. Even Fulgencio Batista's *The Growth and Decline of the Cuban Republic* (1964), the ex-dictator's impassioned defense of his regime, received favorable notice from an anonymous reviewer.

Scientists in America and elsewhere have been outspoken in their criticism of *Mankind Quarterly*,[20] and have focused that criticism invariably upon several specific points: the lack of scientific standards, the intrusion of editorial views in supposedly scientific articles and reviews, and the use of science to defend racist ends. No sooner had the first issue appeared than the Yugoslav anthropologist Bozo Skerlj resigned as an honorary associate editor and repudiated the *Quarterly* for "seem[ing] to show such little concern for facts and to be so distorted by racial prejudice."[21]

A torrent of criticism from other scientists soon followed. A. J. Cain, a demonstrator in animal taxonomy at Oxford, reviewed the first two issues of the *Quarterly* for *Race,* the journal of the Institute of Race Relations (London). "It will be difficult for any serious scientist to read without deep misgivings the first two issues of this new journal," Cain wrote. Some of its articles "are written intemperately, and show besides a method of argument that should never be used in a scientific work, and a lack of information that is surprising." In those articles, "confusion follows close on plati-

20 An exception was the British *Eugenics Review,* which favorably reviewed the first two issues. See "The Mankind Quarterly," *Eugenics Review,* LII (October, 1960), 135.

21 Bozo Skerlj to editor, *Man,* LX (November, 1960), 172–73.

tude" and "overstatement is added to confusion." He concluded, "I can only record that by the publication of this journal, I consider that the scientific study of the races of mankind has not been promoted." [22]

Man, the journal of the Royal Anthropological Institute of London, was equally outspoken in its condemnations. "Few of the contributions have any merit whatsoever," wrote Dr. G. Ainsworth Harrison, who reviewed the first three issues of *Mankind Quarterly,* "and many are no more than incompetent attempts to rationalize irrational opinions." Concerning an article by Editor Robert Gayre, Harrison wrote, "To evaluate the general substance of the paper is impossible unless one is trained in the art of criticizing nonsense." Of the journal as a whole he wrote, "the primary aim of many of the contributions seems to be to elude the facts." Most of the contributions, he thought, are "trivial and third rate. None of the authors rigorously and objectively appraises the limitations of the tests he uses . . . and the few that formulate testable hypotheses appear only to be critical of the evidence which fails to support what they want to demonstrate. The fact that every contribution is concerned with discrediting 'environmentalist' conclusions strongly indicates the editorial policy. What is particularly insidious in a supposedly scientific journal is the use of words with overtones of moral judgment." Harrison concluded his review with an earnest hope "that *The Mankind Quarterly* will succumb before it can further discredit anthropology and do more damage to mankind." [23]

In *Science,* the journal of the American Association for the Advancement of Science, Santiago Genoves of Mexico accused the editors of *Mankind Quarterly* of consciously using "science, or rather pseudoscience, to try to establish postulates of racial superiority or inferiority based on biological differences," and he deplored their efforts. "I have no other purpose," he stated, "than to denounce this attitude of men of science who, with strange antiscientific spirit, distort facts, as Archbishop Wilberforce did a century ago." [24]

Spokesmen for *Mankind Quarterly,* especially the editors and

[22] A. J. Cain, "The Mankind Quarterly," *Race,* II (May, 1961), 78–82.

[23] G. Ainsworth Harrison, "The Mankind Quarterly," *Man,* LXI (September, 1961), 163–64.

[24] Santiago Genoves, "Racism and 'The Mankind Quarterly,' " *Science,* December 8, 1961, pp. 1928–32.

several leading contributors, did not take such criticisms in silence. They responded in kind, and the result was a bitter, name-calling controversy which raged for two or three years and smolders even yet. The principle episode in the controversy was sparked by Mexican anthropologist Juan Comas, who published a critique on *Mankind Quarterly* in an American journal, *Current Anthropology*.[25] Comas described the *Quarterly* as "a supposedly scientific journal whose contents are the cause of profound concern to those interested in racial questions in the biological and anthropological fields as well as in the social field." To substantiate his charge he offered not a general review of the *Quarterly* but a systematic critique of Henry E. Garrett's "Klineberg's Chapter on Race and Psychology: A Review," which appeared in the first issue. Comas sought to discredit Garrett and the *Quarterly* by demonstrating the racism of both. As a result of his effort, he and spokesmen for the *Quarterly* became involved in the recurrent controversy between environmentalists and hereditarians, a fact which increased the significance of their dispute, since they waged it within the context of the larger controversy. *Current Anthropology* submitted Comas' critique of Garrett to twenty scientists, including Garrett himself, R. Ruggles Gates, and Robert Gayre, and published their reactions along with Comas' article. Most of the twenty scientists endorsed Comas' position, though several expressed reservations about his tendency to allow his zealous equalitarianism to intrude unduly into his discussion. The controversy continued through 1962 and 1963, generating more emotion and invective than understanding.[26]

Editors Gayre and Gates assumed the chief responsibility for answering critics of their journal. "The attacks on the Mankind Quarterly," wrote Gates in a letter to the editor of *Man,* "are not based on science at all but have a political basis, having been made mainly by Communists or their fellow travellers. That some are willing to allow their science to be submerged and vitiated by

25 Juan Comas, " 'Scientific' Racism Again?" *Current Anthropology,* II (October, 1961).

26 Comas' original article, the comments by the twenty scientists, and several items in the exchange between Comas and his critics, notably A. James Gregor, Robert Gayre, Henry E. Garrett, and Donald A Swan, were printed by *Mankind Quarterly* in "Anatomy of a Controversy," *Mankind Monographs,* VI (3 parts, Edinburgh, 1963–64).

their political views is one of the tragedies of the period of disturbance through which we are passing." [27] As these remarks indicate, communists as well as equalitarian social scientists have attacked *Mankind Quarterly*, and the attacks from communists, especially those in Iron Curtain countries, were welcomed by defenders of the *Quarterly*.

Gayre made the most systematic response to the attacks. He denied that his journal or any of its contributions were racist or endorsed racial inequality, insisting instead that the *Quarterly* merely refused to accept the "non-sensical assertions" of "a-racist egalitarians." In a revealing statement, he explained the editorial views of his journal: [28]

We wish to state categorically what are the views of the editors on the matter of racial equality. While rejecting egalitarianism as having no warranty in honest scientific expositions and investigations, we do not, on the other hand, subscribe to doctrines of racial *superiority or inferiority*. We believe that just as all individuals within a particular racial stock are different, so is one racial group in relation to another. In respect of some characters various stocks will be superior to others, and in other characters inferior, but in many cases no perceptible differences may be apparent. While environment, both physical and social, may influence these characters, we believe that heredity is by far the most important single factor, and the current fashion to eschew the significance of heredity is a definite disservice to the understanding of what makes for differences in the various characters which distinguish one group from another. Furthermore, we do not presume to judge what is desirably superior or not. We think that within the ambit of the type of civilization erected by the White-Brown stocks or the Yellow races, the Black which has shown no natural predilection to that form of organization will be at a disadvantage in any competition—and is *in that sense* inferior. . . .

With such considerations in mind, no one ought to be surprised if intelligence or other tests *designed primarily for the conditions of life which are those of the Caucasoid stock show* when applied to Negroids, that the Black races are inferior *in these respects*. It would be very odd if that were not the case. But if, in contrast, tests were applied which suited the genius of the Black races, such as those which give due credit in the field of humor, music, art, ability to live a communal life and existence (as distinct from the competitive form of civilization which the Caucasoids tend to erect) feeling for emotional religious expression, or physical abil-

[27] "A propos 'The Mankind Quarterly,'" *Man*, LXII (January, 1962), 13.
[28] [Robert Gayre] "The Mankind Quarterly Under Attack," *Mankind Quarterly*, II (October–December, 1961), 79–84.

ity in boxing, running, and much else, it would be very surprising if the Negroids did not prove themselves superior to the Europeans. Thus we do not believe in *absolute* superiority or inferiority between one stock and another. There are racial differences, and difference implies inferiority or superiority in relation to this or that character involved.

There is, Gayre added, "a middle position between racial equalitarianism and the Nazi doctrines of racial superiority," and in his view it was this middle position which *Mankind Quarterly* occupied.

Gayre's statement reveals the limitations inherent in the views of scientific racists—who did, after all, look upon their racial views as moderate and responsible. It is well enough to speak of racial differences and to deny the existence of absolute racial inequality, but more important are the implications which Gayre and other racists derived from their belief in racial differences and relative racial inequality. It is clear from Gayre's list of things in which Negroes allegedly excel—music, entertainment, athletics, and "communal life"—that his view of the race is not unlike that of paternalists, segregationists, and white supremacists. He states explicitly that Negroes are inferior to whites in ability to meet the challenges of modern western civilization, and the implications of this are clear—Negroes are superior only in qualities that are irrelevant to human progress, which is to say as a practical matter that the race is inferior. And if the purpose of social, political, and economic policies is to preserve civilization and further human progress, it also means that such policies must accept the white man's interests as paramount to the Negro's. Whether Gayre intended it or not, he provided "scientific" justification for racial segregation and exploitation.

Neither the IAAEE nor *Mankind Quarterly* have any influence in scientific circles. Both, however, are well received by racists, segregationists, and political reactionaries. Among the items which the Citizens' Councils list in their official journal as "Citizens' Council Literature" are subscriptions to *Mankind Quarterly*; ten of the thirteen items in the IAAEE Reprint Series; the two items in the IAAEE Monograph Series; volume IV of *Mankind Monographs,* a record of the controversy between Juan Comas and *Mankind Quarterly*; and Ernest van den Haag's "Negroes, Intelligence, and Prejudice," reprinted from *National Review* under an IAAEE imprint.[29] In a recent issue of the John Birch Society magazine *American Opinion,* Dr. Revilo P. Oliver endorsed the IAAEE Reprint Series. "If such reprints are widely distributed," wrote Oliver, a professor of Classics at the University of Illinois, "the 'Liberals,' of course, may have to force the learned and professional journals to exclude articles that do not conform to the Communist line." [30] Professor Oliver recently achieved considerable notoriety by charging that President Kennedy was a communist agent whom the communists themselves assassinated because he procrastinated in his promise to communize the United States.

The endorsements from the Citizens' Councils and Oliver are but two instances of the relationship between segregationists and reactionaries on the one hand, and scientific racists on the other. The efforts of segregationists and reactionaries to apply the ideas of scientific racism to American race policies are themselves an important part of the recent history of scientific racism and are worth discussing in detail.

[29] A recent list of Citizens' Council literature is in *The Citizen,* IX (June, 1965) , 27–28.

[30] Revilo P. Oliver, "Brainwashing," *American Opinion,* VII (November, 1964) , 32n.

7

POPULARIZERS OF SCIENTIFIC RACISM

The recent history of scientific racism consists of two parallel developments. The first was an accomplishment of academic social scientists who, intentionally or not, provided "scientific" data for racists and a "scientific" rationale for segregation and discrimination. The second was an achievement of nonscientists, of popularizers who explained scientific racism to white supremacists and segregationists who in turn sought to make those explanations the basis for racial policy. Both are important elements in the history of civil rights since 1954. The works and speculations of a few academic scientists were of limited significance in themselves and would remain so unless translated into a philosophy of race relations and a program of racial policies. This was the task of popularizers. The story of their achievement is significant in its own right, because it demonstrates the close relationship between segregationists and the social scientists discussed in this study, and illustrates the extent to which the works of the social scientists served the ends of calculating racists. It also explains the efforts segregationists have recently made to apply "science" to race relations.

The efforts were more difficult than might at first appear. Most segregationists do not think in scientific terms. They find the abstractions of science uncongenial; they are more comfortable discussing legal precedents and constitutional interpretations than ruminating in the world of science. Historically, defenders of Southern race policies have been more remarkable for emotion than intellectuality, and few of them ever felt it necessary to think through their racial ideas and formulate a systematic racial philosophy. Traditionally, they found justification aplenty for segregation in their experiences with Negroes. They *knew* the race, they felt, as no other white men ever had. When provoked into defending the "Southern way of life," the essential element of which was first slavery and then segregation, they turned invariably to legal and constitutional arguments, emphasizing the twin doctrines of states' rights and limited (federal) government. Pressed further, they might add that Negroes are not "ready" for integration, that integration violates basic precepts of human decency, Christianity, or "God's way." In any case, they always believed that Negroes prefer segregation and are satisfied with life in the South.

Southern segregationists have usually accepted these arguments as an adequate defense of their racial policies. In effect, they accepted first slavery and later segregation as "right" and "natural" without bothering to develop a rational defense for either. Of course, scientific arguments were always a minor theme in the defense of both, but never more than a minor theme irregularly employed. Southerners have usually ignored scientific justifications for their race policies during periods of racial quietude, turning to science only when outside pressures necessitated a more careful defense of their policies. The antebellum slaveocracy developed a "scientific" defense of slavery only when the abolitionist attack upon the peculiar institution became effective. After 1890 segregationists again turned to science, this time seeking arguments to blunt Northern criticism of new laws and state constitutions disfranchising Negroes, nullifying the Fourteenth and Fifteenth amendments, and legalizing the most rigid kind of racial discrimination. However, once Northerners and the federal government acquiesced in the new policies the Southerners' interest in science diminished. But again after 1954 Southern whites recognized the seriousness of a new challenge to their race policies, and turned once more to science.

The story of this latest effort to use science to defend discriminatory race policies is in part a story of writers, lecturers, and organizers who bridged the gap between academic social scientists and segregationists and white supremacists. The division between the academics and the popularizers, however, is not absolute. Such scientists as Garrett and George are also popularizers, and nonscientists sometimes speak as though they are scientists. It is the popularizers, the nonscientists, who have the most direct impact upon segregationists and white supremacists.

The most significant of the popularizers is Carleton Putnam, a Yankee by birth and inheritance, a Southerner by choice and persuasion. Born in New York City in 1901, Putnam comes from a distinguished New York and New England family and is descended from the Revolutionary War general, Israel Putnam. Educated at Princeton (B.S. in history and politics, 1924) and Columbia (LL.B., 1932), he has spent most of his adult life as an airlines executive. He has been for some time engaged in writing a multivolume biography of Theodore Roosevelt, and more recently, a defense of racial segregation in the South.[1] Though Thomas R. Waring, the archsegregationist editor of the *Charleston News and Courier* has described Putnam as "a dyed-in-the-wool Northerner" and "a Yankee in the true sense of the word," Putnam has in fact spent much of his adult life in the South and the environs of Washington, D.C.

Putnam's emergence as a major spokesman for scientific racists illustrates many crosscurrents in the recent history of scientific racism, including the close relationship between segregation, scientific racism, and political reaction. Though he and his admirers

[1] For a brief account of Putnam's life see W. D. McCain, "Who Is Carleton Putnam?" *The Citizen*, VII (March, 1963), 52–54.

frequently refer to his "science degree," he is not a scientist; his degree is a bachelor of science in history and politics. These references to Putnam's "science degree" are apparently intended to buttress the authority of his scientific preachments, and are another instance of the tendency of racists sometimes to state things in a way that creates a false impression. The fact that Putnam is not a scientist, however, has not inhibited him in his writings on race, nor has it lessened his appeal among segregationists and white supremacists. It has, in fact, been advantageous to him, for it makes him oblivious to the nature and limitations of the scientific process and relieves him of all doubt about the sufficiency of his logic and his evidence.

When the Supreme Court issued the Brown decision, Putnam was not, he says, much concerned one way or another.[2] Gradually, however, casual reading in the public press and the shock of the Little Rock crisis aroused his interest in both the Brown decision and the larger problem of race relations in general. The more he read the more he was aroused. He found the arguments of segregationists cogent, logical, and well presented; those of integrationists "inept" and "lacking in perception." He wondered if no one else saw this. Driven by a growing sense of outrage at the actions and illogic of integrationists, he decided to speak out, to enter the war of words then raging between segregationists and integrationists. His first step was to express his concern in letters to the editors of *Life* magazine and the Memphis *Commercial Appeal*. *Life* ignored his letter, but the *Commercial Appeal* printed it in full. The experience was significant. It convinced Putnam that the national press had closed its mind on race and race relations and erected a "paper curtain" around those subjects to conceal the truth from the American people. In contrast, the appearance of his letter in the *Commercial Appeal* elicited considerable enthusiasm from Southern readers, a fact which further convinced him of the soundness of his own views and the open-mindedness of Southerners, even on the sensitive issue of race relations.

This was a typical reaction of segregationists in similar situations. So convinced are they of their own reasonableness and truthfulness, indeed of their own righteousness, that they are often unable

[2] This author's narrative follows closely that of Putnam himself in his *Race and Reason, A Yankee View* (Washington, 1961), a work which is among other things a self-adulatory account of Putnam's role in defending segregation and spreading the ideas of scientific racism.

to evaluate rationally the views of other people. Putnam was sure that anyone who agreed with him was reasonable, truthful, and righteous, for he was convinced that those terms aptly described his own views. Nor is the reference to righteousness misplaced. A sense of self-righteousness and moral indignation pervades all his writings on race and leads him to the conclusion that his critics are naive, ignorant, immoral, unpatriotic, or all of these. This fact is in part responsible for his failure to provoke a meaningful debate with integrationists, though the shallowness of his ideas, the inconsequence of his evidence, and the disingenuousness of his logic also contributed to his failure. Putnam blamed his failure on the unwillingness of integrationists to debate an issue in which the evidence is against them. Debate, however, is possible only between open-minded men of good will who are receptive to facts and to points of view which differ from their own. Racial topics by their very nature are difficult to debate, whether the debaters be segregationists or integrationists, but Putnam had more difficulty than most men. As a result, he has had more success exhorting the faithful than persuading the skeptical.

In 1958 in the aftermath of the Little Rock crisis, Putnam decided that a direct appeal to President Eisenhower was the best way to dramatize the segregationists' case. Accordingly, he wrote a letter to the President, hoping to convince him of "the reasonableness behind the Southern position." This was the first of several letters from Putnam to prominent public officials, and such letters have since become the chief device for drawing attention to his ideas.

The letter to Eisenhower [3] is a summary of Putnam's objections to the Brown decision and racial integration. In it, Putnam relied very little upon scientific arguments, a fact which indicates that he had not yet realized their usefulness to segregationists. He objected to the Brown decision because it ignored local customs and racial mores in the South, because it represented court-made law and disregarded "the white man's right to freedom of association," because it violated the lessons of history and sought to give Negroes something they had not earned, because it "set back the cause of the Negro in the South by a generation." He told Eisenhower that the integration movement rested upon a false con-

[3] It is printed in Putnam, *Race and Reason*, 5–9.

struction of the Jeffersonian principle of human equality and a misunderstanding of the Christian doctrine of brotherly love. "The command to love your neighbor," he explained, "is not a command either to consider your neighbor your equal, or yourself his equal."

These are standard criticisms of the integration movement, and Putnam's use of them demonstrated his kinship with traditional segregationists. It was axiomatic to him that race relations are the exclusive concern of whites, and that whatever upsets the Southern white man damages "the cause of the Negro." In Putnam's view, the Negro's "cause" was to stay on good terms with white men, not to go around indiscriminately demanding social and political rights. He assumed that the white man's interests are superior to the Negro's, for he also assumed that the South, like the United States as a whole, is a white man's country in which Negroes are permitted to live although without any real voice in primary social or political decisions.

No objection to integration was more important to Putnam than the idea that Negroes have not "earned" the right to equality. "Social status has to be earned," he declared. "It cannot be achieved by legal fiat. . . . Any man with two eyes in his head can observe a Negro settlement in the Congo, can study the pure-blooded African in his native habitat as he exists when left on his own resources, can compare this settlement with London or Paris, and can draw his own conclusions regarding relative levels of character and intelligence—or that combination of character and intelligence which is civilization." This statement has interesting implications. It raises the question, How can Negroes "earn" equal status? What can "clean," God-fearing, hardworking, patriotic, intelligent, middle class Negroes do to "earn" equality? Putnam seems to answer "nothing"—until the "average" Negro matches the "average" white man in the above qualities, and the civilization of Africa equals that of Europe. As a practical matter, this means that individual Negroes can do nothing—but wait and remain segregated. But other questions also arise. Does the emergence of independent Negro nations in Africa count for anything? Does the integration movement itself count for anything? Through this movement Negroes are overcoming all the obstacles and intimidations which the white man's resourcefulness and ingenuity have devised to keep the race down. Is not this movement, so hateful to segregationists, itself a process of "earning" status? Not to Putnam. To him it is a plot by selfish, power-hungry white politicians to "give" special privileges to Negroes in exchange for votes on election day.

President Eisenhower ignored Putnam's letter, a fact which Putnam took to mean that Eisenhower was a part of the national conspiracy of silence against the South and the segregationist point of view. To overcome this conspiracy and get his views before the American people, Putnam sent a copy of the letter to Virginius Dabney, editor of the Richmond *Times-Dispatch,* who printed it and praised it editorially. Other Southern newspapers picked it up, and Putnam was presently inundated with a flood of favorable replies from across the South. At the urging of columnist John Temple Graves of the Birmingham *Post-Herald,* one of the South's most outspoken defenders of segregation, a group of prominent Alabama politicians, among them Albert Boutwell, now mayor of Birmingham, organized a committee to facilitate the distribution of Putnam's letter outside the South. The favorite device of the Putnam Letters Committee, as the group called itself, was to print Putnam's letters in paid advertisements in major newspapers outside the South.[4] Each advertisement included an appeal for funds, which the Committee used to buy still other advertisements in a continuing assault upon the "paper curtain." The effort had an element of the quixotic about it, but it had a certain appeal to thousands of segregationists who derived from it the satisfaction of having participated in a concerted effort to do something about the threat of racial integration.

The response to the Eisenhower letter, the first to be widely printed in non-Southern newspapers, was, according to Putnam, successful beyond all expectations. Within five months, he states, contributions totaled $37,000, and the advertisements continued sporadically over several years. A more important result of the Committee's efforts was the thousands of letters from Northerners and Westerners which, again according to Putnam, overwhelmingly supported his position. "The man and woman in the street in the North," he wrote, "seemed to be on the side of the South," and here was a vast reservoir of good will which Southerners

---

[4] The letter to Eisenhower appeared in the New York *Times,* January 5, 1959.

could exploit in their crusade against integration, and if properly exploited might enable them to win their fight and reverse the Brown decision.

Reverse the Brown decision! That chimera was and remains Putnam's great objective, the Holy Grail he pursues with the ardor and singlemindedness of a medieval knight. Though he is certain that the American people are basically sympathetic to segregation, he is confronted with the stubborn fact that they sometimes act like integrationists. They allow Negroes to vote and attend integrated schools; they follow political, civic, and religious leaders who endorse integration; they support institutions of higher learning in which their children are taught that men are equal and racial segregation is irrational. To reconcile this paradox, Putnam resorts to a favorite device of racists, the plot theory of history. He, too, believes that intellectuals, social scientists, liberals, socialists, and communists have brainwashed the American people into believing against their better judgment that the races are equal and integration is the only rational system of race relations. He therefore warned Americans to beware of "a movement calling itself, here, Communism, there Marxism, somewhere else Socialism," for whatever its name, its objective is always the same, "the subversion of science as well as governments."

Putnam felt compelled to broadcast his convictions, and in March 1959 he expressed them in another letter, this time to Eisenhower's attorney general, William P. Rogers. It was the preparation of this letter that led Putnam to science. He studied the scientific arguments put forth by segregationists and integrationists, read the testimony in the Brown cases, and traced the integrationists' ideas and, indeed, the origins of the equalitarian "conspiracy" back to Franz Boas and the social anthropologists Boas trained at Columbia. Reading Boas' works, he found, was an astonishing experience. "Here was clever and insidious propaganda posing in the name of science," he wrote, "fruitless efforts at proof of unprovable theories," "slippery techniques in evading the main issue," "prolix diversions," "sound without . . . substance." Boas was not simply a poor scientist, he was ludicrous, and while reading his works Putnam was reduced to "laughing out loud."

He decided to pursue the matter further. If he, a nonscientist, saw through Boas' fabrications and insipidness, surely trained scientists did too. To find out for himself, he approached a num-

ber of leading scientists, soliciting their opinions on the works of
Boas and his disciples in social anthropology. He found "professional scientists aplenty" who agreed with his assessment of Boas,
but he also found something else—they would admit their true
feelings in private but not in public. They were inhibited, he decided, by the stranglehold equalitarians have over the academic
and scientific world. "One prize-winning Northern scientist whom
I visited at his home in a Northern city asked me, after I had
been seated a few minutes in his living room, whether I was sure
I had not been followed," he wrote. "Another disclosed in the
privacy of his study that he had evidence he was being checked by
mulattoes at his lectures."

To Putnam, such incidents confirmed his belief that American
science was in an intimidated state. When he first approached the
scientists they were "hesitant, withdrawn and fearful," even those
with national and international reputations. Gradually, however,
their reserve broke down and many of them talked freely, but—
alas!—confidentially, to Putnam. And being an honorable man, he
refuses to violate their confidence; he will not publicly name the
scientists who privately agree with him. "Any public official who
will guarantee their livelihood," he wrote, "can get their names
from me, on one condition—that the scientists themselves agree."

Such a statement can only be taken as a measure of Putnam's
failure to find reputable scientists who agree with his racial views.
Obviously he cannot produce an impressive list of scientists who
support segregation on scientific grounds (though it would be a
simple matter to produce a list of those who condemn it on those
grounds), so he resorts to an unsubstantiated claim that scientists
are cowered into silence or, even worse, into endorsing equalitarianism against their better judgment. His comments about the scientific and academic communities are in notable contrast to the
usual charge by political reactionaries that academic freedom and
tenure are camouflage for intellectual license. If Putnam is correct,
what exists is not academic freedom at all but a degree of thought
control that would do credit to a police state. However, the reader
need only recall the academic appointments of scientists already
discussed in this study to see that Putnam is not entirely correct.
Despite the existence of an equalitarian consensus in the academic
community, there is still a number of social scientists who publicly
dissent from that consensus. The wonder is not that there are no

hereditarians or scientific racists in the nation's colleges and universities, but that there are so many proponents of racial views which are generally discredited.

Putnam's excursion into scientific racism convinced him that the strength of the civil rights movement lay in the fact that the American people have been misled into believing the false scientific claims of equalitarians and environmentalists. Americans have been convinced, erroneously he believed, that "science" has proven the races equal and that heredity has little influence upon character and intelligence. They have therefore decided, also erroneously, that segregation is unscientific, unnatural, and unjust. This conviction is widespread even in the South, Putnam declared, where it has created guilt feelings in many white Southerners who are made to suspect that segregation might after all do violence to scientific truth and thus to justice and "right." Because of this conviction, most Americans are impervious to the appeals of segregationists, especially when their appeals are based on states' rights and constitutional precedents. If segregationists are to succeed, if they are to reach the American people, they must, Putnam concluded, drop their emphasis upon legal and constitutional arguments and turn instead to science. The South can preserve segregation only by convincing the rest of America that equalitarian science is invalid. False sentimentalism and humanitarianism must not be permitted to interfere with the acceptance of scientific truth or with the application of science to race relations. "Any American worthy of the name feels an obligation of kindness and justice toward his fellow man," Putnam told Attorney General Rogers. "He is willing to give every individual his chance, whatever his race, but in those circumstances where a race must be dealt with as a race, he realizes that the level of the average must be controlling, and that the relatively minor handicap upon the superior individual of the segregated race, if it be a handicap at all, must be accepted until the average has reached the point where desire for association is mutual."

Putnam hoped that his letter to the attorney general [5] might embolden intimidated scientists and relieve the consciences of guilt-stricken segregationists. In this letter his major arguments against integration are scientific in nature. He repeated the usual racist

[5] It is printed in Putnam, *Race and Reason*, 21–29.

criticisms of the social science in the Brown decision. A majority of the authorities cited by the Court appear "either to belong to Negro or other minority groups, or to have prepared their studies under the auspices of such groups," he noted. "To expect these groups to present impartial reports on the subject of racial discrimination is like expecting a saloon keeper to prepare an impartial study on prohibition." It was his "considered opinion," he added, "that two generations of Americans have been victimized by a pseudo-scientific hoax in this field, that this hoax is part of an equalitarian propaganda typical of the left-wing overdrift of our times, and that it will not stand an informed judicial test. I do not believe that ever before has science been more warped by a self-serving few to the deception and injury of so many."

To correct the misconceptions in this "hoax," Putnam explained to the attorney general that each race should be measured by its "character-intelligence index." This index he defined as "the combination of intelligence with all of the qualities that go under the name of character, including especially the willingness to resist rather than to appease evil." It "forms the only possible index of the capacity for civilization as Western Europeans know it," he added, "and there is no test for [it] save in observing the native culture in which it results. Such observation does not sustain the doctrine of [racial] equality."

This index, which is central to Putnam's case, is apparently his own contribution to scientific racism. To prove its validity he cited the failure of Negroes in Africa to create a civilization equal to that of modern Europe, a fact which he thought was genetic in origin, though much of his evidence to prove it was historical. Where, he asked rhetorically, is the Negro Shakespeare? The Negro Milton, Edison, Napoleon, Columbus, Lincoln, Beethoven? The Negro city to match London or Paris?

Putnam's discussion of African civilization illustrates the extent to which social darwinism permeates his thinking. "The essential question in this whole [integration] controversy," he wrote, "is whether the Negro, given every conceivable help regardless of cost to the whites, is capable of full adaptation to our white civilization within a matter of a few generations, or whether the record indicates that such adaptation cannot be expected save in terms of many hundreds, if not thousands, of years, and that complete integration of these races, especially in the heavy black belts of the

South, can result only in a parasitic deterioration of white culture, with or without genocide." Negro improvement is a matter of centuries. "Changes in a race occur by mutation and natural selection which involve the gradual elimination of those genes which are unsuited to the surrounding environment," Putnam wrote.[6] "This takes place by mating choices within the race itself and by the dying-off without children of those with a preponderance of unsuitable genes. The process must obviously be a slow one, involving many generations, before the adapting race can hope to achieve equality."

The Putnam Letters Committee printed the letter to Attorney General Rogers in non-Southern newspapers, just as it had the one to Eisenhower, and the response was, says Putnam, overwhelmingly favorable. However, a small minority of those who responded disagreed with Putnam and raised a number of questions which he felt compelled to answer. From their questions he selected those he thought were most significant and prepared answers to them, intending the answers to serve as a general reply to his critics. He decided to publish these answers, hoping thereby to achieve an even wider distribution. The result was *Race and Reason, A Yankee View* (1961), certainly the most widely circulated and probably the most influential defense of segregation written since 1954. It has been especially influential in stimulating among segregationists an interest in scientific racism and awakening them to the possibilities of science as a bulwark for segregation. Published by Public Affairs Press, it reportedly sold more than 100,000 copies within two years. Its circulation has been facilitated by right-wing "patriotic" bookstores as well as segregationist organizations, and some of the latter distribute free copies.

It is a significant book for several reasons. Not only does it detail many standard arguments against integration, but it reflects almost in caricature the intellectual orientation of segregationists. Putnam looks backward nostalgically to the glories of the past, to the days before the American republic was sullied by the New Deal and modern liberalism. In those days, he believes, Americans obeyed the laws of God and nature, lived by moral and ethical absolutes, accepted the inequalities of man, revered the Constitution, and respected legal precedents. There was stability

[6] Putnam, *Race and Reason,* 56.

and order, a reverence for principles, a respect for the ideals which had made this a great nation. In the last thirty years, however, or so Putnam thought, all this had eroded away. Change replaced stability and continuity as the natural order of things; the federal government became a bloated tyrant, twisting the Constitution beyond recognition; moral relativism displaced moral absolutes; labor unions became too powerful; racial and ethnic minorities grew restive, challenging the status and middle class ethic of old Americans. All this alarmed Putnam, and his impassioned alarm is a major reason for his appeal among segregationists. Basically, he is neither a scientist nor a pedagogue, but an exhorter. He tells faithful segregationists and white supremacists what they want to hear, and gives them the assurance which comes from having their racial views rationalized and justified.

Race and Reason is a catechism for "true believers," to borrow Eric Hoffer's telling phrase. It consists largely of a series of questions and answers in which Putnam attempted to refute what he thought were the chief arguments against segregation. Despite the ecstatic praise it has elicited from segregationists, it is unusually simplistic, even for a racist work. In fact, Putnam's evaluation of the works of Franz Boas aptly describes his own: "Here [is] clever and insidious propaganda posing in the name of science, fruitless efforts at proof of unprovable theories," "slippery techniques in evading the main issues," "sound without . . . substance," an approach "so saturated with wishful thinking as to be pathetic." There are, however, no "prolix diversions," for Putnam is an effective writer with a fluid style and beguiling presentation.

One of his basic techniques is to avoid troublesome issues by diverting attention from them through the use of *non sequiturs*. The following examples are typical:

Q. You are preaching a doctrine of white supremacy and allying yourself with lynchers and bombers. Worse, don't you realize that this is the doctrine that led to Hitler's barbaric policies?

A. I am advocating a doctrine of white leadership based on proved achievement, not supremacy in any sense of domination, exploitation, or violence.

In this casual manner he glossed over the harsher aspects of white supremacy. White supremacy can be maintained only by denying Negroes the right to vote, which is to say by dominating and exploiting the race, and the recent rise in Negro militancy seems to indicate that white supremacy can be preserved in the future only by a willingness of whites to resort to violence.

But to return to his answer:

As far as the Negro race is concerned, if it is interested in such cultural elements as our white civilization has to offer, it should realize that to destroy or to debilitate the white race would be to kill the goose that lays the golden egg. . . . Regarding Hitler, can we condemn Christianity because of the atrocities of the Spanish Inquisition? . . . (pp. 55–56)

Q. The NAACP maintains that your comparison of the achievement of great white men with those of Negroes is pointless. They say the same comparison could be made between white men and white women, yet no one claims that women are biologically inferior. They also say that the early Irish immigrants to this country were more shabby and lived in poorer shanties than the Negroes. What is your answer?

A. As to the achievements of women, not even in *Alice in Wonderland* do we find an attempt to equate biological inequivalents. Most women, through history, have been in the home, bearing and rearing children, and to see a Negro man hiding behind a white woman's skirts is just a little sickening.

Concerning the Irish, when the NAACP can point to a Negro city the equal of Dublin or Cork or Belfast, it will be time to discuss it. (p. 59)

Q. Isn't it wrong to injure the self-esteem of any man by reflections on his racial background?

A. No man's self-esteem need be injured by the truth concerning his racial background, any more than an acceptance of innate limitations by people in any sphere need affect their pride. Most of us do not hang our heads in shame if we cannot invent like Edison or write like Shakespeare. . . . (p. 64)

Q. Isn't it unfair to discriminate legally against the exceptional Negro on the basis of a racial average?

A. We discriminate legally against exceptional minors by not allowing them to vote, although certain of them may be more intelligent than many adults. Discriminations of this sort are necessary to the practical administration of human affairs. (p. 64)

Putnam has not answered his own questions. He sometimes dismissed the question as unimportant (e.g., his dismissal of the reference to the Irish), sometimes raised extraneous issues (e.g., his reference to Hitler, Christianity, and the Spanish Inquisition), and sometimes introduced false analogies (e.g., between Negroes and minors). He justifies discrimination against Negroes by pointing out that minors are discriminated against. But the discriminations against minors apply to *all* minors and are temporary. In addition, Negro adults are not minors, nor is intelligence the criterion for American citizenship. Elsewhere Putnam is a staunch advocate of strict construction of the Constitution, and his effort to base the rights of citizenship upon intelligence, which is certainly extra-constitutional, indicates that race, not intelligence or the Constitution, is his principal concern.

His performance is no better on questions relating to science:

Q. While there is no positive scientific proof that the Negro is the equal of the white man, neither is there any positive scientific proof that he is not. Under these circumstances, how can the Negro's inferiority be assumed?

A. It is true that anthropology is not an exact science in the sense that mathematics is, and that its propositions cannot be proved or disproved like mathematical formulae. Nevertheless, the evidence is as clear as the nature of the science permits, and it is all that reasonable men can ask. . . .

"The evidence" to which he referred is the studies of Negro intelligence by H. A. Tanser, Audrey Shuey, and Frank McGurk, and the studies of brain morphology by Wilder Penfield, Ward C. Halstead, and C. J. Connolly. As previously noted, however, the studies by Tanser, Shuey, and McGurk prove only that most Negroes make lower scores than most whites on IQ tests; they do not demonstrate that the lower scores result from innate factors.[7] Penfield and Halstead have repudiated Putnam's use of their works, and have specifically stated that they know of no valid evidence which indicates that Negroes are inferior to whites.[8] Connolly's study also has serious limitations for Putnam's purposes, as physiologist Dwight J. Ingle has demonstrated.[9] Reviewing the studies on brain morphology by F. W. Vint, Robert Bennett Bean, and Connolly, Ingle noted that "the three authors' descriptions of differences did not agree, although each concluded that no morphological feature was found to be exclusively characteristic of either the White or the Negro brain. There is no objective evidence that any of the average differences claimed to exist are marks of inferiority or correlate with intelligence and behavior." So, despite Putnam's statement to the contrary, the evidence is *not* "all that reasonable men can ask."

7 See above, Chapter IV.

8 Halstead and Penfield's letters to the editor of *Perspectives in Biology and Medicine* are quoted in Ingle, "Comments on the Teachings of Carleton Putnam."

9 Ingle, "Comments on the Teachings of Carleton Putnam," 30, *et passim.*

Putnam made his most ambitious use of science in replying to this question: "The NAACP asserts that there is virtually unanimity among scientists on the biological equality of the Negro. Is this true?" He phrased the question ingeniously, attributing the belief in "biological equality" to the NAACP, not to scientists, which was itself enough to discredit the question among segregationists. The phrase "biological equality" is itself ingenious. What does it mean? It could mean that there are no valid biological reasons for racial discrimination, but Putnam apparently intended his use of it to suggest that the races are biologically identical. Certainly the manner in which he used it obscured the distinction between racial differences and racial inequality. By confusing racial equality and biological sameness, he undertook to discredit the former by ridiculing the latter.

Putnam's answer to the question was emphatic. "It is not. There is a strong northern clique of equalitarian social anthropologists under the hypnosis of the Boas school which . . . has captured important chairs in many leading northern and western universities. This clique, aided by equalitarians in government, the press, entertainment, and other fields, has dominated public opinion in these areas and has made it almost impossible for those who disagree with it to hold jobs." Those who do disagree "have been forced largely into the universities of the South where they are biding their time." What was his authority for this? "My files," he wrote, "provide ample proof of this."

Unfortunately for his case, this is no proof at all. If he has proof, his obligation to produce it transcends his respect for those timid scientists he claims to protect. For if Putnam's racial views are correct, the integration movement *is* a threat to Western civilization, and the necessities of civilization outweigh the convenience of a few spineless scientists. But apparently for Putnam and many of his readers, the allegations were sufficient in themselves. "In a moral sense," he wrote, "we are confronted with what might almost be called a trilogy of conspiracy, fraud and intimidation: conspiracy to gain control of important citadels of learning and news dissemination, fraud in the teaching of false racial doctrines, and intimidation in suppressing those who would preach the truth." Despite Putnam's assurance on this point, it might be argued that his references to conspiracy, fraud, and intimidation are more applicable to such areas as Mississippi, the state in which Putnam is most influential, than to areas where equalitarian social science is widely accepted. One need only recall the stranglehold of segregationists upon the University of Mississippi, the pressures brought upon Professor James Silver there,[10] the racism that fills the columns of many Mississippi newspapers, and the intimidations against anyone in the state who deviates from orthodoxy on racial matters. Zealous segregationists are at least as insistent upon orthodoxy and conformity as are zealous integrationists. Certainly no area of the country has more zealously guarded its school children from unacceptable racial views than has the deep South.

Putnam has still other scientific authorities to offer. He cited three obscure works in French, G. Lefrou's *Le Noir D'Afrique* (1943), G. A. Heuse's *Biologie du Noir* (1957), and J. Millot's *Biologie des Races Humaines* (1952), which he assured his readers "are considered authoritative by our leading physical anthropologists." From these works he extracted quotations describing Negroes in most unflattering terms. Lefrou, for example, repeated the long-discredited idea that the intellectual development of Negroes ends at puberty. "There are two quite distinct stages in the intellectual life of the Negro," he wrote, quoting another French author. "As a child he is amiable, gentle, gracious, spontaneous and docile. He appears very precocious, more precocious by all odds than the great majority of European children. He understands and easily assimilates many things. At the date of puberty a radical metamorphasis takes place. A sharp arresting of development occurs and even a slight regression. The intellectual progress of the Negro is rapid during the first ten or twelve years, next it slows down, becomes stationary, then proceeds slowly, diminishing during some fifteen years. Finally a rapid enfeeblement occurs." Lefrou's views are based upon the idea that Negroes are more primitive than whites and closer to animals on the evolutionary scale. Like animals, the idea runs, their infancy is brief; they reach physical maturity quite early, but their intellectual development is arrested by the advent of puberty, when the sutures of the brain are said to knit together so firmly that the physical growth of the brain is halted completely. Adult Negroes are thus physically—and sexually—mature but intellectually adolescent, children with the physical and sexual appetites of grown-ups.

10 See James Silver, *Mississippi, The Closed Society* (New York, 1964).

Lefrou, Millot, and Heuse, plus Nathaniel Weyl (who is not a scientist), and biologist Garrett Hardin of the University of California, Santa Barbara,[11] are the "nonequalitarian anthropologists" cited by Putnam. His "science" is therefore much weaker than that of such writers as George, Garrett, Shuey, and McGurk. *Race and Reason* is important to the history of scientific racism not because of the amount of empirical data it offers (which is none at all) or the array of scientific authorities it quotes (which is anything but impressive), but because four important scientific racists wrote a laudatory introduction to it. The four were Henry E. Garrett, Wesley C. George, editor Robert Gayre of *Mankind Quarterly*, and R. Ruggles Gates. They were "in complete accord" with Putnam's science and endorsed "his balanced presentation of genetic and environmental factors in the area of both racial and individual biology." [12]

They also agreed with Putnam's "estimate of the extent to which non-scientific ideological pressures have harrassed scientists in the last thirty years." Like Putnam, they thought this pressure "often [resulted] in the suppression or distortion of truth" and was responsible for the widespread acceptance of equalitarianism. "Man must be guided by science, but scientific thought must not be molded to preconceived political ideas," they declared, molding their own scientific thoughts to preconceived political ideas. "Statesmen and judges today frequently take positions based upon an inadequate knowledge of the facts so far as they relate to the nature of man," they continued. "We do not believe that there is anything to be drawn from the sciences in which we work which supports the view that all races of men, or all ethnic groups are equal and

11 See Garrett Hardin, "The Competitive Exclusion Principle," *Science*, April 29, 1960, pp. 1292–97. It is difficult to see why Putnam cites this article to support his position. There is no racism in it, merely a discussion of the "competitive exclusion principle," an ecological hypothesis which suggests that in nature complete competitors cannot coexist. Hardin suggests that the principle has parallel implications for economics, genetics, and ecology. "As a result of recent findings in the fields of physiological genetics and population genetics, particularly as concerns blood groups, the applicability of both the inequality axiom and the exclusion principle is rapidly becoming accepted," Hardin wrote. He used the word "inequality" to refer to differences which favor survival in nature. He did not give it social and racial significance, or imply that it had any.

12 Putnam had written, for example, that "intelligence is almost entirely a matter of heredity." *Race and Reason*, 58.

alike, or likely to become equal or alike, in anything approaching the foreseeable future. We believe on the contrary that there are vast areas of difference within mankind not only in physical appearance, but in such matters as adaptability to varying environments, and in deep psychological and emotional qualities, as well as in mental ability and capacity for development."

Putnam hoped *Race and Reason* would accomplish two objectives: awaken America to the evil consequences of integration and lead the South to a new and better strategy in defending segregation. Integration is evil, he believed, because it leads inevitably to racial amalgamation, which in turn will be disastrous because Negroes have "no inborn capacity for Western civilization." Furthermore, he wrote, "It is not the South which is committing a moral crime against the Negro in maintaining segregation, but the North which is committing a moral crime against the South in forcing integration."

One test of the cogency of Putnam's logic is to take his admonitions concerning Negroes and apply them to segregationists in Mississippi, among whom *Race and Reason* was well received. "The capacity for a free civilization involves many attributes," Putnam wrote, "self-control (which, among other things, includes resistance to emotionalism), self-reliance, self-responsibility, willingness to bear the burdens of others without casting upon others the burdens one should bear one's self, willingness both to accept the verdict of majorities and to concede the rights of minorities, willingness to obey the law even when it hurts, willingness to support rather than to raid a treasury, emphasis upon the importance of the individual." Judging by the recent history of race relations in Mississippi, most Mississippi segregationists are not notable for "self-control" or "resistance to emotionalism." Nor is "self-reliance, self-responsibility, [and] willingness to bear the burdens of others without casting upon others the burdens one should bear one's self" the best way to describe their exploitation of Negroes. The reference to a "willingness . . . to accept the verdict of majorities and to concede the rights of minorities" is even more to the point. Mississippi segregationists have shown little concern for the rights of the Negro minority in their midst, nor are they willing to accept "the verdict of majorities" in those areas of the state where Negroes outnumber whites. Like John C. Calhoun before him, Putnam forgot that there are several kinds of majorities and minorities, and to be valid a defense of majority rights must be applicable to all majorities and consistent with the rights of all minorities. The admonition to Negroes "to obey the law even when it hurts" is particularly ironic in view of Putnam's defense of Mississippi, a state which has systematically subverted or ignored not only the *Brown* decision but the Fourteenth and Fifteenth amendments and the civil rights acts of 1957, 1960, 1964, and 1965. Finally, it should be noted (according to the Library of Congress Legislative Reference Service) that for every $218 paid by Mississippians in federal taxes, the federal government spent $327 in the state in 1959–61. And of every $1,000 in Mississippi income, $286 came from the federal government. It would seem that Mississippians do not always live up to Putnam's admonitions to support rather than raid the public treasury.

Segregationists have heaped lavish praise upon both Putnam and *Race and Reason*. An official of the Citizens' Councils described the latter as a "brilliant" work which "filled an aching need." [13] Dr. W. D. McCain, president of the University of Southern Mississippi, who reviewed *Race and Reason* for *The Citizen* reported in the spring of 1963 that the book had been reviewed 658 times, 544 of which were favorable, fourteen noncommittal, and one hundred unfavorable. However, he added, thirty-two of the unfavorable reviews appeared "in Negro newspapers which could scarcely be expected to view the book objectively." [14]

The impact of *Race and Reason* cannot be fully measured by counting favorable reviews, most of which were apparently in Southern (white) newspapers. More significant was the response of political and educational leaders in some areas of the deep South. Governor Ross Barnett of Mississippi was so impressed that he proclaimed October 26, 1961 "Race and Reason Day" in his state.[15] *Race and Reason* is "a significant and valuable new book" which "meets a long-recognized need in improving communications between patriotic Americans, informing responsible Northern citizens of the viewpoint on race relations held by loyal Southerners,

[13] W. J. Simmons, "The Reason for 'Race and Reason,'" *The Citizen*, VII (March, 1963), 5.

[14] McCain, "Who is Carleton Putnam?" 53–54. See also Garrett, "Facts vs. Opinions on 'Race and Reason,'" 7–12. For a favorable review by a Virginia attorney see Stuart Campbell's review in *American Bar Association Journal*, XLVIII (June, 1962), 567.

[15] His proclamation is printed in *The Citizen*, VI (November, 1961), 4.

and the reasons therefor," Barnett proclaimed. It has "made an important contribution towards creating in the North an understanding of the South's problems, attitudes and actions in the matter of race relations, and has brought together in authentic form the pertinent facts in a manner which Southerners have found most helpful." He urged Mississippians to observe "Race and Reason Day" by reading and discussing the book, by calling it "to the attention of friends and relatives in the North, and by participating in appropriate public functions, thereby demonstrating the appreciation of the people in our state for Mr. Carleton Putnam and for his splendid book."

By all accounts "Race and Reason Day" was a notable occasion. A number of civic, political, and business leaders arranged a testimonial banquet to honor Putnam, and more than five hundred guests paid twenty-five dollars a plate for dinner and the privilege of hearing an address by the guest of honor.[16] In a speech entitled "This Is the Problem," Putnam repeated the major ideas in *Race and Reason* and urged white Mississippians to renewed efforts to overcome the "paper curtain" of Northern ignorance and indifference. *"You have a completely indoctrinated society in the North!"* he told the Mississippians, and "on that indoctrination the integration movement rests." In peroration he added, "The *fight* is your affair! Do the best you can! I'll put it in the words of George Washington himself: 'Erect a standard to which the wise and honest can repair. The event is in the hands of God.'"

There is no evidence that God was impressed by Putnam's plea, but much evidence that segregationists were. Shortly before "Race and Reason Day" in Mississippi, the Louisiana State Board of Education adopted the following resolution:

WHEREAS, There is increasing evidence that the science of biology and anthropology are being distorted and perverted to serve the purposes of certain pressure groups whose aims are inimical to the customs, mores, and traditions of this Nation, and

WHEREAS, An eminent American scholar has written a book that exposes the flagrant distortion and perversion of scientific truth by so-called social anthropologists and socialistically oriented sociologists, and

WHEREAS, The State Board of Education has the legal and moral responsibility of prescribing the curricular experience offered in the schools of

[16] Carleton Putnam, "This is the Problem," *The Citizen*, VI (November, 1961), 12–23.

the State which, in the judgment of the Board, will best prepare students for their duties and responsibilities as citizens of the United States, and

WHEREAS, It is the consensus of this Board that selected mature students in certain schools would profit from the careful reading and study of the book RACE AND REASON, A YANKEE VIEW, by Carleton Putnam . . .

THEREFORE BE IT RESOLVED by the Louisiana State Board of Education, that the State Department of Education take such steps as may be necessary to bring this book to the attention of Louisiana school administrators and teachers. . . .

The Board also recommended *Race and Reason* to "selected college personnel," including deans, instructors, students enrolled in courses in anthropology, sociology, and psychology, and a mandatory course in communism vs. Americanism, and certain high school students selected on the basis of "maturity, sincerity, and dependability." [17]

Scientists have been less impressed by *Race and Reason*. Not long after the Louisiana Board of Education passed the above resolution, the Committee on Science in the Promotion of Human Welfare, an affiliate of the American Association for the Advancement of Science, condemned *Race and Reason* as scientifically invalid.[18] "We know of no scientific evidence which can challenge [the] axiomatic principle" that "all citizens are to be regarded as equally entitled to the benefits of citizenship," they continued. "The assertion that such evidence exists ignores the rule of relevance and the limitations inherent in our knowledge of the complex interactions among social groups. In addition, by fostering the illusion that the social decisions about interracial relations can be determined by 'objective scientific fact,' it shields the individual's conscience from a confrontation of the grave moral issues which at present confound the relations among racial groups." The available scientific evidence, they concluded, "cannot properly support a challenge to the principle of human equality, which is assured by the Constitution of the United States." Putnam was unimpressed by the committee report. "It is a tissue of fallacies and confusion," he declared, "put forward by men of no special qualification in the pertinent disciplines of anatomy and phys-

17 See [Margolis] "Science and Segregation," *Science,* December 8, 1961, pp. 1868–69. For an account of efforts to get the Virginia Legislature to pass a resolution endorsing *Race and Reason,* see New York *Times,* February 18, 1962, p. 62.
18 "Science and the Race Problem," *Science,* November 1, 1963, pp. 558–61.

ical anthropology, who have acted with transparent political motivation." [19]

The American Anthropological Association and the American Association of Physical Anthropologists also condemned Putnam's views as unscientific. "The American Anthropological Association repudiates statements now appearing in the United States that Negroes are biologically and in innate mental ability inferior to whites," read a resolution adopted by the Association in 1961, "and reaffirms the fact that there is no scientifically established evidence to justify the exclusion of any race from the rights guaranteed by the Constitution of the United States." [20] The physical anthropologists were equally emphatic. "We, the members of the American Association of Physical Anthropologists, professionally concerned with differences in man, deplore the misuse of science to advocate racism," read a resolution adopted in 1962. "We condemn such writings as *Race and Reason* that urge the denial of basic rights to human beings." They also expressed sympathy for "those of our fellow teachers who have been forced by misguided officials to teach misguided race concepts that have no scientific foundation," and they affirmed again "that there is nothing in science that justifies the denial of opportunities or rights to any groups by virtue of race." [21] This resolution is especially significant in view of Putnam's charge that equalitarianism had no real support from physical anthropologists, whose discipline was most directly concerned with the physical aspects of race.

Several scientific journals reviewed *Race and Reason,* all unfavorably. Gordon Allen of the Public Health Service reviewed it for *Eugenics Quarterly,* the journal of the American Eugenics Society, and noted that Putnam wrote "with dangerous persuasiveness." But he added, Putnam's "facts and . . . logic are not very sound scientifically," for he "repeatedly violates scientific standards of accuracy." And "alleged scientific justification for dealing with Negroes as a race stems from a mistaken notion of the genetic

[19] Putnam, "Science and the Race Problem," *Science,* December 13, 1963, pp. 1419–20.

[20] "Science and Segregation: The American Anthropological Association Dips into Politics," *Science,* December 8, 1961, pp. 1868–69. For Putnam's response see his letter to the editor, *Science,* March 16, 1962, pp. 966–68; and New York *Times,* December 2, 1961, p. 47.

[21] "American Physical Anthropologists Condemn Racism," *Current Anthropology,* III (October, 1962), 445.

nature of individual and racial differences," wrote Allen. "Putnam evidently regards races as absolute and clearly homogeneous divisions of mankind instead of the arbitrary classification on a continuum that they are. Ignoring the particulate nature of heredity, Putnam infers that each individual carries the genetic qualities of his entire race and that all his genes are, in a sense, marked. The facts indicate that, for the most part, Whites and Negroes share the same genes and differ mainly in the relatively frequency of those genes. Each individual has his own assortment of genes, his own genotype. With respect to the sort of hereditary adaptation to civilization, an individual's manifest traits are the best guide to his genotype. These may be a poor guide, but the traits of preceding generations are even poorer and remote ancestry can add no information at all." [22]

Theodosius Dobzhansky, one of the nation's foremost geneticists, reviewed *Race and Reason* for the *Journal of Heredity*.[23] Noting that Senators Richard Russell of Georgia, Harry Byrd of Virginia, and Strom Thurmond of South Carolina had praised the book, he described it as "a political tract combatting the desegregation decision of the Supreme Court," and not a work of science. "By no stretch of its meaning can Putnam's book be said to be 'scientific,' " Dobzhansky wrote. "Race prejudice arises from emotion not from reasoning, although time and again it has sought to shore itself up with pseudo-science." [24]

The refusal of scientists to accept his premises infuriates Putnam, but does not lead him to re-examine his premises or con-

[22] Gordon Allen, review of *Race and Reason, Eugenics Quarterly*, VIII (June, 1961) , 105–07. For a rejoinder to Allen see Henry E. Garrett, "Comment on Gordon Allen's Review of Putnam's Race and Reason," *ibid.*, (December, 1961) , 218–20; and Allen, "Reply to Garrett Concerning Putnam's Race and Reason," *ibid.*, 221–22.

[23] Theodosius Dobzhansky, "A Bogus 'Science' of Race Prejudice," *Journal of Heredity*, LII (July-August, 1961) , 189–90.

[24] There are numerous other instances of adverse comment on *Race and Reason* by scientists. "The evidence cited by Putnam is without scientific value," writes physiologist Dwight J. Ingle, in "Racial Differences and the Future," *Science*, October 16, 1964, pp. 375–79. See also Julian H. Steward, letter to the editor, *Science*, March 16, 1961, pp. 964–66; Stanley Diamond, "Race and the Ideology of Race," *Current Anthropology*, III (June, 1962) , 285–88; Donald C. Simmons, "Scientific Racism," *New Republic* (January 5, 1963) , 9–10. See also the symposium edited by Princeton sociologist Melvin M. Tumin, *Race and Intelligence*, in which sociologist Ralph H. Turner of University of California at Los Angeles; anthropologist Sherwood L. Washburn of the University of California, Berkeley; psychologist Silvan S. Tomkins; and testing expert Henry

clusions. He has aroused a great deal of controversy but no debate; he has generated much heat but no light. From his own point of view, nothing constructive has come from his controversies with scientists. He has merely encouraged them to denounce his works and refute his claims. Putnam versus the scientific community in America is no even match. Even David faced smaller odds in battling Goliath, and Putnam is no David.[25]

Putnam is by no means the only significant popularizer of scientific racism. Among the others the most accomplished writer is James Jackson Kilpatrick, whose *The Southern Case for School Segregation* (1962) is the most literate defense of segregation published in recent years. Editor of the Richmond *News Leader* and a nationally syndicated newspaper columnist, Kilpatrick is both less extreme in his views and more effective in expressing them than are most other apologists for segregation.

His use of science[26] parallels Putnam's. He praises *Mankind*

C. Dyer condemn *Race and Reason*. For the most systematic refutation of *Race and Reason* see Ingle, "Comments on the Teachings of Carleton Putnam." See also Putnam, "A Reply to Dwight Ingle," *Mankind Quarterly*, IV (1963), 43–48.

25 Putnam's career as a dispenser of scientific racism continues even today. The National Putnam Letters Committee is still active, still dispensing his letters and speeches. In 1962 he addressed the Louisiana Attorney General's Conference for District Attorneys, and told an audience that included Louisiana Governor Jimmy Davis and members of the state Supreme Court that equalitarian propaganda has "infiltrated the life sciences since New Deal days." Putnam, "The Road to Reversal," *The Citizen*, VII (March, 1963), 23–34. In 1963 he told the Putnam Letters Club in a Lincoln Day address that "genetic racial differences in intelligence, character and behavior are the basic reality of life." Putnam, "These Are the Guilty," *ibid.*, 36–51. "These Are the Guilty" appeared also in *Mankind Quarterly*, IV (July–September 1963), 12–27. Putnam's most recent letter to a prominent official was to the late President Kennedy following the integration crisis at the University of Mississippi in 1962. See New York *Times*, October 3, 1962, p. 33. See also criticisms of this letter by Columbia University anthropologist Morton H. Fried, *ibid.*, October 10, 1962, p. 46; and the reply to Fried from Henry E. Garrett and Wesley C. George, *ibid.*, October 24, 1962, p. 38. See also Putnam's letters to Dwight Ingle, Margaret Mead, and David W. Kendall, special counsel to President Eisenhower, in *Three Letters on Science and Race* (National Putnam Letters Committee, undated). The latest statement of Putnam's views is his *Framework for Love, A Study of Racial Realities* (National Putnam Letters Committee, 1965).

26 Kilpatrick, *The Southern Case for School Segregation*, 43–93. See also Kilpatrick, "View from a Southern Exposure," in Robert A. Goldwin (ed.), *100 Years of Emancipation* (Chicago, 1963), 103–28.

Quarterly (it was launched by "a group of distinguished anthropologists, psychologists, and social scientists, rebelling against the obstinate attitude of the [Ruth] Benedict-[Ashley] Montagu school") ; denounces "Liberal social anthropologists" and "the entire school of Franz Boas"; singles out Kenneth Clark, Otto Klineberg, Juan Comas, Gunnar Myrdal, and UNESCO for special villification; and praises the works of Frank McGurk, Wesley C. George, Robert M. Yerkes, H. A. Tanser, and Nathaniel Weyl. He reserves his highest encomiums for Carleton Putnam, who has, he says, "driven the Liberal anthropologists practically to apoplexy by the unfair tactic of reading their works and taking them seriously— something no layman is expected to do. The rule is that non-anthropologists must treat anthropologists respectfully, even when anthropologists write nonsense."

A curious but striking inconsistency runs through Kilpatrick's treatment of scientific racism, and destroys whatever effectiveness his arguments might otherwise have. The ideas of scientific racism would seem to be no more valid than the premises upon which they rest, and their most important premise is that heredity is far more significant than environment in determining the ability and character of an individual and a race. Without this premise scientific racists have virtually no case. It is astonishing, therefore, that after reviewing the controversy between hereditarians and environmentalists, Kilpatrick dismissed it as unimportant. Segregationists "have regularly overestimated the factors of heredity and underestimated the factors of environment," he wrote. "Their position would be improved if they simply acknowledged that the question of the Negro's innate inferiority has not been proved and hence is still open." Later he adds, "In terms of the problem immediately at hand, the question of whether the Negro's shortcomings are 'innate' seems to me largely irrelevant anyhow. The issue is not likely to be proved to the satisfaction of either side any time soon; it may not be susceptible of proof at all. Whether [the characteristics of Negroes] are inherited or acquired, they *are*."

In view of this dismissal of so vital a subject, Kilpatrick's unstinted praise of scientific racists is paradoxical. "The evidence put together by Shuey and McGurk is solid, dispassionate, unbiased, and overwhelming," he wrote in a typical passage. In point of fact, however, if the works of Miss Shuey and McGurk are valid they demonstrate beyond doubt that heredity *is* vastly more important than environment in determining the intelligence of Negroes. It was the intention of those authors to demonstrate the relative significance of heredity and environment upon racial intelligence and the validity of their works rests in part upon whether they achieved that goal. If their works are "solid, dispassionate, unbiased, and overwhelming," they settle the heredity-environment controversy, and if they do not settle the controversy it is difficult to see how they merit such unstinted praise.

His inconsistency on this point is puzzling, but only at first appearance. Kilpatrick is steeped in the lore and mythology by which segregationists have traditionally defended Southern race policies, and that lore and mythology emphasize not science but states' rights and strict construction of the Constitution. In his defense of segregation, Kilpatrick, who had a leading role in resurrecting the doctrine of interposition in the years immediately following the Brown decision, falls into the trap Putnam warned against. He consumes his energies discussing states' rights and constitutionalism because, in the final analysis, he is not convinced of the significance of the scientific arguments he employs. "The ruins of Zimbabwe are a long way from Prince Edward County, Virginia, and the finest analysis of electroencephalic findings among the Zulus is of small importance in teaching a class of Alabama sixth-graders," he writes. "The arguments of anthropology are of interest to the South, and I would not wish to leave any impression that would minimize their importance; the fear of ultimate racial interbreeding, encouraged by prospective generations of desegregated and integrated school systems, is a very real fear in the South and not an imagined one. If these Negro characteristics *are* innate, the white Southerner sees nothing but disaster to his race in risking an accelerated intermingling of blood lines. And even if these Negro characteristics are not innate, the white Southerner wants no intimate association with them anyhow."

Kilpatrick's inconsistency went unnoticed by segregationists and scientific racists. Henry E. Garrett, who spent a vast amount of time and energy attempting to prove the predominance of heredity over environment, favorably reviewed *The Southern Case for School Segregation* for *Mankind Quarterly*. "This book," he wrote, "should be required reading for every young American lawyer and law student." He made no mention of Kilpatrick's ambivalence on the heredity-environment controversy.[27]

Nathaniel Weyl, best known as a spokesman for conservative, anticommunist political causes, is another prominent popularizer of scientific racism. More systematic in his treatment of scientific authorities than either Putnam or Kilpatrick, he is also probably less influential. Three of his works are significant, *The Negro in American Civilization* (1960), *The Geography of Intellect* (1963), which he wrote in collaboration with another prominent political conservative, Professor Stefan Possony of the Hoover Institute on War, Revolution and Peace at Stanford University, and *The Creative Elite in America* (1966), in which he repeats and expands many of the views he expressed in earlier works.

The Negro in American Civilization is broader in scope than *Race and Reason* or *The Southern Case for School Segregation*. It does not, however, introduce any new ideas and need not be reviewed here.[28] *The Geography of Intellect,* however, is not so readily disposed of. It is a remarkable work, and to read it is at once frightening and fascinating. It is many things—a collection of racist and nativist ideas, some of them no longer fashionable even among racists; an anticommunist tract written by two prominent conservatives; a mixture of truths and half-truths, common sense and nonsense, *non sequiturs* and irrelevancies. It is a distillation of several facets of racist thought, and in the words of Martin Mayer in *Commentary,* it provides integrationists and egalitarians with "a relatively complete list of what it is we shall overcome." [29]

Weyl and Possony begin with the plausible assumption that brainpower is the most vital human asset in the twentieth century. They also assume, more questionably, that the brainpower necessary to maintain and advance modern civilization "does not exist, either actually or potentially in the requisite qualities among all nations, peoples and races." North Europeans and Jews, they

[27] Henry E. Garrett, review of *The Southern Case for School Segregation, Mankind Quarterly,* III (April–June, 1963), 264–65.

[28] Psychologist Frank C. J. McGurk wrote an introduction to Weyl's *The Negro in American Civilization,* describing the work as a "refreshing antidote" to the "one-sided environmentalist argumentation" which "could serve as a basic reference text in any scientific consideration of race and race difference."

[29] Martin Mayer, "Race and Ability," *Commentary,* XXXVIII (July, 1964), 61–63.

think, possess it in considerable quantities, other Europeans and Mongoloids in lesser amounts. Latin Americans and Arabs have even less, and Negroes virtually none at all. Christian peoples have more than non-Christians (except Jews, who have most of all), and Protestants have more than Catholics. "The I.Q. distributions of Protestant nations," the authors remark solemnly, "tend to be markedly higher than those of Catholic nations."

The chief purpose of *The Geography of Intellect* was to demonstrate the truth and significance of the ranking of ethnic groups noted above. In doing this, Weyl and Possony give considerable attention to Negroes. To demonstrate the inferiority of the race they cite an odd assortment of authorities, from Sir Francis Galton to anthropologist Carleton Coon, from Thomas Jefferson to David Hume and Montesquieu. Negroes, they write drawing heavily upon the ideas of darwinian racists, lack "personality integration" and "capacity for sustained thought or introspection at any level." Negroes are unable "to reason coherently, to maintain attention or even a consistent emotional reaction"; their most conspicuous characteristics are "imitativeness, lack of originality, passivity and childish self-aggrandisement."

Other groups, especially Latin Americans and Arabs, are not much better. "Negro Africa, the Middle East, Latin America, and Southeast Asia are genetically unpromising," the authors wrote. In Latin America "the predominant character structure seems to be deficient in drive and this helps explain the lack of consistent progress in most of the area. Islam and Negro Africa are much clearer examples of cultural systems which create mentalities poorly adapted for successful functioning within the matrix of Western civilization." The problem is largely genetic, but partially environmental, and the latter fact offers a ray of hope. "If a free enterprise economy is allowed to be introduced into Latin America," predict Weyl and Possony, "dynamism toward the physical environment will tend to supplant the exercise of power toward individuals and, in the process, the traditional character structure of the Latin Americans will inevitably be modified."

The chief threat to the future of Western Civilization, or so Weyl and Possony believe, lies in the fact that democracy, communism, and false concepts of equality have led nations to pursue policies which are basically dysgenic. The "application of pseudo-egalitarian ideology to political, social and economic life" downgrades excellence and exalts mediocrity, and the population explosion of recent years is the result of "rampant reproduction" among "mentally incompetent" groups. To neutralize these threats, Weyl and Possony urge the nations of the world to seek out and nurture their "elites," the creative minorities who sustain and advance civilization. "Genetic factors play a major role in the rise and fall of civilizations," they insist, and if mankind is to avoid a genetic crisis, eugenic policies must be formulated and consciously followed. "Perhaps the voluntary artificial insemination of women with the sperm of geniuses," they suggest, "will eventually arrest the genetic impoverishment of the human race."

But they foresee major obstacles to the adoption of such policies. International communism promotes "dysgenic deterioration and catastrophe" as a means of achieving world revolution. Everywhere, "science is distorted . . . by a nihilism of values, by the dogma of equality as applied to nations, races, peoples, histories, art forms and civilization." The civil rights movement threatens national cohesion by asserting the claim to equality of "an ethnic group which is deemed below the national standard." "Egalitarian levelers preach that all men are equal in talent and relentlessly propagandize for indiscriminate miscegenation." The result is "miscegenation of the suicidal sort," mating "based on whim or sexual desire, which breeds the best with the worst and thus produces the mediocre."

It would be easy to believe that Weyl and Possony are jesting, that they intended this volume to be a satire on racists and racism. Apparently this was not the case, however, for they write with a sense of gravity that is devoid of humor, and offered *The Geography of Intellect* as a serious work of science. But how can one take seriously a work which uses the results of the 1960 Olympic Games to demonstrate the musculature of racial and ethnic groups and the "apparent geographic and ethnic concentration of prowess in sports?"

The Geography of Intellect has apparently had no influence upon scientific racists. While Weyl's other work, *The Negro in American Civilization,* is distributed by the Citizens' Councils and often cited by racists, *The Geography of Intellect* is systematically ignored. It seems too much to say that it is so patently absurd that racists are undeceived by it. An anonymous reviewer in *Mankind Quarterly* described it as a "major contribution" of "catholic" scope and "provocative of much new thought," and added, as if to reassure himself, that it "must be treated seriously." [30] But such remarks were atypical.

Perhaps segregationists ignored *The Geography of Intellect* because of the slurs it inadvertently casts upon Southerners. "There is reason to believe that hot climates shape human evolution in ways which inhibit, or at the very least do not adequately stimulate, the growth of mental capacity," wrote Weyl and Possony. They referred here to the evolution of Negroes in the heat of Africa, but since they wrote in general terms, their statement might have been taken personally by Southerners. When Caucasians are exposed to heavy work in great heat, the authors continued, "little blood gets to the brain, which may be why it is difficult for some white men to do creative work in hot weather." Again, Southern whites might have taken this personally; they might have understood it to mean that Southerners are lazy and shiftless. "These facts may provide a clue to the observed differences between the mental performance of Negroes, on the one hand," declared Weyl and Possony, "and Caucasians and Mongolians, on the other." And to overly sensitive Southern whites these "facts" might also provide a clue to the "observed differences" between the mental performances of Northern and Southern whites, such as Horace Mann Bond gleaned from the studies used by Audrey Shuey in *The Testing of Negro Intelligence*.[31]

Carleton Putnam, James Jackson Kilpatrick, and Nathaniel Weyl are perhaps the most influential popularizers of scientific racism. Each wrote an important summary of scientific racist ideas, and apparently each was widely read by segregationists across the South. But if the ideas of scientific racism were to achieve maximum acceptance among segregationists, the task of dissemination could not be left to chance. Nor was it. The Citizens' Councils of America, with headquarters in Jackson, Mississippi, assumed a major part of that task, and in recent years has been the most active agency disseminating scientific racism among segregationists in the South. *The Citizen* and its predecessor as official journal of the Councils, *The Citizens' Council,* contain numerous articles

[30] Unsigned review of *The Geography of Intellect, Mankind Quarterly,* IV (April–June, 1964) , 223–24.

[31] See above, Chapter IV, Tables I and II, pp. 80 and 81.

by and about scientific racists. The Councils also distribute many items in the literature of scientific racism, and statements by Council spokesmen indicate they consider scientific arguments a major facet of their defense of segregation.

Perhaps the best illustration of the latter fact is the attention Council leaders give science when addressing audiences outside the South. One of the Councils' leading spokesmen is W. J. Simmons, editor of *The Citizen*. In the last several years Simmons has traveled throughout the nation spreading the Councils' racial views, and often devoted a part of his addresses to scientific racism. An address to the students of Carleton College, Northfield, Minnesota, on May 15, 1962, was typical. Among the subjects Simmons discussed on that occasion was "the equalitarian dogma" which, he told the students, "originated with the Boas school of social anthropologists." To refute this dogma, he cited the works of several of the more important scientific racists and several scientists who are not racists but who have pointed out the existence of significant differences between races. "The objective and carefully worded statements" of these scientists, Simmons declared, "confirm the experience of 34 million white people in the South, who have lived with the [race] problem all their lives." [32]

Simmons made more systematic use of scientific racism in "Race in America: The Conservative Stand," an article he wrote for Huston Smith's symposium, *The Search for America* (1959). Here he sought, among other things, to disprove the "claim that is being made today: that 'science' has shown that there are no significant differences among the races." By phrasing the "claim" in this manner, Simmons misrepresented it, but in doing so he sought, perhaps, to enhance the plausibility of his own position. He cited the works of R. Ruggles Gates, Pitirim Sorokin, Henry E. Garrett, Frank McGurk, and Audrey Shuey to prove that racial differences do exist, but added in a moment of candor that "the question of race differences and their significance is far from having been settled in the research laboratories." By this admission he hoped perhaps to make his readers forget that the only real justification

[32] W. J. Simmons, "The Race Problem Moves North," distributed by the Citizens' Councils of Jackson, Mississippi. Simmons repeated the same ideas in an address to the organizational meeting of the greater Los Angeles Citizens' Council, Los Angeles, California, June 30, 1964; also available from the Citizens' Councils of Jackson.

for segregation is the conviction that "the question of race differences and their significance" *has* been settled, and in the manner described by scientific racists. To concede that the issue is still unsettled is to admit that innate racial differences have not been scientifically demonstrated.

Simmons' admission was a tactical device sometimes used by racists to disarm an unfriendly audience by saying in effect, "We segregationists make no dogmatic claims about Negro inferiority; we only dispute the dogmatic claims of equalitarians." Among segregationist audiences, however, this mask of open-mindedness was dropped; in fact, it *had* to be dropped. Imagine a spokesman for the Citizens' Council telling an audience of Mississippi segregationists that the issue of Negro inferiority "is far from having been settled in the research laboratories!"

Despite his attention to scientific racism, Simmons seems not to have taken science too seriously. Like Kilpatrick, he went through the ritual of discussing scientific racism—just as Putnam had admonished segregationists to do—but he clearly felt the basic issue lay elsewhere. "Even if science were to prove the races to be absolutely equal in potential—which we must emphasize it has not—such a finding would in no way affect the practical aspects of race relations," Simmons wrote, "for these are rooted in social attitudes which are totally unrelated to any kind of scientific premise whatsoever. Social attitudes arise from the everyday experiences of generations which crystallize in time into customs and folkways. It is these rather than the abstractions of the scientist that guide men's actions. . . . The fact is that these [folkways] motivate people and direct their actions, even if, being 'of the spirit,' they cannot be measured in test tubes or by slide rules. Society is a living organism, not a formula." Simmons, however, ignored his own advice. Society is indeed "a living organism" and, like everything else about it, the folkways of segregation are not immune to change.

In their efforts to spread the ideas of scientific racism, segregationists have received little assistance from national news media. Among national news magazines only *U.S. News and World Report* has given them any support. Though its editors also print articles by equalitarians and integrationists, *U.S. News and World Report* has on a number of occasions included articles which incorporate the views of scientific racists. The magazine pays scientific racists the considerable compliment of treating their ideas as a point of view as worthy of serious consideration as that of equalitarians, and by so doing enhances the plausibility and attractiveness of those ideas among segregationists. This fact is especially significant because *U.S. News and World Report* is the only national news magazine which has any sympathy for southern segregationists on the issue of racial integration.

This should not be misunderstood. There is no explicit racism in *U.S. News and World Report*. It is the pattern of its treatment of Negroes, segregationists, and racial controversies that is significant. This magazine, edited by one of the nation's leading conservatives, David Lawrence, printed Frank McGurk's article purporting to prove that Negroes are innately inferior to whites in intelligence; reprinted Henry E. Garrett's "The Equalitarian Dogma"; interviewed Garrett on the consequences of racial intermarriage; and presented each of these as the views of responsible scientists.[33] It has also printed a number of articles comparing intelligence test scores of whites and Negroes in segregated school systems in the South. Each of these articles showed Negroes scoring much lower than whites, but in none of them did the author explain the complexities of this subject or discuss the influence of environment upon the test results. Nor did they explain the attitudes of psychologists toward racial intelligence. As a result the articles left the impression that Negroes do poorly on IQ tests because they are innately inferior to whites, and that widespread integration in the schools will inevitably lower educational standards and "hold back" the progress of whites.[34]

Taken together, the discussions of Negroes, civil rights, and school integration which have appeared in the last dozen years in *U.S. News and World Report* give a distinctly distorted view of those subjects, and the distortions do a disservice to Negroes. Civil rights advocates are often presented in an unfavorable light, while segregationists are treated sympathetically. One who reads nothing but this magazine is likely to believe that Negroes are

[33] McGurk, "A Scientist's Report on Race Differences"; Garrett, "One Psychologist's View of 'Equality of the Races,'" and Garrett, "Racial Mixing Could Be Catastrophic."

[34] See for example W. T. White, "What Dallas School Tests Show," *U.S. News and World Report*, September 21, 1956, p. 98; "Achievement Tests," *ibid.*, August 31, 1956, p. 8; and "Do Mixed Schools Lower Classroom Standards," *ibid.*, February 3, 1956, pp. 38–40.

unready for integration because of the criminality, immorality, and illiteracy or marginal literacy among the race; that Southern whites know best how to handle race relations in the South; that there is a bona fide debate among reputable scientists over questions of racial equality; that the South's position in civil rights disputes is more constitutionally correct than that of integrationists; that many civil rights leaders are potentially, if not actually, dangerous radicals, while most Southern white political leaders are responsible statesmen dedicated to constitutional government and orderly progress for both races.

Among national journals of opinion only *National Review,* edited by William F. Buckley, Jr., has opened its pages to scientific racists. Again, there is no explicit racism, only an occasional statement of views which segregationists find appealing. Editorially both the *Review* and its editor condemn segregation, racism, and white supremacy, but they also publish—and apparently take seriously—such articles as "Intelligence or Prejudice?" [35] in which Ernest van den Haag makes thinly veiled pleas for school segregation.

As one would expect of a writer in Mr. Buckey's journal, van den Haag is more sophisticated than other scientific racists, more elusive, more circumspect. The most prominent sociologist who has identified himself with segregationists and scientific racists, van den Haag was born in The Hague and educated in Europe and the United States, receiving a Ph.D. from New York University. He is a practicing psychoanalyst, a professor of social philosophy at his alma mater, and a lecturer in the New School of Social Research. In 1960 he published a critique of Kenneth Clark's testimony in the Brown cases, which he described as "pseudo-scientific" and "misleading," and accused Clark of deliberately misrepresenting his own research. Denying that he was himself a segregationist, van den Haag declared instead that he accepted the "common-sense view that Negroes are humiliated and frustrated by segregation." However, he found much to criticize in the Brown decision as well as in Clark's testimony. "It is mainly the compulsory feature that makes me uneasy," he wrote of the decision. "Though the end be laudable, the means do not suit it . . . compulsory congregation is objectionable and not the proper remedy for the at least equally

[35] Ernest van den Haag, "Intelligence or Prejudice?" *National Review,* December 1, 1964, pp. 1059–63.

objectionable compulsory segregation its [sic] replaces." He explained further, "The imposition of congregation by the Court in Washington will hardly make the local white children compelled to go to school with Negro children (or their families which influence them) receptive to the ideals to be fostered, nor will the circumstances help them perceive the actual individual Negro as distinguished from the stereotype, or generate the open mind and warmth the new school mates want." [36]

In "Intelligence or Prejudice?", which appeared in *National Review* in 1964, van den Haag's purpose was to dispute the booklet, *Race and Intelligence, A Scientific Evaluation* (1963), in which sociologists Melvin Tumin and Ralph H. Turner, anthropologist Sherwood L. Washburn, psychologist Silvan S. Tomkins, and testing authority Henry C. Dyer had criticized the works of Garrett, Shuey, and other scientific racists. Should the public schools be integrated? he asked himself. "Mixed education now would impair the education of Negro and of white children," he answered. "The white children obviously require for optimum education maximum utilization of their present performance abilities," while Negro children "require whatever can be done to increase their performance in view of the deficient environment of the past." This means, "at least for the time being, [that] the needs of Negro children would be met best—i.e., to their advantage and without disadvantage to others—by separate education geared to meet the obstacles presented by lack of opportunity and unfavorable environment." Van den Haag is "in favor of improving the quality of

---

[36] Van den Haag's criticisms of the Brown decision are themselves open to challenge. They are inconsistent with much of the research on the effects of integration in newly integrated high schools. See for example Robert Coles, *The Desegregation of Southern Schools: A Psychiatric Study* (New York and Atlanta, 1963). They ignore the dynamic factor in the integration process; racial attitudes, in other words, are not static. They also place the Brown decision on the same moral level with laws and customs by which Southern whites enforce segregation. They do, however, permit van den Haag to have things both ways. They enable him to endorse racial integration and at the same time castigate the Brown decision as no better than the racist policies of segregationists. Van den Haag's views on racial segregation seem to reflect a profound misunderstanding of the nature of segregation in the South. In *Education as an Industry* (1956), for example, he suggested that the ideal solution to the problem of segregated education would be to provide three school systems which would afford all students a free choice between all-white, all-Negro, and integrated schools. The efficacy of such a system in the deep South would of course be problematical.

education for all," but "this can be done only if pupils are separated according to ability. . . . And this means very largely according to race."

There remains, however, the troublesome fact of racial overlap. Logically it might be argued that if van den Haag's interest is really intelligence and quality education rather than racial policy, he would favor a system which segregated students according to ability instead of race, or perhaps a system which would permit Negro children of exceptional ability to attend otherwise all-white schools. But he opposes both these systems. "I think this could demoralize the remaining Negro children and could be hard also on the transferred child," he said of the latter. "Nonetheless, if both the white and Negro children (and/or parents) desire it, this objection would be greatly weakened." He concluded that "Negroes and whites should be educated separately, unless there is evidence in specific cases that the learning of neither group suffers from congregation and that neither group objects. Instruction in schools for Negroes should attempt to remedy the disadvantages suffered by students coming from a culturally deprived home environment." But this, he added, "cannot be done except by separate education." Van den Haag thus inverted the rationale and logic behind the Brown decision and the school integration movement. He assumed that segregation, not integration, is the natural state of race relations, and shifted the burden of proof from segregationists to integrationists.

Van den Haag's discussion of school integration in *National Review* is even more revealing when compared to editor Buckley's criticisms of New York Congressman Adam Clayton Powell and others whom Buckley described as "racists" during his abortive campaign for mayor of New York City in 1965. "Racists are those who treat people primarily as members of a race," wrote Buckley in November 1965. [37] Only nine months earlier van den Haag had written the following in Buckley's journal: "mixed [i.e., integrated] education now would impair the education of Negro and white children"; "segregation by color . . . is educationally rational"; and "it would be cruel to sacrifice children to egalitarian ideolo-

[37] William F. Buckley, Jr., "Harlem is in New York City," *National Review*, November 2, 1965, p. 979.

gies." [38] By Buckley's own definition, van den Haag would seem to be a racist, and one who used Buckley's journal to disseminate his racism.

Through such individuals as Carleton Putnam, James Jackson Kilpatrick, and Nathaniel Weyl, such organizations as the Citizens' Councils, and such magazines as *U.S. News and World Report* the ideas of scientific racists filter down to the American public. In the process of being adapted to the uses of some of the more emotional segregationists, those ideas are sometimes grossly distorted and oversimplified. Often, however, the difference between the ideas developed by academic social scientists and the implications drawn from them by segregationists and white supremacists is a matter of degree and emphasis, rather than kind. More often than not the academic social scientists seek no more than a plausible defense for the status quo in race relations, and specifically disassociate themselves from the violence and intimidation by which Ku Klux Klansmen and other extremists preserve segregation. But the matter is not so simple. The social scientists cannot by a simple disclaimer completely disassociate themselves from the uses to which their ideas are put by extremists, especially when the uses are clearly implied in the ideas themselves. Extremists who quote the social scientists are often doing no more than carrying the social scientists' ideas to a logical and natural conclusion.

In 1957 the Citizens' Councils prepared "A Manual for Southerners," which they hoped would be used in the elementary schools of Mississippi. Among the portions written for fifth and sixth graders were the following scientific justifications for segregation:[39]

First of all, let's see how we know so much about the races being different. Many famous scientists have studied the races of man for hundreds of years. These scientists have ways they can weigh and measure the skeletons and brains of the different races. And all of these men agree that the black, yellow, red, and white men are very different from each other. Scientists have studied the habits of the different races. They find that men's habits can be grouped by races. The white man has certain habits

[38] The last three statements are in van den Haag's follow-up to the original article. See "Intelligence or Prejudice? Some Letters and a Reply," *ibid.,* February 9, 1965, pp. 101–02.

[39] *The Citizens' Council,* II (June, 1957), 3; *ibid.,* (July, 1957), 3.

that are very different from the black man's. Some of these habits that scientists study are:

1. The way a race worships its God
2. The kind of laws a race makes for itself
3. The kind of music a race likes
4. The kind of art that a race makes
5. The things a race thinks are right and wrong.

. . . The white man is very civilized, while the pure Negro in Africa is still living as a savage. . . .

. . . Negro children [in Washington, D.C.] were way behind white children in their school work. This is because white children can learn faster than Negroes can. So the children could not do the same work in the same grade. This made them feel unhappy.

The students were tested to see how fast they could learn school work. These tests showed that the white children can go much faster in their learning and work. When the races are mixed in school, the white children do not get as much education as they usually get. The whites have to wait for the Negroes to catch up.

Sustained exposure to such ideas, even when expressed less categorically, has conditioned the American people to accept the arguments of scientific racists and made their descriptions of Negroes more plausible. In fact, one of the chief advantages enjoyed by racists in their efforts to spread scientific racism is the fact that white Americans have been predisposed by their racial experiences to believe that Negroes are in fact inferior to white men. The attitudes of white Americans toward Negroes (and those of Negro Americans toward whites as well) have always reflected the relative status of the two races in this country. When Negroes were slaves whites assumed that slavery was the natural condition of the race. When segregation replaced slavery, that, too, became in the eyes of whites the natural condition of Negroes. Today, in most areas of the country, but especially in the South where the ideas of scientific racism are most popular, Negroes still occupy the most inferior places in life. Of the large ethnic groups in America, they are still the most poverty stricken, ignorant, and backward, and conform less to the social mores and moral code of the American middle class. The social, economic, educational, and political status of the race seems, at first glance to confirm what scientific racists were saying all along. It is this fact which makes white Americans, especially Southerners, susceptible to the preachments of scientific racists, and it seems logical to conclude that the susceptibility will disappear only when Negroes achieve equality and full integration into American life.

8

EFFORTS TO REVERSE THE BROWN DECISION

Segregationists were interested in science for practical rather than ideological or even scientific reasons. They were attracted to science, or rather to scientific racism, not because they felt it necessary to prove Negroes inferior to whites or that segregation is the best racial policy—they believed these things already. What they sought from science was a basis for telling the American people that there are valid, rational grounds for racial separation, especially in areas of social relations affecting courtship and marriage.

But these were general objectives, and segregationists were slow to understand that science could be useful to them in more concrete ways. Not until the early 1960's did they realize, and then rather suddenly it seems, that through science they might accomplish the most illusory of all their hopes, reversal of the Brown decision. By that time they had abandoned all expectation of reversing the decision on legal or constitutional grounds. Given the makeup of the Supreme Court, there was no possibility that the decision would be reversed on those grounds. A new strategy was called for, and segregationists who took a second look at the Brown ruling remembered earlier charges that it rested not upon law and constitutional precedent but upon works and theories of a few social scientists. Urged on by Carleton Putnam and others, they became convinced that social science was the Achilles heel of the Brown ruling. A challenge based upon science, they decided, might succeed where those using states' rights and constitutional literalism had failed. Thus the two elements in the story of scientific racism converged. Academic social scientists joined segregationists in a concerted effort to overturn the Brown decision. The shift of emphasis from legalism to science, however, was a change in tactics only; the ultimate goal—to destroy the legal basis of the civil rights movement—remained the same.

Perhaps the most striking fact about the shift was the grounds upon which it rested. When the Brown decision was announced in 1954, segregationists were unanimous in denouncing the Supreme Court for accepting nonlegal testimony and citing in footnote eleven social science authorities, some of whom were not discussed in the lower courts. Senator Richard B. Russell, of Georgia, complained that "the Court admittedly substituted psychology for law" and subjected the rights of the states and the liberties of the people "to findings of amateur psychology." Senator James O. Eastland, of Mississippi, was even more outspoken, denouncing not only the Court's use of "the unprecedented, unsound, and irrelevant authority of a group of recent partisan books on sociology and psychology" but also its use of authorities who were "left-wingers of the first order," "Communists or near-Communists." [1]

The latter charge by Eastland became a major theme among segregationists, who sought to discredit the social science by "exposing" the political views of the social scientists. On May 26,

[1] *Congressional Record*, 83rd Cong., 2nd Sess., C, Pt. 6 (May 27, 1954), 7252; and *ibid.*, Pt. 9 (July 23, 1954), 11522, 11525.

1955, Eastland, who was chairman of the Senate Judiciary Committee and its Subcommittee on Internal Security, delivered a lengthy speech in the Senate detailing his criticisms of the Court and urging a sweeping investigation of communist influences behind the Brown decision. The Senate and the American people, read a resolution which he urged his colleagues to adopt, "are now entitled to know beyond doubt and peradventure the complete extent and degree of Communist and Communist-front activity and influence in the preparation of the pseudo 'modern scientific authority' which was the sole and only basis for the decision of the Supreme Court." Accordingly, the resolution would order an inquiry into "the extent and degree of participation by individuals and groups identified with the Communist conspiracy, Communist-front organizations, and alien ideologies, in the formulation of the 'modern scientific authority' upon which the Supreme Court relied in the school integration cases." [2] In offering his resolution, Eastland told the Senate that the Supreme Court had been "indoctrinated and brainwashed by leftwing pressure groups." The Court had attempted "to graft into the organic law of the land the teachings, preachments, and social doctrines" of Karl Marx, he charged, and the effort was "part and parcel of the conspiracy to divide and destroy this Government through internal controversy." Only once before in the Western world had courts of law "resorted to textbooks and the works of agitators to sustain [their] decision[s]," Eastland continued, " . . . when the courts of Nazi Germany accepted 'Hitler's racist laws.' "

Despite the emotionalism and irrelevancy of much of the segregationist criticism, the Brown decision did raise fundamental questions concerning the use of expert nonlegal testimony in the courts, and it provoked a controversy on this issue among lawyers and legal theorists. The ruling offered lawyers (and social scientists) a rare opportunity to study the use of expert social science testimony in the courts, and debate such complex items as relevancy and admissibility of evidence, personal bias among social scientists, and the fact that social science opinion sometimes changes even on the most important subjects. The Brown decision itself pointedly illustrated the changes in social science opinion in the two

[2] The resolution is printed in *Congressional Record,* 84th Cong., 1st Sess., CI, Pt. 6 (May 26, 1955) , 7120.

generations since the Court issued the Plessy ruling in 1896. In that year the separate-but-equal concept conformed to the racial views which predominated among social scientists but by 1954 the concept seemed hopelessly racist and unscientific. Then, too, the lawyers and social scientists encountered such difficult questions as the relative weight to be given expert testimony which disputed clearly established judicial interpretations. Did not the use of social science in the Brown decision introduce an undesirable, even dangerous, relativism into the law and violate the principle of *stare decisis?* Did not the decision introduce instability and uncertainty and threaten the principle of the rule of law as opposed to the rule of man? Might not the decision, by its own logic, be overturned should a majority of the Supreme Court at some time in the future personally favor segregation? Finally, and here scientific racists came in, might not the expert opinion which the Court accepted in the Brown decision be disputed, perhaps even refuted, by experts equally competent to those who testified in the lower courts and/or were cited in footnote eleven? Such questions are important ones, and their discussion in the law quarterlies is another measure of the impact of the Brown decision and of the intellectual crosscurrents it aroused.

Several distinguished legal theorists, among them Edmond Cahn of New York University and Charles L. Black, Jr., of Yale, both professors of jurisprudence, dismissed the social science testimony and the authorities cited in footnote eleven as of no influence upon the Court and no significance in the decision. Both Cahn and Black endorsed the decision itself and supported the principle of racial integration, but they considered the social science evidence presented by Clark and others too weak to be a satisfactory basis for so important a decision and so vital a principle. A sturdier basis was needed, which they found in legal and constitutional precedents. They argued impressively that the decision was fully consistent with constitutional guarantees of the Fourteenth Amendment and a long list of judicial decisions.[3]

Since Cahn was a staunch integrationist, his vigorous criticism of the social science testimony was especially appealing to scientific

---

[3] Edmond Cahn, "Jurisprudence," *New York University Law Review,* XXX (January, 1955), 150–69; and Charles L. Black, Jr., "The Lawfulness of the Segregation Decision," *Yale Law Journal,* LXIX (January, 1960), 421–30.

racists, and they quoted him frequently. "I would not have the constitutional rights of Negroes—or of other Americans—rest on such flimsy foundation as some of the scientific demonstrations in [the Brown testimony]," Cahn wrote. The social scientists who presented the evidence "are fine, intelligent, dedicated scholars," he continued, "yet one can honor them as they deserve without swallowing their claims." Their evidence simply did not prove their conclusions, though their conclusions were, in Cahn's judgment, plain common sense. Common sense and everyday observation manifest the harmful effects of segregation upon Negroes to anyone with an open mind, but neither doll and drawing tests nor any other social science experiment had ever objectively demonstrated the nature or scope of those effects. The testimony in the Brown cases had thus been superfluous, no more than a painstakingly elaborate ritual. The Court had not been "taken in" by the social scientists, as segregationists charged. On the contrary the Court had relegated the so-called experts to a footnote, and the footnote itself was merely a sop to those who had testified.

Legal experts who were also segregationists agreed with Cahn and Black that the social science evidence in the Brown cases was inadequate and misleading. They were unconvinced, however, by Cahn and Black's assertions that there was sufficient legal and constitutional authority for the Brown decision. Lawyers such as Eugene Cook, attorney general of Georgia, and William I. Potter of Missouri, thus attacked the decision as legally and constitutionally incorrect as well as scientifically unsound. The Brown decision did not hold that the separate-but-equal doctrine was bad law, they wrote in the *American Bar Association Journal*,[4] it held instead that the doctrine was bad sociology. The decision rested solely on social science, or more accurately on "pseudo-socioscience" which the Court accepted in disregard of the facts of the cases. Like Cahn and Black, Cook and Potter thought the social science testimony was an insufficient basis for overturning the hoary separate-but-equal principle and destroying the legal basis for race relations in a quarter of the nation. They, too, thought the social sciences too young, too imprecise, too changeable to be safely

[4] Eugene Cook and William I. Potter, "The School Segregation Cases: Opposing the Opinion of the Supreme Court," *American Bar Association Journal*, XLII (April, 1956), 313–17.

used for such purposes. "Should our fundamental rights rise, fall or change along with the latest fashions of psychological litera- ture?" they asked. "How are we to know that in the future social scientists may not present us with a collection of notions similar to those of Adolf Hitler and label them as modern science?"

The whole affair was troubling to Cook and Potter, who saw in it a grave threat to the orderly processes of law. "Under elementary and elemental law," they wrote, "a court may not consider treatises in a field other than law, unless the treatises them- selves are the very subject of inquiry. The doctrine of judicial notice extends only to those things of common knowledge that lie without the realm of science." This narrow view of the judicial process served Cook and Potter as a basis for their defense of racial discrimination and a focus for their attack upon the Court.

What has become of the accepted tests of constitutionality of statutes?
What of the rule that a distinction in legislation is not arbitrary and not violative of the equal protection of the Fourteenth Amendment if any state of facts reasonably can be conceived that would sustain it? . . .
What of the rule that 'legislative determinations express or implied are entitled to greater weight,' and that validity must be shown 'by things which will be judicially noticed, or by facts established by evidence,' and that 'the burden is on the attacking party to establish the invalidating facts'; that 'being a legislative judgment, it is presumed to be supported by the facts known to the legislature unless facts judicially known, or proved, preclude that possibility'? [5]

The position of Cook and Potter was substantially that taken by Southern segregationists and political leaders in their fight against the Brown decision and public school integration. It had the distinct advantages of being defensible upon the high ground of principle, including the principle that this is a government of law and not of man, and of showing respect for the certainty and continuity of law.

It had, however, gotten segregationists nowhere, for the Supreme Court disagreed with them concerning the admissibility of social science evidence in integration cases. Accordingly, they began to shift their ground, admitted the relevancy of social science, and resolved to beat integrationists at their own game. They would seek out their own social scientists, amass their own evidence, and built a scientific defense for segregation. In so doing, however, they

[5] *Ibid.*

compromised their principles and, in effect, accepted the contention of the NAACP that scientific knowledge has an important contribution to make in illuminating constitutional issues. But, characteristically, they let their zeal overcome their reason, and carried the idea too far. They then adopted a course which placed no limitation on the use of science in court and would in fact make science the master of law. Thus, their position was not the same as that of the NAACP in the Brown cases. "The Constitution should not be wedded to any social science any more than to a school of economics," Jack Greenberg, who later succeeded Thurgood Marshall as chief counsel for the NAACP, had written in defense of the Brown decision. "On the other hand, constitutional interpretation should consider all relevant knowledge. The Constitution turned on a moral judgment; but moral judgments are generated by an awareness of facts." [6] This view would circumscribe the role of social science and make it an auxiliary of law. Greenberg would have social science serve, not dominate, the law.

But segregationists, having convinced themselves that social science could be made to serve their ends, proposed to give it a much larger role. In cases in which they used social science to argue for a reversal of the Brown decision, the most important of which were *Stell v. Savannah-Chatham County Board of Education* and *Evers v. Jackson Municipal Separate School District*,[7] they based their arguments exclusively upon social science, and demanded that the Constitution be interpreted to suit their science. Accepting the tenets of scientific racism as completely valid, they insisted that "science" has proven Negroes inferior to whites in critical areas of intelligence and educational capacity, and insisted that public policy incorporate that fact. They demanded that constitutional interpretation conform to scientific facts, at least as they understood those facts.

Their position has important and fascinating implications. Apparently, segregationists, or at least those who handled the Stell

[6] Jack Greenberg, "Social Scientists Take the Stand: A Review and Appraisal of their Testimony in Litigation," *Michigan Law Review*, LIV (May, 1956), 953-70.

[7] Civil Action No. 1316, U.S. District Court for Southern District of Georgia; Civil Action No. 3379, U.S. District Court for Southern District of Mississippi.

and Evers cases, would make the meaning of the Constitution dependent upon science, and this without reservation. They would, in effect, make the constitutional guarantees of American citizenship dependent upon the latest findings of science. Carried to its logical conclusion this would reserve the rights of citizenship to those who can demonstrate scientifically that they belong to a racially—and why not ethnically?—superior group. If segregationists can "prove" that Negroes are racially inferior and thereby justify denying them the rights and privileges of citizenship, why cannot someone else do likewise for other minorities? Why cannot Anglo-Americans in the Southwest segregate Mexican-Americans and deprive them of the right to vote, and New Yorkers do likewise for their Puerto Rican minority? The implications in this for all non-Caucasians in America are manifest—their civil rights are at the mercy of anyone who "proves" them inferior to North Europeans. In their efforts to overturn the Brown decision, segregationists and scientific racists resorted to an expediency which, if followed to a logical conclusion, would make mockeries of the Constitution and American citizenship. But they did not expect to take their views so far. All they wanted was a return to the status quo before 1954, that is to the days before Earl Warren became chief justice of the Supreme Court and the federal government began meddling seriously in the racial affairs of the South.

Perhaps the real significance of the use of social science in the Stell and Evers cases was due to the willingness of segregationists to take from public officials, and thus the American people themselves, the chief role in interpreting the Constitution and defining the rights of citizenship. This role they would reserve for scientists, a fact which is especially remarkable since they placed no limitations on science, or, at least, on their own science. They accepted at face value the evidence and conclusions of scientific racists, and thought it axiomatic that an "inferior" race was not entitled to equality in American life. In view of the fact that the overwhelming weight of scientific evidence and opinion was against them, this position was, for their own self-interest, extremely shortsighted. Scientific racists cannot match in number or prestige the scientists and social scientists who endorse the equalitarian-environmentalist point of view, nor can they match in quantity or quality the amount of scientific evidence and opinion which disputes racist claims. In a fair contest before an impartial court, scientific racists are bound to lose, and their willingness to challenge integrationists on scientific grounds was a measure of their political and legal myopia and their desperation as well.

An equally striking fact about the use of science in the Stell and Evers cases was the violence segregationists did to their professed constitutionalism. Elsewhere they assumed the stance of unwavering political conservatives and professed to believe in strict interpretation of the Constitution. They attacked the Brown decision as court-made law which ignored a long line of legal precedents, and they never tired of reminding the Court that Congress had passed no law (before 1964) requiring integration of the public schools. In Stell and Evers, however, they turned completely around and urged the court to read into the law another principle which Congress had never passed—that the meaning of the Constitution depends upon scientific knowledge. Certainly Congress has never made the rights of the citizen dependent upon intelligence, brain size, or evolutionary development. The Fourteenth Amendment does not say specifically that racial segregation is unconstitutional, but it does state that all citizens are entitled to equal protection of the laws, and the Supreme Court has responsibility for interpreting that general principle in specific cases. It would seem farfetched indeed to argue that the principle includes, either implicitly or explicitly, a test of intelligence, brain size, or evolutionary development. It would seem even more farfetched for such an argument to come from strict constitutionalists.

The use of science in the federal courts was an expediency on the part of segregationists which destroyed whatever effectiveness they might otherwise have derived from posturing as men of principle. They talked solemnly and endlessly about freedom, individual rights, and self-government, but they would deprive Negroes of all these things, and for reasons beyond the power of the race to control. They would promote freedom, liberty, and individualism by depriving Negroes of constitutional rights and liberties already enjoyed by other Americans, and by denying the federal government the power to intercede for the race. It would be easy to believe that their primary concern was not liberty, individual rights, or constitutional government, but racial segregation and white supremacy. Despite their libertarian rhetoric, what they really sought was legal and constitutional justification for racial discrimination. They were fond of saying that Negroes have no "civil right" to integrated schools. The question remains, however, where did whites get their "civil right" to segregated schools?

The decision to use science to challenge the Brown decision in the federal courts was a result of the urgings of such men as Carleton Putnam, Henry E. Garrett, and R. Carter Pittman, the last a prominent Georgia attorney who is an articulate defender of segregation and a prominent spokesman for the Citizens' Councils.[8] On several occasions Putnam urged segregationists to challenge the Brown ruling on scientific grounds, promising them full cooperation from scientific racists. "I think I could assure you now that if a serious attempt were planned to reverse the Brown decision," he told the annual state Attorney General's Conference for District Attorneys in Louisiana in February, 1962, "I could name you a score of scientists who would be willing to testify— men who would come from abroad as well as Americans." [9] In October he broached the subject again in his open letter to President Kennedy in the aftermath of the crisis which followed James Meredith's enrollment in the University of Mississippi. "The cause of our trouble lies in the incomplete and partisan nature of the evidence on which the Supreme Court decision of 1954 was based," he told Kennedy. "Since 1954 much has become apparent concerning that evidence," and "much new evidence has also come to light." The best summary of this new evidence, he added, is George's *The Biology of the Race Problem.* "I would ask that you personally read the [George] report," he wrote the President, "and do what you can to clear the way to the Supreme Court for a new case based upon it, as well as upon voluminous other evidence now being assembled in various cases soon to be initiated in the lower courts." [10]

The cases to which Putnam referred included the Stell and Evers cases, *Brown v. School District 20 of Charleston County,*[11] and *Armstrong v. The Board of Education of the City of Bir-*

[8] See for example R. Carter Pittman, "Equality Versus Liberty: The Eternal Conflict," *American Bar Association Journal,* XLVI (August, 1960), 837–80. Pittman was a member of the Honorary Advisory Board of *The Citizen.*

[9] Putnam, "The Road to Reversal," 24.

[10] Putnam to President Kennedy, printed in New York *Times,* October 3, 1962, p. 33.

[11] For a summary of this case see *Southern School News,* September 1963, p. 22.

mingham,[12] in each of which social scientists or educators testified that segregated schools are preferable to integrated schools on both scientific and educational grounds. The Stell case was by far the most significant of these cases, for in it segregationists made their most concerted effort to refute the social science testimony in the Brown cases and to present, comprehensively and systematically, their own scientific evidence against integrated schools.

In its origins, the Stell case was not unlike dozens of other cases brought by Negroes to speed school integration in the South. For years after 1954 the school board of Savannah and Chatham County, Georgia, had done nothing to implement the Brown decision; on the contrary, members of the board used every tactic imaginable to thwart the decision, and ignored persistent pleas of Negroes for integrated schools. After repeated rebuffs from the board, a group of Negro parents went into the federal district court in Savannah in 1962 and asked Judge Frank M. Scarlett to enjoin the board from continuing to segregate the schools by race. Their complaints were typical. They charged that Negro schools in Savannah and Chatham County were inferior to white schools, especially in variety and quality of educational experiences offered students. By segregating children by race, they also charged, the school board was violating the Brown decision and depriving Negroes of rights guaranteed by the Fourteenth Amendment. The board routinely denied the charges, contending instead that a recent building program had equalized Negro schools and recently implemented pupil placement policies had ended the policy of racial segregation in the schools.

This pupil placement policy was the cornerstone of the board's defense. In the early 1960's, as the Supreme Court began methodically striking down all laws, ordinances, and administrative procedures which made distinctions based on race, the states and school districts in the South officially abolished those laws, ordinances, and procedures, and in their stead adopted pupil placement policies designated to perpetuate segregation without mentioning race. Such policies were transparently discriminatory, at least in the way they were applied, but they were accepted, if only in principle, by the Supreme Court, and soon became the chief means of preserving school segregation in the South. Accord-

12 Civil Action No. 9678, U.S. District Court for Northern District of Alabama.

ing to the policy then in effect in Savannah, the school board assigned each pupil to a particular school not on the basis of race
but on an elaborate set of educational, psychological, and sociological guidelines which included the following: "The scholastic aptitude and relative intelligence or mental energy or ability of the
pupil; the psychological qualification of the pupil for the type of
teaching and associations involved; the effect of admission of the
pupil upon prevailing academic standards at a particular school;
the psychological effect upon the pupil of attendance at a particular
school; . . . the home environment of the pupil; the maintenance
or severance of established social and psychological relationships
with other pupils and with teachers; . . . the ability to accept or
conform to new and different educational environment; [and] the
morals, conduct, health and personal standards of the pupil." [13]
The expressed purpose of these guidelines was to drop race as the
basis for pupil placement, but as interpreted by the Savannah-
Chatham County school board they resulted in assignment of *all*
Negroes and *all* whites to racially separate schools. The board insisted that this was coincidence, not design, and Judge Scarlett,
who heard the case, was unperturbed by the claim.

After Negro plaintiffs filed their action, a group of white parents
petitioned to intervene in the case, alleging that the school board
did not adequately represent the interests of their school-age children. It was the intervenors who transformed the Stell case into
an instrument for challenging the Brown decision on scientific
grounds. Their attorneys were R. Carter Pittman, Charles J.
Bloch, of Macon, Georgia, a prominent constitutional lawyer and
outspoken segregationist,[14] and George S. Leonard, of Washington,
D.C. Pittman and Bloch had both criticized the Supreme Court
for using expert, nonlegal testimony in the Brown decision, and
were vocal champions of states' rights and strict constitutionalism.
Now, however, they joined scientific racists in an effort to interpret
the Constitution by expert, nonlegal testimony of their own, and
for their purposes the Stell case was ideal. The most systematic,
recent study of comparative racial intelligence was Robert T. Osborne's report on the public schools of Savannah, and his conclusions were all Bloch and Pittman could ask.[15]

[13] Quoted in Savannah *Evening Press*, July 1, 1963.
[14] See Charles J. Bloch, *States Rights: The Law of the Land* (Atlanta, 1958).
[15] See above, pp. 83–87.

According to their petition to enter the Stell case, the inter-venors were "Whites, sharing a common biological origin, cultural heritage and consciousness of kind," who objected to their children being "forcibly compelled to associate with plaintiffs and others of their ethnic group in the common schools" of Savannah and Chatham County.[16] Their petition, plus the briefs and arguments they presented to the Court, are together the best exposition of the ideas of scientific racism this author has seen. The briefs reflect a substantial knowledge of the literature and ideas of scientific racism, and their use of science is far more effective than that in most segregationist writings. The emotionalism and invective which mar so much of the literature of scientific racism are notably absent. Authors of the briefs made a conscientious effort to discuss all major points of disagreement between scientific racists and equali-tarians, and though they were far from successful in proving their case, their presentation was systematic and thoughtful. They sought to reopen all the issues the Brown decision had ostensibly settled, and their effort was clearly a serious one. They hoped—and ex-pected—to take their case all the way to the Supreme Court and make it a *cause celebre* in the struggle against school integration.

Their petition to the Court was a resume of racist arguments against integrated schools, and emphasized the relevance of those arguments to the public schools of Savannah. They first pointed to Osborne's study, which they used as authority for contending that the intelligence and educational achievement of white and Negro children in Savannah are so disparate that "extensive racial inte-gration will seriously impair . . . academic standards and educa-tional opportunities" in white schools. Next, they noted the high rate of immorality among Negroes, which, they insisted, made widespread integration unthinkable. "Existing group differences in socio-moral and behavioral standards in Savannah and Chatham County are of such a magnitude that extensive racial integration will seriously impair prevailing socio-moral standards in the now all-White schools," they declared. "The rates of emotional instabil-ity, behavioral delinquency, illegitimacy and venereal diseases among Negro children and their parents are vastly greater than

[16] Record on Appeal from the U.S. District Court for the Southern District of Georgia (Savannah Division) to the U.S. Court of Appeals for the Fifth Circuit, *Stell v. Savannah-Chatham County Board of Education*, Civil Action No. 1316, Pleas and Answer of Intervenors.

among White children and their parents." Finally, intervenors insisted that white-Negro differences are organic in nature. "Racial differences in physical mental, psychical, and behavioral traits between plaintiffs and petitioners are, to a large extent, genetically determined and are a natural result of the biological processes of race formation," they wrote, emphasizing the debt of scientific racists to darwinism. "The origin and formation of the various races of mankind . . . resulted from differential and adaptive selection of hereditary variations (arising from mutations and genetic drift), in reproductively isolated populations." The differences thus begun were "perpetuated and stabilized through continued isolation and inbreeding of the major races over long periods of time," and are manifested today in the "anatomical, psychological, and bio-chemical traits" of each race. As a result, there are "significant differences in cerebral morphology and physical constitution which are structurally related to racial differences in mental, psychical and behavioral traits," and which "constitute a rational basis for segregation of races in schools, particularly among the young and immature."

To demonstrate this "rational basis" for segregation, intervenors summarized the teachings of "modern social science," emphasizing their implications for racial and educational policy. The ultimate justification for school segregation, they told the Court, is a deeply embedded "consciousness of kind" which instinctively leads individuals to prefer associating with members of their own race. "Selective associational or racial preference is a universal human trait, which manifests itself in a variety of cultures and at a very early age," intervenors declared, and it "may have a genetic basis, arising out of the biological processes of race formation." It is natural and healthy to prefer association with one's own race, especially during the formative years of childhood and adolescence, for only in this way can "optimal personality development and social maturity" be achieved. Such association produces "a more stable self-concept, fulfills in-group identity needs, and provides an atmosphere more conducive to optimum social growth and maturity." To force children of widely differing racial groups into integrated schools impairs the personality development and self-image of individuals of both groups, and at critical points in their physical and emotional growth.

By making "consciousness of kind" into an instinctive trait, the intervenors created for themselves the same problems that had plagued other racists on this point. It is difficult to understand why "a universal human trait" which "may have a genetic basis" needs reinforcing by environmental controls such as mandatory racial segregation in the public schools. If there is in fact an instinctive preference for one's own race, it is difficult to understand why Negroes go to such lengths to integrate the schools and why so many whites endorse their efforts. Moreover, if the desire to associate with one's own kind is instinctive, it seems paradoxical that school integration would produce the problems intervenors foresaw: "serious sex problems due to the lower moral standards of Negroes," "interracial social intercourse, interracial dating, [and] interracial dancing." Apparently the instinctive consciousness of kind did not preclude such problems. The intervenors seemed to say that Negroes have an unnatural sexual affinity for whites, and whites in turn, or at least those of public school age, are unable or unwilling to resist the Negroes' advances.

Another logical inconsistency was implicit in the intervenors' description of Negro schools. They repeatedly assured the Court that Negro schools in Savannah and Chatham County were equal to white schools. Yet one of their basic arguments against integration was that educational standards in white schools would deteriorate if significant numbers of Negro pupils were admitted. They warned that Negro pupils would bring with them "a severe increase in disciplinary problems resulting from the more prevalent use of violence, vile profanity, lascivious sexual behavior, thefts, vandalism, cheating, lying, and other anti-social conduct." Now if these are in fact the behavioral traits of Negro pupils, it would be difficult to imagine how Negro schools could be equal to white schools. The same argument applies to the assertion that Negro pupils are significantly below whites in educational achievement. If this is indeed the case, the educational level of Negro schools is necessarily below that of white schools, and the educational opportunities they offer must be proportionally lower.

In discussing Negro schools, intervenors came perilously close to suggesting that ignorant, unintelligent, antisocial, and criminally inclined students be shunted off into segregated schools where society can forget them. It seems not to have bothered them that social, sexual, disciplinary, and academic problems existed in Negro schools. Their concern was to keep those problems out of white schools. Conditions in Negro schools, they seemed to say, are a problem for Negroes, not for society at large. They said in effect that if Negroes are unintelligent and antisocial, so be it. Society can do nothing about problems which are genetically determined; it can merely recognize those problems and refuse to exacerbate them through unnatural schemes such as racially integrated schools. It follows from this that there is little hope that Negroes will improve their lot, but intervenors felt that what hope there is comes from segregated schools. There, Negroes can fraternize with members of their own race, develop "more substantial self-concepts and a lesser rejection of their own race . . . suffer less frustration and repressed hostility," and, hopefully, "exhibit greater race pride and solidarity." It seems ironic that such benefits will come from associating with other Negroes, a group which are, in intervenors' words, prone to "violence, vile profanity, lascivious sexual behavior, thefts, vandalism, cheating, lying, and other anti-social conduct." If associating with such a race will adversely affect white pupils, it seems illogical to say it will have the opposite effect upon Negroes themselves.

Technically, the effort to overturn the Brown decision rested upon the contention that the decision constituted a finding of fact rather than a ruling of law. In layman's terms this means that the decision enunciated no new interpretation of the Fourteenth Amendment to the effect that racial segregation is per se a violation of the equal protection clause. Instead, the Court merely found that the individual Negro plaintiffs in the Brown cases had been denied equal protection of the laws by certain specific actions of their local school boards. The Brown decision, in other words, had no general applicability; it applied only to individuals and school boards involved in the Brown cases. It enunciated the law in those cases, not the law of the land. Every case involving racial segregation must therefore be decided on its own merits and according to facts presented in testimony in the case itself. A Negro seeking admittance to a white school must first prove in court that his attendance in an all-Negro school deprives him, specifically and individually, of equal protection of the laws, and the court must decide his case on the merits of the evidence he himself presents. A case in 1963 could not be decided on the basis of evidence available in 1954, any more than the Brown cases were decided by evidence available in 1896. In 1963 intervenors in the Stell case demanded a "new appraisal of the facts" just as the NAACP had in 1954.

To accomplish their purpose, they had to prove, first, that the Brown decision rested upon factual error and, second, that the facts presented in the Stell case dictated a new finding which would in effect set aside the Brown ruling. The Brown testimony was full of "subjective value judgments" which were "unrelated to any objective findings," they told the Court, singling out the testimony of Robert Redfield and Kenneth Clark as especially weak and deceptive. As for the appendix to appellants' brief, it was a statement "signed but not sworn to, by 32 so-called 'Social Scientists' . . . none of whom had any first-hand knowledge of the problems discussed" in the Brown cases. "In 1963 there is serious academic and intellectual dissatisfaction with the sociological materials underlying the Brown decision," they declared. The "modern authority" in that decision was "obviously written in order to establish 'favorable social and economic theories' and to create a climate which would make possible the decision that was finally reached in Brown." In other words, equalitarians had conspired to produce a body of social science literature endorsing racial integration, and having done so they went to court demanding that public school segregation be abolished, citing their own works in justifying the demand.

A major portion of intervenors' brief was a list of scientific works supporting their views. Those works, the most substantial of which they included as exhibits in their brief, included items by Ernest van den Haag, Robert T. Osborne, Henry E. Garrett, Audrey M. Shuey, Frank C. J. McGurk, Nathaniel Weyl, E. Raymond Hall, Cyril Burt, R. Ruggles Gates, J. C. Carothers, and others.[17] As these names indicate, the brief was a distillation of

17 The exhibits included van den Haag, "Social Science Testimony in the Desegregation Cases—A Reply to Professor Kenneth Clark"; Osborne, "Racial Differences in Mental Growth and School Achievement: A Longitudinal Study"; Osborne, "School Achievement of White and Negro Children of the Same Mental and Chronological Ages"; Osborne, "Racial Difference in School Achievement"; Garrett, "Klineberg's Chapter on Race and Psychology: A Review"; Garrett, "The Equalitarian Dogma"; Garrett, *Great Experiments in Psychology* (New York, 1951); Shuey, *The Testing of Negro Intelligence;* McGurk, "Psychological Test Score Differences and the Cultural Hypothesis"; McGurk, "A Scientist's Report on Race Differences"; Weyl, *The Negro in American Civilization;* Hall, "The Zoological Subspecies of Man"; Burt, "The Inheritance of Mental Ability"; Gates, *Human Genetics;* Carothers, *The African Mind in*

the scientific racism of recent years, and the Stell case is best understood as a culmination of that racism. It was an attempt to use the men and works already discussed in this study to reverse the Brown decision and thereby reinterpret the Constitution. Had the intervenors been successful, the Stell case would have done for segregationists what the Dred Scott decision did for slaveholders in 1857. It would have read segregation and white supremacy into the law of the land and deprived Negroes of many rights enjoyed by other Americans.

On the basis of the authorities listed in their brief, intervenors concluded that *"the bulk of available scientific evidence and modern authority in 1963 support the view that race is a valid unit of classification for educational purposes and that the operation of separate schools on the basis of race and color is a reasonable decision."* [18] In truth, however, "the bulk of available scientific evidence and modern authority" was not summarized by intervenors. In no sense was their brief a survey of the "available scientific evidence and modern authority" on the subject of race. It was instead a discussion of carefully selected authorities who directly or indirectly agreed with them concerning school segregation. The authorities were not representative of scientific opinion in the relevant disciplines, and to the extent that their data were valid, they did no more than prove that races differ physically and Negroes have inferior schools.

Like other racists, intervenors inevitably encountered the troublesome problem of overlap. In every characteristic, from intelli-

Health and Disease; David C. Rife, *Heredity and Human Nature* (New York, 1959) ; and Carleton Coon, *The Origin of Races* (New York, 1962) . In addition the exhibits included several articles which purported to prove that the average Negro brain is inferior to the average white brain. These were Raymond Pearl, "The Weight of the Negro Brain," *Science,* November 9, 1934, pp. 431–34; H. L. Gordon, "Amentia in the East African," *Eugenics Review,* XXV (January, 1934) , 223–35; F. W. Vint, "The Brain of the Kenya Native," *Journal of Anatomy,* LXVIII (January, 1934) , 216–23; and James H. Sequeira, "The Brain of the East African Native," *British Medical Journal,* I (March 26, 1932) , 581.

[18] Record on Appeal from the U.S. District Court for the Southern District of Georgia (Savannah Division) to the U.S. Court of Appeals for the Fifth Circuit, *Stell v. Savannah-Chatham County Board of Education,* Civil Action No. 1316, Supplemental Brief and Argument in Support of Motion to Intervene and for other Relief in Behalf of the Petitioners Named in the Original Motion. Emphasis in original.

gence to illegitimacy, from emotional stability to venereal disease, they found significant statistical overlapping. In their view, school segregation by ability grouping would be "reasonable if the *only* difference between the two ethnic groups were an overlapping statistical distribution of a *single* trait subject to precise measurement—such as IQ scores—and if the role of observable physical differences in social progress were ignored." Whites and Negroes differ in many psychological and behavioral traits, they pointed out, and "it is the *totality* of such differences, not any *one single* difference, that must be carefully considered in any evaluation of school segregation by parents and school officials. This is the same principle of frequency probabilities which underlies insurance rate classifications. . . . Race is the most convenient and rational classification for the operation of separate schools, since the race, not the individual, is the unit of inheritance and evolutionary change."

To clinch their argument for segregated schools, intervenors resorted to an analogy often used by racists. "An 'unintellectual' farm boy 'knows' that if you train breeds of rabbit dogs with breeds of bird dogs, pen them together, hunt them together and bring them up in the same environment, none of them will be worth killing either as rabbit dogs, bird dogs, or coon dogs," they wrote. "The knowledge that one may not send different breeds of dogs to the same school is simple for the farm boy but it becomes 'difficult and complicated' for many of those sheltered from realities." Such false analogies abound in racist literature. Intervenors are apparently saying that whites and Negroes are to be educated for different purposes, just as rabbit dogs and bird dogs are trained for different tasks, and they should therefore be educated separately. The fact is, however, that they are not educated for different tasks. The public schools of America attempt to stimulate their students intellectually, to prepare them for college and professional or vocational training, to impart to them an understanding of and appreciation for the moral, political, and economic principles of society, and to help them become better citizens. Nowhere do they attempt to train Negroes into whatever is the human equivalent of rabbit dogs and whites into the equivalent of bird dogs. The two races do not have separate roles in American society, though segregationists sometimes assume that they do. In their analogy with bird dogs and rabbit dogs, intervenors illustrated, perhaps inadvertently, their real feelings about the Negro's place in American society. They assumed that the Negro's role is separate and distinct from the white man's, and the function of the public schools is to prepare them for their separate roles.

The highlight of the Stell case was the testimony of Robert T. Osborne, Henry E. Garrett, Clairette P. Armstrong, Wesley C. George, and Ernest van den Haag. Their testimony naturally invites comparison with that in the Brown cases. Witnesses in the two cases touched upon many of the same topics, but the Stell testimony was broader in scope, shallower in content, and notably less convincing. The chief empirical data introduced in the case were from Osborne's study of intelligence and educational achievement in Savannah schools, which, according to Osborne himself, proved that segregation was necessary for quality education. Each of the witnesses discussed his own views of race and race relations, and in the process summarized the major ideas of scientific racism and assured the Court that those ideas are scientifically valid.

Garrett's testimony was the most wide ranging. He warned that school integration was evil, for the Negro's intelligence was vastly inferior to the white man's. "The differences between the negro [sic] and white are mostly within the realm of what you'd call abstract intelligence," he testified, "that is, the ability to deal with numbers, pictures, diagrams, blueprints, words, things of that sort, those things which made European Civilization and never have made a civilization in Africa in five thousand years. That, I call abstract intelligence and that is where the negro falls down." [19] He divided intelligence into three categories: abstract or scholastic, social ("the ability to get along with people"), and mechanical-motor ("the ability to deal with things with your hands"). "Could you approximate for me the differences between the two [races] so far as your experience goes in those three [categories]?" he was asked by an attorney for intervenors. "Well, I think the great difference comes in the abstract and the verbal side," he replied. "In social adaptability I don't know of any specific studies but my guess, maybe it's educated, I don't know, would be there isn't any great difference. In the mechanical-motor, I just don't know. I have read a lot of stories about how Africans fail to put oil in the motors and ruin them and all that kind of thing. I don't know how much that means." In the transcript of proceedings,

19 *Ibid.*, Transcript of proceedings, 127–65.

there is no indication that the attorney, or the Court either, found anything extraordinary in this candid admission of ignorance by an "expert" witness.

Garrett's most important contribution to the intervenors' case was to relate the ideas of scientific racism to educational policy. The following exchange indicates his usefulness to segregationists (and, incidentally, the calibre of the Stell testimony) :

Q. Would the differences in these three types of ability you have discussed, Dr. Garrett, indicate to you the desirability of any different educational treatment in negro schools as against white schools?

A. Well, I am not an educator and I can't say. I think I know what I might do if I had a free hand, but I would prefer to let somebody, who is an educator, testify on that. I will say that if you should integrate massively that you ruin the white schools. . . .

Q. Well, in what way would it ruin them?

A. It would pull the achievement level down one to three grades through the elementary school and it would do so in the high school.

Q. In other words, your congregated schools would be pulled back from one to three grades on the average?

A. And neither group would be happy. One group would be challenged above its ability level and the other group would not be challenged enough.

Q. In psychology is there any normal reaction to that type of congregation, where you have two socially coherent groups mixed together?

A. It's frustration, of course, and frustration leads to aggression and aggression leads to broken windows and muggings and crime.

Q. And this effectively is the result of bringing the groups together?

A. Right.

Q. Under classroom conditions?

A. Right. . . .

Q. And adversely affect the education of both groups?

A. Yes. And I would like to say, too, that I am a friend of the colored man. I have never said that he was inferior. I say that he doesn't do some things as well as the white man. . . .

Q. Tell me, Dr. Garrett, what evidence is there that segregation per se causes injury to the negro students?

A. There is no evidence.

Nor, he added for good measure, is there "any possibility" that environmental factors account for the racial differences which Osborne reported in his study of Savannah schools.

Intervenors' third witness, Dr. Clairette P. Armstrong, was even more outspoken. She testified that school integration is "very detrimental" to Negro children because of racial differences in intelligence. In her study of truancy in New York City, *660 Runaway Boys* (1932), she found that 37 percent of Negro truants blamed their truancy on "the school situation," a fact which she took to mean that school integration increases frustration in Negro pupils who learn less rapidly than their white classmates. Racial differences in intelligence, she told the Court, are "organic" and "innate," and indicate that Negroes are inferior to whites. "Do you think that negroes are innately inferior to whites, is that your testimony?" she was asked. "There is a spread, of course, from the lowest to highest," she answered, "but the averages, on the average, the means are different, so that from my own experience I would say that it is an inferiority." [20] Under cross examination, she disputed statements that the poor performance of Negro pupils in Savannah could be caused by inferior schools. "A child, a bright child," she averred, "can teach itself to read, irrespective of anybody or anything." Intelligent children of either race can and do attain high levels of educational achievement regardless of the quality of their schools or educational experiences. The problem of Negro children, she stated, is not poor schools but lack of innate ability. If her argument is valid for Negroes, however, it should be equally valid for whites, in which case the alleged antisocial behavior of Negro pupils will not interfere with the education of whites in integrated schools.

Dr. Wesley C. George testified next, and his testimony was a summary of *The Biology of the Race Problem*. The only biological scientist to testify for intervenors, he was asked to describe the physiological and morphological differences between whites and Negroes and explain their practical significance. The most important difference, he testified, is the disparity in average brain weight of Negroes and whites. "Brain weight in large groups of people is indicative of the relative capacity of those races of people for learning in the higher mental processes," he explained. Intelligence is determined by brain weight, and brain weight, like skin color, is inherited. The relevance of this for educational policy is obvious:

Q. Now, Doctor [George], I will ask you to state whether or not, in your

20 *Ibid.*, 176–86.

opinion, differences between whites and negroes in intelligence and in ability to absorb an education are due to genetic factors?

A. That is my belief.

Q. Doctor, in your opinion would the placing of negroes in an environment created by white children and white teachers or, in other words, mixing them in the schools, would that eliminate innate differences in intelligence and in behavioral traits?

A. Not in the hereditary traits. The hereditary traits are the basis of our behavior. . . .

Q. Where two distinct races of mankind are unalterably different, as you say they are, is there any way . . . by mixing the groups together, that those differences can be changed to the benefit of both groups?

A. None has ever been demonstrated and I don't think that any exists.

Such was the social science testimony in the Stell case. Perhaps its chief weakness resulted from the tendency of witnesses to read more into their data than was actually there. They acted on the premise that regardless of the specific limitations of their evidence, its totality made it reasonable to assume that racial differences are genetic in origin. Thus, they concluded, it is reasonable to assume that Negroes are racially inferior to whites in intelligence and educability, and to insist that social and educational policies incorporate that assumption. Witnesses in the Brown cases, on the other hand, felt that since Negro inferiority had not been demonstrated, it could not be assumed, and that in any case the rights of citizenship are not dependent upon intelligence, brain size, or evolutionary development.

Attorneys for the NAACP made no effort to refute the Stell testimony. Mrs. Constance Baker Motley, who directed the plaintiffs' case, called no witnesses to dispute those who testified for intervenors. In brief cross examinations, she pointed out that the witnesses represented a tiny minority of social scientists, and their so-called scientific evidence was only a subterfuge for discrimination and white supremacy. She objected repeatedly to the introduction of social science testimony in the case, but her objections were invariably overridden by Judge Scarlett. Mrs. Motley took the position, which resembled that of segregationists in the Brown cases, that social science testimony was specious and irrelevant since the Supreme Court had already decided the constitutional issues involved in the case. The issue was clear-cut, she felt; the district court and the Savannah-Chatham County school board are both bound by the Brown decision. Confident that her position was constitutionally as well as scientifically correct and would be affirmed by higher federal courts, she told Judge Scarlett that he had no alternative but to order the school board to integrate the schools of Savannah forthwith.

Judge Scarlett, who had a long record of using his court to nullify the Brown decision and harass the civil rights movement, disagreed with Mrs. Motley. Throughout the case he cooperated fully with intervenors. He accepted at face value the testimony of their witnesses, and used it as the basis for his ruling.[21] In the course of his ruling, he cited Osborne, Miss Shuey, Garrett, McGurk, Miss Armstrong, van den Haag, H. A. Tanser, R. Ruggles Gates, Robert Bennett Bean, George A. Lundberg, Carleton Coon, and others, and summarized the arguments used by intervenors and their witnesses. There is no indication in his ruling that he asked himself whether the evidence presented by intervenors did in fact represent "the teachings of modern social science." His ruling gives the impression there are *no* valid scientific data and opinion contrary to that offered by intervenors.

As a judge, Scarlett felt it imperative to offer a legal rationalization for using the intervenors' evidence to declare the Brown decision inapplicable to the schools of Savannah. He turned, therefore, to the segregationists' contention that the Brown decision rested upon a finding of fact rather than a conclusion of law. "The existence or non-existence of injury to white or black children from integrated or segregated schooling is a matter of fact for judicial inquiry and was so treated in Brown," Scarlett ruled. "The factual nature of the finding of injury through segregation in Brown opened the door to the proof which intervenors have made in this case." He found then, as a fact, that racially segregated schools in Savannah and Chatham County were not discriminatory and did not deprive Negroes of the constitutional guarantee of equal protection of the laws. "All the evidence before the Court was to the effect that the differences in test results between the white and negro students is attributable in large part to hereditary factors, predictability resulting from a difference in the physiological and psychological characteristics of the two races," he continued. "The

21 *Ibid.*, Opinion and Judgment. The Opinion and Judgment in the case is circulated in pamphlet form by the National Putnam Letters Committee. It is also printed in *Race Relations Law Reporter*, VIII (Summer, 1963), 514–28.

evidence establishes and the Court so finds that of the twenty-point difference in maturity test results between negro and white students in Savannah-Chatham County a negligible portion can be attributed to environmental factors. Further no evidence whatsoever was offered to this Court to show that racial integration of the schools could reduce these differences. Substantially all the differences between [white and Negro] children is inherent in the individual and must be dealt with by the [school board] as an unchangeable factor in programming the schools for the best educational results."

Scarlett also found that the results of school integration would be as intervenors had described. "The congregation of two substantial and identifiable student groups in a single classroom, under circumstances of distinct group identification and varying abilities would lead to conflict impairing the educational process," he declared. "It is essential for an individual to identify himself with a reference group for healthy personality development. Physical and psychological differences are the common basis of group identification, indeed they compel such self-identification. To increase this divisive tendency, it has been established without contradiction, that selective association is a universal human trait; that physically observable racial differences form the basis for preferential association and that patterns of racial preference are formed and firmly established at a pre-school age."

Scarlett felt the chief sufferers from integration would be Negro pupils. "Failure to attain the existing white standards," he wrote, "would create serious psychological problems of frustration on the part of the negro child, which would require compensation by attention-creating antisocial behavior." Later he added that "whatever psychological injury may be sustained by a negro child out of his sense of rejection by white children is increased rather than abated by forced intermixture, and this increase is in direct proportion to the number and extent of his contacts with white children." Nor could this difficulty be eliminated by integrating only the brightest Negro children into otherwise all-white schools. Bright Negroes transferred into white classrooms "would not only lose their right of achievement in their own group but would move to a class where they would be inescapably conscious of total social rejection by the dominant group." There they would be torn between the desire to associate with white classmates and the rejection they could regularly expect from them. The effects of such a policy would be "even more injurious" to children left in all-Negro schools, who would lose the benefits of associating with the best members of their race. "The Court finds," wrote Scarlett, "that selective integration would cause substantial and irremovable psychological injury both to the individual transferee and to other negro children."

Scarlett's ruling was welcomed by segregationists and scientific racists. *The Citizen* hailed it as "a good first step on the road to reversal" of the Brown decision. "Judge Scarlett's decision," read an editorial in the official journal of the Citizens' Council, "could go far toward replacing with reason and sanity the madness which has afflicted race relations in this country under the baneful policy of pro-Negro racism adopted by the Eisenhower and Kennedy administrations." [22] Judges on the Fifth Circuit Court of Appeals were less impressed. They peremptorily reversed Scarlett's decision and reprimanded him for "a clear abuse" of his discretionary powers as a judge. They directed him to grant forthwith the relief asked by Negro plaintiffs by directing the school board to integrate the public schools of Savannah and Chatham County. Scarlett did as ordered; the board obeyed his order and the schools of Savannah were integrated, at least tokenly, without serious incident.

The Stell case had been for naught.

Segregationists soon made another effort to use social science evidence to reverse the Brown decision, this time in *Evers v. Jackson Municipal Separate School District,* a case involving an effort to integrate the schools of Jackson, Mississippi. The evidence in this case, named, interestingly, for Darrell Kenyatta Evers, daughter of murdered NAACP leader Medgar Evers, was less systematic and inclusive than that in Stell, but it covered substantially the same ground and need not be repeated here.[23] In the Evers case Federal District Judge Sidney C. Mize heard testimony from several social scientists, among them Frank McGurk, and from several educators and nonscientists whose testimony was intended to supplement that of the social scientists. Mississippi Congressman John Bell Williams, a member of the 1957 House subcommittee which

[22] "A Good First Step on the Road to Reversal," *The Citizen,* VII (May, 1963), 2, 25.

[23] It is summarized in *Southern School News,* June 1964, p. 14.

"exposed" the alleged evil effects of school integration in Washington, D.C., predicted similar conditions in Jackson if the schools there were integrated. Kirby Walker, superintendent of Jackson public schools, testified that integration would produce massive educational problems because of racial differences in learning ability and educational achievement. James Gooden, a Negro, who was assistant superintendent for Negro schools in Jackson, testified that segregated schools are in the "best interest" of both races.

The late Judge Mize used his "Opinion" in the Evers case to summarize the ideas of scientific racism and to plead for a reversal of the Brown decision. "There is no known scientific study showing the existence of injury resulting to Negro children through separate education," Mize wrote. On the contrary, "separate classes with teachers of the same race are academically superior[,] . . . maintain a better disciplinary status," and "substantially diminish the number of delinquents and drop-outs in the schools." He concluded that "integration—not segregation—injures the Negro school child."

But having accepted the arguments of scientific racists, Mize faced a legal problem. "It is conclusive that the existing assignment of children in the schools of Jackson constitutes a reasonable classification," he declared, and to change to integrated schools "would substantially destroy the present levels of academic achievement in the school district and deny to [whites] the equality of educational opportunity, which they are entitled to have." But having so found, he could go no further. The Fifth Circuit Court of Appeals had already rejected Scarlett's ruling in the Stell case, and for Mize to disregard the Brown decision in deciding the Evers case would be both futile and foolish, and earn for him a reprimand from the Court of Appeals. He understood this. He would have to uphold the Brown decision, but not before denouncing it thoroughly. That decision, he declared, rested "upon the determination of . . . a fact, as distinguished from the declaration of a rule of law" and legally it did not apply to the schools of Jackson. Neither the school board nor the school children of Jackson had been represented in the Brown cases, and according to the doctrines of *res judicata* and *stare decisis* are not bound by the Brown decision. The due process clause of the Fourteenth Amendment requires that the school board and school children of Jackson have the same opportunity to be heard in court as those school boards and children involved in the Brown cases.

But having said this, Mize refused to declare the Brown decision inapplicable to Jackson. The Appeals Court ruling in the Stell case, he declared, was "contrary to the facts and the law applicable thereto," but because of it he felt compelled to order the schools of Jackson to integrate. In so doing, however, he vented his despair over the Brown decision and the domination of the federal courts by integrationists. "In the opinion of this Court," he wrote, "the facts in this case point up a most serious situation, and, indeed, 'cry out' for a reappraisal and complete reconsideration of the findings and conclusions of the United States Supreme Court in the *Brown* decision. . . . Accordingly, this Court respectfully urges a complete reconsideration of the decision in the *Brown* case." Until that is accomplished, however, the schools of Jackson must integrate. The effort to reverse the Brown decision on scientific grounds had failed.[24]

24 U.S. District Court, Southern District of Mississippi, Jackson Division, Civil Action No. 3379, *Evers v. Jackson Municipal Separate School District*, Opinion.

9

SINCE THE STELL CASE

The Stell case was the high-water mark of scientific racism, and its outcome left the movement in a state of suspension and indecision. Racists had expected the case to go to the Supreme Court and become a *cause celebre* in their controversy with integrationists. Their expectation, however, was never realized, and Judge Mize's disposition of the Evers case reflected their disappointment and frustration too. They understood at last that the federal courts offered them no hope, and many of them apparently concluded that the whole excursion into scientific racism had been worthless.

Suddenly, however, their prospects brightened. Nineteen sixty-four was a presidential election year, and in the early months of the campaign the outlook for segregationists seemed to take on new hope. A "white backlash" against Negroes and the civil rights movement appeared as if from nowhere, gaining strength from race riots in Philadelphia, Rochester, and Harlem. Governor George Wallace of Alabama entered the Democratic presidential primaries in Wisconsin, Indiana, and Maryland and polled a significant minority vote in each state. Most important of all, segregationists saw, or thought they saw, in the presidential candidacy of Barry Goldwater an opportunity to blunt the civil rights movement, especially after he voted against the Civil Rights Act of 1964.

The hopes, however, were illusory. Goldwater conservatives and arch-segregationists suffered stunning political defeats everywhere except the deep South. Instead of slowing the process of integration, Goldwater's candidacy was in many respects a blessing in disguise for Negroes and the civil rights movement. The Senator unwittingly contributed to the defeat of many conservatives, and his own defeat not only demoralized the Republican party but demonstrated the potency of Negro voting and the political short-sightedness of his failure to disassociate himself completely from segregationists. Because their hopes were so high during the campaign, scientific racists were dejected by its outcome, which followed fast upon their defeats in the Stell and Evers cases. So widespread was their dejection that since the fall of 1964 they have undertaken no new offensive against integration or the Brown decision and published no new major works.

This does not mean that the dangers represented by the revival of scientific racism in the last decade have disappeared, or that segregationists have lost interest in science. On the contrary, the dangers are still quite real and segregationists remain interested in science. In October, 1965, Henry E. Garrett repeated the salient ideas of scientific racism in *The Citizen,* describing anew the ill effects he foresaw from school integration. Three months later, he addressed the annual leadership conference of the Citizens' Councils, which met to explore methods of circumventing school integration, including establishment of private schools under Council sponsorship.[1]

---

[1] See Henry E. Garrett, "How Classroom Desegregation Will Work," *The*

Today scientific racism remains potentially dangerous not because it offers a likely basis for reversing the Brown decision or convincing national leaders that races are unequal and segregation should be the law of the land. The danger lies instead in several factors which lend credibility to the ideas of scientific racism and enhance their appeal among white Americans. Given the proper catalyst, these factors might again at some future time induce the nation to make "science" the basis of its racial policies. Lest this be misunderstood, let it be repeated: today scientific racism is only a potential danger, but potential dangers sometimes become real.

Among the factors which account for this, several are especially significant. The attitude of many white Americans toward Negroes is still permeated with racism; segregation frequently prevents meaningful contact between the races and thereby perpetuates racial stereotypes; many respected and influential nonracists sometimes express anti-Negro views; ultraconservative groups provide scientific racists with powerful political allies; and the low status of Negroes in American life continues to provide ostensibly objective evidence to support the racist characterization of Negroes.

In 1965 public opinion analyst Louis Harris posed the following question to a cross-section of white Americans: "I want to read off a list of things about coming into contact with Negroes. . . . I wish you would tell me if you personally would or would not object to [the items in the list]." The figures below are percentages of those who objected to various forms of contact with Negroes:[2]

	Nation	North	South
Working next to a Negro on the job	10%	7%	24%
Sitting next to a Negro on a bus	13	8	24
Sitting next to a Negro at a lunch counter	17	11	47
Sitting next to a Negro in a movie theater	20	14	50
Own children going to school with Negroes	20	13	53

Citizen, X (October, 1965), 4–17; and Medford Evans, "The Leaders of the Leaders," *ibid.,* (November, 1965), 8–9. For the most recent detailed criticism of the social science authorities cited in the Brown decision, see Peter A. Carmichael, *The South and Segregation* (Washington, 1965), 108–75. The Court's "presumption that 'modern authority' has established new grounds giving new meaning to equal protection of the laws proves illusory," wrote Carmichael, who is a philosophy professor at Louisiana State University.

2 Los Angeles *Times,* October 18, 1965, p. 4.

	Nation	North	South
Using same restroom as Negroes	25	18	58
Trying on the same suit or dress that a Negro has tried on in a clothing store	31	24	64
Having a Negro family as your next-door neighbor	37	30	71
Close friend or relative marrying a Negro	85	82	98
Your own teen-age daughter dating a Negro	92	90	100

As these figures demonstrate, white Americans, Northerners as well as Southerners, have deeply embedded prejudices against close contact with Negroes. It is to these prejudices that scientific racists appeal when they speak of "consciousness of kind" and instinctive preferences for one's own ethnic group, and when they insist that school integration is bound to cause "trouble" and Negroes are better off in schools of their own.

The strength of this white prejudice against close contact with Negroes is due in part to the fact that many, maybe even most, white Americans lead lives which for practical purposes are completely segregated. Many, perhaps most, white, middle-class Americans have no contact with Negroes except Negroes who are menials, servants, or in similar low-status occupations. They have no social contact with middle-class Negroes; they rarely work with members of the race, at least not as equals; nor do they worship with them. They rarely see Negroes in movies or on television in situations in which race is not important; and when they read about them in the newspaper, the Negroes are likely as not protesting something—picketing, sitting-in, or otherwise behaving in a manner that the middle class regards with suspicion or alarm.

The result is that whites do not know Negroes. They have few occasions to question their stereotyped views of the race, and those views persist even today, as the Harris survey pointedly revealed. "I want to read some things that have been said about Negroes," Harris also asked his cross-section of white Americans. "For each, tell me if you tend to agree more or disagree more with each statement." The results, expressed in percentages of those who agreed more, were as revealing as the replies to his first question:

	Nation	North	South
Negroes tend to have less ambition	58%	54%	80%
Negroes smell different	54	48	86

	Nation	North	South
Negroes have looser morals	53	48	77
Negroes laugh a lot	50	44	79
Negroes have less native intelligence	41	36	65
Negroes keep untidy houses	36	33	53
Negroes breed crime	33	30	50
Negroes care less about the family	32	29	46

Two years earlier, in 1963, Harris found that 41 percent of white Americans and 61 percent of white Southerners believed "Negroes want to live off the handout"; while 31 and 51 percent respectively believed "Negroes are inferior to whites." [3]

The characteristics in this list are the same as those ascribed to Negroes by scientific racists. Harris' survey, though it cannot be taken at face value because the interviewees were not asked whether the conditions are racial in nature, is nevertheless a striking illustration of the extent to which anti-Negro ideas permeate American thought.

Another reason for the potential dangers of scientific racism stems from the fact that anti-Negro ideas are found in the works of many notable authors (who usually wrote before 1954) who are not racists and make no plea for anti-Negro racial policies. This fact is significant since it enables racists to quote a variety of authors who are untainted with conscious racism, for example, Albert Schweitzer and Arnold Toynbee.[4] Similarly, they find such a standard reference work as *Encyclopedia Britannica* helpful to their cause. Under the entry "Races of Mankind," the 1964 edition of

[3] See William Brink and Louis Harris, *The Negro Revolution in America* (New York, 1964), 140–41.

[4] In relating his African experiences, Schweitzer often expressed views not unlike those which once inspired Victorian imperialists to shoulder the white man's burden. "The negro, then, under certain circumstances works well, but— only so long as circumstances require it," he wrote in *On the Edge of the Forest Primeval* (New York, 1922). "The negro is a child, and with children nothing can be done without use of authority. We must, therefore, so arrange the circumstances of daily life that my natural authority can find expression. With regard to the negroes, then, I have coined the formula: 'I am your brother, it is true, but your elder brother.'" *ibid.*, 83, 95. In his monumental *Study of History*, Toynbee, whom most Americans probably consider the greatest historian of this generation, wrote as follows: "It will be seen that, when we classify mankind by colour, the only one of the primary races, given by this classification, which has not made a creative contribution to any of our twenty-one civilizations is the Black Race." Toynbee, *Study of History* (London, 1934), I, 233.

the *Britannica* discusses Negroes in language somewhat akin to that of racists.[5] "In addition to woolly hair all these people have the following characters in common: dark skin sometimes almost black, broad noses, usually a small brain in relation to their size," the entry read. "In the skeleton there is a smoothness of contour which even in adults often recalls the bony form of a child, and among some members of the group the forehead has that prominent and smooth form which is so characteristic of the infant of our race." Though this appeared in the 1964 edition of *Britannica,* it was written about 1930 and reflects the racial views popular in the first quarter of the twentieth century. Of the dozen authorities listed in the bibliography, the most recent was published in 1928 and the oldest, William Z. Ripley's completely antiquated *Races of Europe,* was published in 1899. The author, L. H. Dudley Buxton, treated race solely as a means of dividing mankind according to physical features, and nothing in the article indicates scientists have learned anything about race in the last generation. Editor-in-chief of the 1964 *Britannica* was Harry L. Ashmore, a well-known liberal champion of civil rights and racial integration now with the Center for the Study of Democratic Institutions in Santa Barbara, California. Scientific racists could and did use Ashmore's name to enhance the authority and respectability of ideas expressed in "Races of Mankind."

Among scientists who are not racists there are a handful whose works directly serve the needs and interests of scientific racists. Racists often cite nonracist scientists to buttress their racism, but their use of authorities such as Wilder Penfield, Garrett Hardin, and Curt Stern is a bald deception which is obvious to anyone familiar with the works of those men. The same, however, cannot be said of their use of works by Carleton S. Coon, one of the nation's most eminent anthropologists, a past president of the American Association of Physical Anthropologists and formerly Curator of Ethnology and Professor of Anthropology at the University (of Pennsylvania) Museum in Philadelphia. Author of several major works of anthropology and ethnology, Coon is not a racist as that term is used here. He has repeatedly criticized racists and segregationists and emphasized his belief in the innate equality of races. "Neither in the field of hereditary potentialities concerning the

[5] "Races of Mankind," *Encyclopedia Britannica,* (1964 ed.), XVIII, 864A.

over-all intelligence and the capacity for cultural development, nor in that of physical traits, is there any justification for the concept of 'inferior' and 'superior' races," read a 1965 statement on race signed by Coon and several other scientists of international reputation. "The biological data (given in the report) stand in open contradiction to the tenets of racism. Racist theories can in no way pretend to have any scientific foundation." [6] Despite his endorsement of these views, Coon had three years earlier, in *The Origin of Races* (1962), published an hypothesis ideally suited to the needs of scientific racists.

To substantiate their ideas of racial inequality and Negro inferiority, scientific racists rely heavily upon the theory of evolution or some variation thereof. According to that theory, racial differences represent adaptations to the physical environment in which each race evolved. This theory, however, is not entirely satisfactory to racists, even with their own interpretation of it. It assumes that mankind was originally one, that races and ethnic groups have a common biological heritage, and racial differences, although not exactly superficial, are only part of the story of race. It is thus possible to accept both the evolutionary hypothesis and the unity of mankind, and on the basis thereof to defend the brotherhood of man and challenge the idea that race mixing is biologically harmful. What racists needed was a "scientific" theory disputing the biological unity of mankind from which to argue against both race mixing and the brotherhood of man.

Coon supplied such a theory. Not intentionally, to be sure; but the conclusions racists drew from his theory were logically drawn and did no violence to his hypothesis. Coon theorized that all mankind descended from a common ancestral species, *Homo erectus,* which evolved into *Homo sapiens* not once but five times and into five separate races. These races are Caucasoid, Mongoloid, Congoid (most African Negroes), Capoid (Bushmen and Hottentots), and Australoid (Australian aborigines), and the prototypes of each emerged before the evolution to the *sapiens* state. Not only did each race enter the *sapiens* state separately, according to Coon's theory, but just as important for racists, each did so at a different time. Using evidence provided by fossils, fire remains, and primitive human tools, Coon theorized that Caucasoids

[6] Los Angeles *Times,* October 2, 1964, p. 4.

reached the *sapiens* state approximately 250,000 years ago, or perhaps 200,000 years ahead of the Congoids, from which American Negroes descended. The significance of this difference was obvious to racists, just as it was to Coon, who spelled it out in detail. "It is a fair inference . . . that the subspecies which crossed the evolutionary threshold into the category of *Homo sapiens* the earliest have evolved the most," he wrote, "and that the obvious correlation between the length of time a subspecies had been in the *sapiens* state and the levels of civilization attained by some of its populations may be related phenomena." [7]

Had Coon set out consciously to formulate a theory to fit the needs of scientific racists, he could hardly have done better. "Caucasoids and Mongoloids who live in their homelands and in recently colonized regions, such as North America, did not rise to their present population levels by accident," he wrote. "They achieved all this because their ancestors occupied the most favorable of the earth's zoological regions."

Racists have widely praised and just as widely exploited Coon's theory. Virtually every major work of scientific racism published in the last few years endorses the theory and uses it as evidence for racial inequality and Negro inferiority. Carleton Putnam wrote an article for *The Citizen* lauding *The Origin of Races* as definitive proof of Negro inferiority. Nathaniel Weyl reviewed it for *National Review* and praised its "massive evidence," "dispassionate scholarship," and "challenging conclusions." Coon had, according to Weyl's review, demonstrated "the reality of race." [8]

Despite the enthusiasm of racists, Coon's theory "has not been widely accepted" by American scientists. This at least is the conclusion of a survey made by *Science News Letter*. Anthropologist Frederick S. Hulse of the University of Arizona characterized Coon's theory as an "extreme opinion" with "no evidence of any nature to support it." Theodosius Dobzhansky thought the possibility that mankind had evolved from *Homo erectus* to *Homo sapiens* on five separate occasions "vanishingly small"; and Ashley Montagu dismissed Coon's theory as "far-fetched" and "quite out of harmony with the biological facts." [9]

[7] Carleton S. Coon, *The Origin of Races* (New York, 1962) , ix–x.

[8] Carleton Putnam, "Evolution and Race: New Evidence," *The Citizen,* VI (July–August, 1962) , 7–10; and Nathaniel Weyl, "The Reality of Race," *National Review,* January 15, 1963, pp. 33–35.

[9] "Theory on Negro Origin," *Science News Letter,* November 3, 1962, p.

Coon's theory, like the views of Schweitzer and Toynbee quoted above, contributes to the authority of and potential danger from scientific racism. Of even greater significance in this respect is a number of well-organized and well-financed pressure groups which espouse, in varying degrees of intensity and effectiveness, views which parallel those advocated by scientific racists. These are political or "educational" groups which inhabit the extreme right wing of American politics. Among them are a few significant groups such as the Citizens' Councils and John Birch Society, several less significant ones such as the Ku Klux Klan and National States Rights party, and a flock of others such as the Liberty Lobby, Dan Smoot's followers, and the National Eugenics party. These groups do not always agree with each other or with scientific racists, and each has its own ax to grind, but they do share certain philosophical assumptions about politics, society, and mankind which have significance for racial policy. The policies they endorse do not in the final analysis differ significantly from those advocated by scientific racists and white supremacists.

The relationship between scientific racism and ultraconservatism, however, is not always as obvious as this statement perhaps suggests. Individuals and groups on the right-wing fringe of American politics are not necessarily racists; in fact many of them have no—or very little—interest in race and race relations and rarely if ever discuss racial topics. Others, however, are racists and are preoccupied with race relations, and they look upon ultraconservatism as an instrumentality for preserving segregation. The confluence of ultraconservatism and scientific racism results from the common political and economic views they share, views which if translated into public policy would have the effect of perpetuating segregation, white supremacy, and the second-class status of Negroes in America. This is often true whether individual ultraconservatives are overt racists or not. Spokesmen for the John Birch Society, for example,

---

285; Theodosius Dobzhansky, "Possibility that Homo Sapiens Evolved Independently 5 Times Is Vanishingly Small," *Current Anthropology*, IV (October, 1963), 360, 364–66; and Ashley Montagu (ed.), *The Concept of Race* (New York, 1964), 229. Coon has summarized his views in "New Findings on the Origin of Races," *Harper's Magazine*, CCXXV (December, 1962), 66–74; and "What is Race?" *Atlantic Monthly*, CC (October, 1957), 103–08. His theory would seem to be completely superseded by the fossil remains recently discovered by anthropologist L. S. B. Leakey and others in southern Africa. See, for example, Robert Ardrey, *African Genesis* (New York, 1961).

insist that the Society is not racist, that it in fact advocates equal rights and opportunities for all Americans. The fact remains, however, that the Society urges policies which, if adopted, would destroy the civil rights movement and close the avenues of protest which have been most efficacious for Negroes. Spokesmen for the Society have advocated reversing the Brown decision, rescinding most of the civil rights legislation passed in recent years, revoking most of the executive orders and administrative policies through which the federal government seeks to eliminate racial discrimination, "restoring" public schools to local control, and impeaching Earl Warren. They object, they insist, only to the tactics of the civil rights movement, only to unconstitutional actions by the federal government, unconstitutional civil rights laws, infringement upon the property rights and personal liberties of white Americans, and "communist infiltration" of the civil rights movement.

But they cannot disassociate themselves from the obvious consequences of policies they advocate, policies which would effectually destroy the civil rights movement and preserve the racial status quo. In the view of spokesmen for the Birch Society, every effective tactic utilized by Negroes in the civil rights movement is "unconstitutional," "socialistically inspired," or part of a "communist conspiracy." Wrote John Rousselot, public relations director of the Society, "The overwhelming proportion of 'civil rights' agitation is manipulated from behind the scenes by Communists, Communist sympathizers, or fellow travellers." [10] If Rousselot is correct, if most civil rights "agitation" is in fact communist controlled, then communists are responsible for much of the success of the civil rights movement, for the "agitation" led directly to the successes. The Birmingham riots produced the Civil Rights Act of 1964, the Selma march, the Voting Rights Act of the following year. For Rousselot to give communists credit for achievements as popular as these are among Negroes would seem to be, from his own standpoint, extremely shortsighted. But his shortsightedness is not intentional; it is instead a result of his effort to oppose the civil rights movement on ostensibly nonracist grounds. Racists would destroy the effectiveness of the civil rights movement by shouting "Negro inferiority" and "equalitarian conspiracy"; Rous-

[10] John Rousselot, "Civil Rights, Communist Betrayal of a Good Cause," *American Opinion*, VII (February, 1964) , 10.

selot and other ultraconservatives would accomplish essentially the same end by shouting "unconstitutional" and "communist domination."

The convergence of scientific racism and ultraconservatism is more than a coincidence of economic and political ideas, more than guilt by association. On numerous occasions in recent years ultraconservatives have directly and indirectly endorsed the ideas of scientific racists; and though they assiduously avoid saying that Negroes are racially inferior to whites, that is the clear and logical inference of what they do say. Dr. Revilo P. Oliver, formerly an associate editor of *American Opinion,* the magazine of the John Birch Society, and a prominent spokesman for the Society, endorsed the IAAEE Reprint Series, and it is reasonable to assume that he accepts the racism which is the chief ingredient of those reprints.[11] Medford Evans, a frequent contributor to *The Citizen* and a leading spokesman for the Citizens' Councils, is a contributing editor of *American Opinion.* In a recent typical installment of his column, "From the South," a regular feature in *American Opinion,* Evans denounced the Brown decision and lauded the establishment of private schools as a device for thwarting school integration in the South. The Brown decision, he wrote, is "perhaps the most racist ruling since the fall of the Third Reich," for it held that Negro schools are per se inferior to white schools.[12]

Some of the most characteristic ideas of scientific racism often appear in Birch Society literature. Earl Lively, Jr.'s *The Invasion of Mississippi* (1963), an account of the crisis which followed James Meredith's enrollment in the University of Mississippi, repeats many of those ideas. So also does Rosalie M. Gordon's *Nine Men Against America* (1958), an attack upon the United States Supreme Court and part of the evidence the Birch Society uses in its campaign to impeach Chief Justice Earl Warren. These works are items in the American Opinion Reprint Series and circulate widely in ultraconservative circles. The social science incorporated in the Brown decision, wrote Lively, "is rank opinion and conjecture and should not be given the dignity of consideration as 'scientific' thought. . . . The psychological and sociological opin-

11 Revilo P. Oliver, "Brainwashing," *American Opinion,* VII (November, 1964), 32n.
12 Medford Evans, "From the South," *American Opinion,* VIII (November, 1965), 67.

ions put forth in this case by the Court and its 'authority' are a far cry from anything 'scientific' " There is "some reason to doubt," he added later, "that the individuals referred to by the Court were selected for their abilities in their pseudo-scientific fields. Rather, examination of their works and the records of their personal conduct indicates that their interest in the case at hand was more political than academic." The contributors to Myrdal's study, for example, "represent a cross section of the leadership of the Communist movement that uses the Negro question as an issue for promoting revolution. They are Communists, fronters, ultra-liberal do-gooders, and professional agitators. Many are Negroes." Essentially the same views have been expressed by Robert Welch, founder and president of the Birch Society. In *The Politician* Welch credited unnamed communist conspirators with "forcing through the anti-segregation decision of the Supreme Court, which [they] certainly planned as far back as when [they] had Gunnar Myrdal brought over here to write his mammoth book." By that decision the communists made "it practically impossible for the coalition of conservative southern Democrats and conservative Republicans ever to be reestablished with the same strength again." [13]

The most illuminating example of ultraconservative "science" in Birch Society literature is an article which appeared in *American Opinion,* December, 1964, in which Revilo P. Oliver applied the principles of genetics, as he understood them, to history and some of the problems facing mankind today.[14] Like scientific racists, Oliver believes the study of genetics is inhibited by "liberal intellectuals" who allegedly find it necessary to suppress genetic truth. The truth they suppress, or so Oliver believes, demonstrates beyond dispute that heredity is the predominant influence in life,

13 Earl Lively, Jr., *The Invasion of Mississippi* (Belmont, Mass., 1963), 41–43; Rosalie M. Gordon, *Nine Men Against America* (Belmont, Mass., 1961), 39–46; Robert Welch, *The Politician* (Belmont, Mass., 1964), 65, cxx; and Welch, "A Letter to the South on Segregation," (no imprint). For typical discussions of the civil rights movement in Birch Society literature see Medford Evans, "Mississippi, the Long Hot Summer," *American Opinion,* VII (November, 1964), 7–18; Scott Stanley, Jr., "Revolution, the Assault on Selma," *ibid.,* VIII (May, 1965), 1–10; and Alan Stang, *It's Very Simple: The True Story of Civil Rights* (Belmont, Mass., 1965).

14 Revilo P. Oliver, "Biology, History and the Historians," *American Opinion,* VII (December, 1964), 63–83.

and he thinks this truth is vitally important for national survival. "All of the evidence thus far available," he wrote, "indicates that intelligence is as completely and unalterably determined by genetic inheritance as [are] physical traits," which are themselves "genetically determined beyond possibility of modification or alteration except by physical injury or chemical damage." Behavioral traits are thus innate and transmitted by heredity. There is "evidence", for example, "that makes it seem extremely probable that criminal instincts are inherited." Individual differences are products of "differences in genetic strains," and he declared, "All men are born unequal."

Individual differences add up to group differences, and these in turn produce cultural differences. Accepting this basic idea of scientific racism, Oliver concluded that cultural differences are genetically determined. "Historians who try to account for the rise and fall of civilizations by describing political, economic, philosophic, and religious changes without reference to genetic changes in the population are simply excluding what *must* have been a very important factor," he declared. "The continuity of a culture depends on a more or less instinctive acceptance of the common values of that culture," and instincts are inherited. This means, as scientific racists have repeatedly emphasized, that behavior is genetically, not culturally, determined and that every civilization reflects the genetic composition of the people who created it. Oliver avoided any mention of race, or at least any mention that could be literally construed to mean that races, as opposed to groups, of men are unequal.

He went to great lengths to explain "the scope of genetic forces in the continuity of a civilization," basing much of his explanation upon Lothrop Stoddard's *Revolt Against Civilization* (1922). Stoddard's volume, which the Freeland Products Company of New Orleans had recently reprinted in a paperback edition, was one of a number of similar works published around World War I. It combined racism, nativism, and popular notions about genetics in a manner designed to alarm "old Americans" with scare stories about an allegedly imminent "genetic crisis" in the world, a crisis supposedly caused by "race suicide" (that is, low birth rates) among genetically fit groups and promiscuous and uncontrolled breeding among the unfit. Stoddard feared that inferior racial and ethnic groups—"undermen" he called them—working through bolshevism and other dysgenic philosophies were destroying civilization, which he equated with the world supremacy of North Europeans.

After praising Stoddard's analysis as cogent, illuminating, and still timely, Oliver offered another authority on the same subject, Elmer Pendell's *The Next Civilization* (1960). Professor Pendell, of Jacksonville State College in Jacksonville, Alabama, offered a thesis similar to Stoddard's, but he treated it even more simplistically and with more abandon. (For example, he advocated organizing voluntary eugenic associations and "heredity corporations" and using artificial insemination to overcome the threat of eugenic catastrophy.) The real obstacle to eugenic reform, said Oliver in substantial agreement with Pendell, is the leftist-dominated government of the United States, which is consciously pursuing dysgenic policies. "The United States is now engaged in an insane, but terribly effective, effort to destroy the American people and Western civilization by subsidizing, both at home and abroad, the breeding of the intellectually, physically, and morally unfit," wrote Oliver, "while at the same time inhibiting, by taxation, and in many other ways, the reproduction of the valuable parts of the population—those with the stamina and the will to bear the burden of high civilization." These policies are threatening national survival and the future of civilization, and unless they are reversed in the near future it will be too late. "The reproduction of the superior stock" must be encouraged, and "the multiplication of the inferior" checked, but this can be achieved only by extreme measures. "We must use at least the taxing power of government, if not its power of physical coercion," Oliver declared, "to induce or compel the superior to have children and to prevent the inferior from proliferating." But even these measures, he conceded despairingly, offer little hope for the United States. Even if the leftist-dominated government in Washington could be induced to adopt eugenic policies, the decisions concerning who would and would not have children would be made by "a Senator Fulbright, a Walt Rostow, an Adam Yarmolinsky, a Lyndon Johnson, or a Jack the Ripper."

The real solution to genetic problems, he added, does not lie where most geneticists think it lies—in selective breeding of individuals of high IQ. A high IQ is important but is not sufficient by itself; it is only one of the qualities necessary for the advancement of civilization. Many so-called geniuses, for example, Einstein and the poet Shelley, are "in their judgement of social and political problems, virtually morons." Oliver labeled such persons "mattoids," a term he applied to anyone gifted in one area but feebleminded in other qualities equally important to the advancement of civilization. Many geniuses, he declared, suffer from "moral insanity," and are greater threats to civilization than the masses with low intelligence. The danger is not that "civilization is going to collapse from sheer lack of brains to carry it on"; the fact is that civilization "is now collapsing faster and harder from a superabundance of brains of the wrong kind." The danger is diabolical geniuses such as Stalin and Mao Tse-Tung, not a deficiency of brainpower in the masses.

Oliver ended his lamentation on a pessimistic note, which only emphasized the cataclysmic nature of his forebodings. Americans will "soon be drowned in the flood" caused by "the terrible multiplication of the populations of Asia and Africa," he warned in the manner of a latter-day Jeremiah. "The minority of the earth's inhabitants that is capable of creating and continuing (as distinct from aping) a high civilization" faces the distinct possibility of being exterminated.

Dan Smoot, editor of the *Dan Smoot Report,* is another ultra-conservative whose views parallel those of scientific racists. The Brown decision, Smoot wrote on one occasion, is based upon "the opinions of modern sociologists and psychologists, the chief of which [sic] was Gunnar Myrdal, a Swedish socialist with a communist front record, who, in a book called *An American Dilemma,* had proclaimed his utter contempt for the Constitution of the United States." The decision is one of a series in which Earl Warren has endeavored "to stretch the meaning of the Fourteenth Amendment, because the communists and socialists whom he cites as modern authorities think this should be done." On another occasion, Smoot cited Audrey Shuey's *The Testing of Negro Intelligence,* and Garrett's introduction to it, as proof that equalitarian and integrationist ideas do not coincide with the "findings of scientific" research. "It is obvious that Western civilization was produced by whites," he wrote in citing Garrett and Miss Shuey; but like Oliver he refused to say flatly that Negroes are inferior to whites. "For primitive living under harsh physical conditions, the black man is obviously better adapted than whites," he wrote, "but for living in the white man's civilization, whites are obviously better adapted than negroes [sic]." In other words, Negroes are not absolutely inferior; they are not inferior in everything, only in things that count.[15]

The community of interest between racists and ultraconservatives is a two-way street. Ultraconservatives accept many of the ideas of racists, and racists in turn accept many of the views of ultraconservatives. The social and political views expressed in Nathaniel Weyl and Stefan Possony's *The Geography of Intellect* and Carleton Putnam's *Race and Reason* to mention two notable examples, are the same as those expressed in the literature of ultraconservatism. This aspect of the relationship between racism and ultraconservatism is illustrated in an address which William J. Simmons delivered to the organizational meeting of the Greater Los Angeles Citizens' Council in the summer of 1964. [16] Amid the racism which constituted the larger part of his address, Simmons, who is editor of *The Citizen,* sprinkled his reactionary political views. The Citizens' Councils, he began, are concerned about two things—racial integration and the growth of "an all powerful Federal government [which] is taking us down the road to tyranny, with the resulting loss of our personal freedom." Both are threatening the future well-being of America and both result from essentially the same thing—"the wave of equalitarianism which started in our educational system, especially teachers' colleges like Columbia, before World War I." This wave spread slowly at first, "until the shock of the great depression and the advent of the New Deal provided a fertile ground for its proliferation." To Simmons, the New Deal was the instrumentality through which liberals, equalitarians, and intellectuals had conducted their assault upon traditional American ideals and institutions. Since Franklin Roosevelt's presidency, he remarked, "the nation has been managed from Harvard, with occasional ideological assists from Columbia."

New Dealers and their intellectual and political heirs, Sim-

15 See *Dan Smoot Report,* January 30, 1961, p. 35; and July 13, 1963, p. 222. For the most detailed ultraconservative indictment of social science as a tool of socialist-communist conspirators see *The Great Deceit: Social Pseudo-Sciences* (1964) , a Veritas Foundation study published under the supervision of Archibald B. Roosevelt and Zygmund Dobbs.

16 William J. Simmons, address to the Organizational Meeting of the Greater Los Angeles Citizens' Council, June 30, 1964, available from the Citizens' Councils of Jackson, Mississippi.

mons continued, served the interests of America's enemies, both foreign and domestic, in a variety of ways. They "saved Stalin from internal collapse by extending diplomatic recognition and thereby helped him obtain loans which tided him over"; and their aid to international communism continues even yet, its most recent expression being the limited nuclear test ban treaty of 1963. They are also responsible for the systematic attacks upon American business and industry which are part of a larger effort to undermine faith in free-enterprise capitalism. "The concept became ingrained in several generations of college students that profit was evil," Simmons declared. Business is "taxed unmercifully" to finance a burgeoning federal government and "stifled by regulations as the insatiable thirst for power of those in control in Washington [grows] apace." Labor unions have been coddled until their leaders have become political as well as economic tyrants.

In Simmons' view the most sinister of all New Deal policies, one which latter-day liberals have expanded far beyond the original designs of New Dealers, was the attack upon "the race which had developed the most advanced and most highly industrialized country in the world." This was, he felt, an integral part of the liberal assault upon free enterprise, states' rights, the Constitution, and the moral, religious, and social ethic of the middle class. The effectiveness of the attack was due in part to deception, to managed science as well as managed news, and in part to seductive slogans such as "peace," "equality," and "civil rights." The real nature of the attack, however, is indicated by the fact that "peace" and "civil rights" are today "the two top priority objectives of the Communist Party." The American government, Simmons said in peroration,

is today controlled by liberals or collectivists, or welfare staters, or whatever. Now why is this group able to maintain itself in power? Because primarily of the fact [sic] that the white conservatives are divided into conflicting political and sectional groups and the white liberals hold the balance of power through the leverage of the negro bloc vote. This is obvious in the heavy voting Northern states, and it is coming to be more of a factor in the Southern states. It was the negro vote in the South as well as in the North, for instance, that elected the present Democratic Administration. Hence the combined drive by the Administration and the negro pressure groups to force Southern states to register hundreds of thousands of unqualified negroes.

To get this bloc vote, the liberals promise more and more special privileges for negroes in the form of 'civil rights' bills, which not only would give them social and political preference, but economic as well.

The only way in which politicians have ever held the negro bloc vote is through an ever ascending rate of taxing whites and spending on negroes. Of all aspects of the welfare state, this is one of the most immoral, for it subsidizes laziness and waste at the expense of industry. Such brazen redistribution of the wealth amounts to no less than stealing.

It is not within the purview of this study to detail the views of "equalitarian" or "environmentalist" scientists. It seems appropriate, however, to comment in general terms upon certain of their major objections to scientific racism.

The basic error of racists is their misunderstanding of the concept of race. In their view, "race" is a fixed, permanent entity from which the individual inherits not only certain identifiable physical features, but equally identifiable mental, moral, and behavioral traits as well. There exist, then, or so racists believe, such things as "Negro intelligence," "Negro morality," and "Negro personality," and these are in large part racially and genetically determined. "Psychic" traits, in other words, are produced by evolution and transmitted in the genes in the same manner as skin color, hair texture, and facial configuration. From these assumptions racists reason that each race can be measured—and judged—by the culture it produces, the society it creates, the morality and intellectual achievement its members display. This means, among other things, that the improvement of Negroes in crucial areas such as IQ test scores and social behavior is largely beyond the power of Negroes themselves, or whites either, to accomplish. Improvement must await the long, slow processes of evolution. Eventually, perhaps, Negroes will reach the levels already achieved by whites, though even here the logic of racists is discouraging, for as Negroes evolve upward whites will presumably do likewise. The prospects of Negroes ever catching up would appear to be hopeless.

To equalitarians "race" is not nearly so powerful or static a force. It is instead a "process, a series of temporary genetic conditions always in process of change," and races are best defined as "populations which differ in the relative commonness of some of their genes," or as "genetically isolated mating groups with distinctive gene frequencies." [17] According to these definitions, races differ rela-

[17] Ashley Montagu, *Man in Process* (New York, 1961), 91–92; L. C. Dunn and Theodosius Dobzhansky, *Heredity, Race and Society* (New York, 1946), 108; and Pettigrew, *A Profile of the Negro American*, 59.

tively, not absolutely, and the difference is in the frequency of certain genes. Genes (and the chromosomes which contain them) are the mechanism through which heredity operates, but they are not racial in nature. "Negro genes" do not differ in kind from "white genes." An individual Negro does not inherit a set of "Negro genes" which, by racist logic, would give him "Negro intelligence," "Negro morality," and "Negro personality." Though intelligence, morality, and personality are each influenced to some unknown but considerable degree by heredity, the influence operates on an individual, not a racial, basis. In every race there is a vast reservoir of genes, but an individual inherits only a minute number of those in his racial gene pool. Every individual (except identical twins), regardless of race, has a unique combination of genes and is a unique human being with distinctive characteristics and potentialities. His traits and abilities are his as an individual, not as a member of a race. There is a complete overlap of personality and morality types, as well as range of mental ability, among the basic racial groups.

Nor is the genetic composition of a race static. In the case of American Negroes there has always been a steady infusion of "Caucasian genes" so that perhaps one-fourth of the Negro's gene pool today consists of "alien genes." This has immense significance for the claims of racists, and their failure to take it sufficiently into account is a notable weakness in their ideology. It pointedly illustrates the difference between biological and social definitions of race. Natural selection, mutation, and genetic drift also operate to alter the genetic composition of racial groups, and thereby contribute decisively to the dynamic of race, to the constant reshuffling and recombination of genes, to the "process" mentioned above.[18]

Besides misconstruing the nature of race and inheritance, racists also misunderstand intelligence, which is vastly more complicated—and fascinating—than they believe. They look upon intelligence, as upon race, as fixed and static, and in large measure racially determined. But the evidence is massive and wholly convincing [19] that intelligence is individual and plastic. "Intelligence is not merely an inherited capacity, genetically fixed and destined to

[18] This subject is explained in layman's terms in Theodosius Dobzhansky, *The Biological Basis of Human Freedom* (New York, 1958); Dobzhansky, *Mankind Evolving* (New Haven, 1962); and Ashley Montagu (ed.), *The Concept of Race* (New York, 1964).

[19] See for example Pettigrew, *A Profile of the Negro American*, 100–35.

unfold in a biologically predetermined manner," wrote Harvard psychologist Thomas F. Pettigrew. "It is a dynamic, on-going set of processes that within wide hereditary limits is subject to innumerable experiential factors." [20]

The racists' approach to intelligence, like their approach to race in general, is curiously fatalistic. They have an almost blind faith in IQ test scores, and in interpreting those scores they invariably assume that IQ is static and innate intelligence will develop regardless of environment. Here also they ignore a vast amount of evidence which indicates, convincingly, that this is not the case. In the famous Demonstration Guidance Project in Junior High School 43 in New York City, to cite one example, striking improvements in IQ test scores and scholastic performance were achieved by a massive guidance and remedial program. When the project began in 1956 only 26 percent of the students in Junior High 43 had IQ test scores of 110 or better, a distinctly below-average group. Three years later this percentage was 58. In 1956 2.5 percent of the students had IQ scores of 140 or over; six years later 12 percent achieved that level.[21] Similar though less spectacular results have been achieved in the Higher Horizons project, also in New York City, the "Banneker Group" in St. Louis, and the integrated schools of Washington, D.C.[22]

Washington, D.C., provided the most rigorous test yet made of the effects of massive integration in the public schools. The schools in the nation's capital were integrated immediately following the Brown decision, and psychological and achievement tests in the first year of integration revealed an appalling situation. The average scores of students were far below national averages in every category tested, a fact which racists took as proof that Negroes are intellectually inferior and that integration inevitably lowers educational standards. A flood of newspaper and magazine articles "exposed" the situation; a congressional subcommittee dominated by Southern racists "investigated" Washington schools and recommended that "racially separate public schools be reestablished."

20 Pettigrew, *A Profile of the Negro American*, 107.
21 See the testimony of Dr. John Theobald, New York City School Superintendent, in U.S. House of Representatives, Committee on Education and Labor. *Hearings on Integration in Public Education Programs*. 87th Cong., 2nd Sess., March 1–April 16, 1962, 288–89.
22 See the discussion in Pettigrew, *A Profile of the Negro American*, 125–29; and Charles E. Silberman, *Crisis in Black and White* (New York, 1964), 255–307.

The disparity in achievement between white and Negro students, the subcommittee declared, is too great for integrated schools to be effective. Integration, they found, creates discipline and sex problems which interfere with the learning process and produces morale problems for both teachers and students.[23]

The District Superintendent of Schools, Dr. Carl F. Hansen, however, was not dissuaded from the facts of the case. Integration had not lowered standards in District schools, he felt, it had merely revealed the stark inferiority of Negro schools. To him, the solution was not resegregation but improvement of school services and standards so as to raise the performance of all pupils, Negro as well as white. And this he accomplished. After 1955, when the schools were first integrated, there was steady improvement in the performance of Washington students on standardized aptitude and achievement tests; by 1960 their performance approached national averages in most areas tested. The significance of this is underscored by the fact that it occurred while the percentage of Negroes in the schools was steadily increasing, and in spite of the fact that the student population in Washington is decidedly atypical. Not only is the percentage of Negroes unusually large (81.5 percent in 1961) but a majority of the students are from the central city and a disproportionately small minority from affluent suburbs. "A brief summary of the [achievement test] results will show, where comparative data are available, a general upgrading of achievement levels since 1955," reported Dr. Hansen in 1960. "This has occurred during a period of steady increase in the percentage of Negro pupils, testifying to the capacity of the Negro pupil to respond to educational opportunity." [24]

It is obvious, then, that Negroes are as educable as whites and that integration does not itself lower educational standards, though it does reveal the inferiority of Negro schools. This, again, is an all-important point which racists invariably ignore. Negro schools *are* inferior, and grossly so, whether in the rural South or the

[23] U.S. House of Representatives, Committee on the District of Columbia. *Report of the Subcommittee to Investigate Public School Standards and Conditions and Juvenile Delinquency in the District of Columbia* (Washington, 1957) , 47.

[24] Carl F. Hansen, *Addendum: A Five-Year Report on Desegregation in the Washington, D.C., Schools* (New York, 1960) , 19. There is a detailed report on the improvement in test results in U.S. House of Representatives, Committee on Education and Labor. *Hearings on Integration in Public Education Programs.* 87th Cong., 2nd Sess., March 1—April 16, 1962, pp. 382–402.

ghettoized North and West. A few years ago, to cite one example, James B. Conant found that the total appropriations per pupil in Chicago averaged 21 percent less in all-Negro schools than in all-white schools.[25] The inferiority of Negro (and slum) schools, however, is not due solely to money expended; other factors not statistically measureable are also involved. The total school environment is more significant than expenditure per pupil. Negro (and slum) schools seem generally to have poorer and less experienced teachers than white suburban schools, or the teachers in Negro and slum schools rarely make the same demands upon their students. White suburban schools are oriented toward preparing students for college, and they accordingly insist upon respectable levels of achievement. In slum and Negro areas, the community, the parents, the school board, the teachers all expect little of students, and the students soon come to expect little of themselves. As Kenneth Clark has said repeatedly, Negro children do not learn because they are not taught, and they are not taught because no one expects them to learn.[26] A vicious cycle exists, and as a result the prophecy that Negro and slum children have low intelligence and little educability is self-fulfilling.

The principal weakness of scientific racism, however, is not its scientific deficiencies, though these are serious enough to discredit it; the principal weakness is the logical fallacy inherent in the idea that civil rights and race relations are genetic problems which are best approached through an understanding of the Negro's genetic inheritance and evolutionary development. Racial policies are first and foremost social policies and must be treated as such if they are to be solved. The American Negro is what he is today because of social, not genetic, reasons. He makes lower IQ scores than whites, earns less money, is more likely to commit certain crimes and deviate from middle class standards of morality and personal conduct. But these are products of racial discrimination and class differences and are irrelevant to the composition of his gene pool. Scientific racists refuse to recognize this fact, and as a result are unable to understand the real nature of the race problem. In fact, they are themselves an important element in that problem.

25 Cited in Silberman, *Crisis in Black and White,* 263.
26 See Clark, *Dark Ghetto* for a discussion of this aspect of the problem.

INDEX